In memory of my father, Frank L. Smith
1913-1977

Whose untimely death, through human eyes,
Gave birth to my ministry as a Christian author
And compelled me to think deeply about life on the other side of life

TABLE OF CONTENTS

INTRODUCTION

Could someone please tell me why, of all my books, this one has caused so many quizzical looks on the faces of those who have asked me what I'm writing? "It's about death and afterlife," I've been answering each time for months now. With but few exceptions, I keep getting this incredulous look, as if to say, "You're kidding, aren't you?" Or, "How could you possibly know what's on the other side of death?" Or (literally, in one case), "Are you a prophet?"

Have we really come to the point where it should be surprising that a Christian author would explore the subject of what happens after death from the source book of all his other writings—the Bible? Sure, there are unanswered questions about the "other side" which at times leave us frustrated and bewildered. But there is a wealth of information in Scripture which seems to go virtually unnoticed in our rush to get to the parts which affect "the here and the now." Then again, what could possibly affect the "here and now" more than the future prospect of death, towards which each one of us is hurtling at this very moment?

Along with other authors, I'm sure, I find it frustrating that my readers often begin at the end of the book and work their way back towards the front. This book in particular should not be read that way. Each chapter builds on the previous one. Later chapters are written on the assumption that important bases have already been covered earlier in order for them to make sense. That said, the very value of thinking about the afterlife comes in "knowing the end of the story first and working backwards." How can we hope to properly embrace the temporal until we have grasped the eternal? By seeing the future first, we can better appreciate the present.

Whether or not we like to think about it (and mostly we don't), the defining moment of your life and mine will be the split-second instant we each die. At that point, either we will cease to exist altogether, or we will continue on in some form undoubtedly shaped and molded by the lives we have lived up to that point. Naturally, just as with life itself, our deaths and what will happen beyond them is a great mystery. Even if we come anywhere close to capturing what we can know about it, the afterlife will always remain a mystery. Yet, it is not a mystery about which we are completely clueless. Indeed, in sheer volume of text, as well as in specific teaching, God has revealed far more than many casual readers of the Bible suspect. Unless one is prepared to make a serious study of the subject, it is easy to slip past profound insights right before our eyes.

My own interest in the subject first began when, as a young District Attorney, I watched a number of autopsies as part of homicide investigations. I never could get over the fact that the cold, lifeless corpse lying there on the stainless steel table had been so very much alive and animated only hours before. And there was also that unforgettable comment as the pathologist was slicing through one victim's brain. "It's a normal, healthy brain," I vividly recall him saying. With equally sharp recall, I remember asking myself: "How could a person have a 'normal, healthy brain' and yet be dead? Isn't who we are essentially a matter of brain function?" Didn't Descartes just about have it right in his observation: "I think; therefore I am"?

And then there was the phone call informing me that my father had died—all too suddenly at the relatively young age of 63. From that day onward, my time on earth has seemed far more compressed. Even now, it's hard to escape the thought that, if I live to be no older than my father, I have little more than five years left in this world. Call me a "short-timer." That's certainly how I've come to see life, even if the Lord should grant me many more years on earth.

There is also sheer intellectual curiosity about how so many people can have such widely divergent views about death, afterlife, and the end of time—even people reading the same Scriptures. Can all those theories simultaneously be true, and, if not, what is the truth? And how can we know for sure, especially in light of what, upon first impression, appear to be any number of conflicting passages on the subject?

Although I was prepared to encounter the standard afterlife controversies in the process of my study, I confess I had not anticipated how closely afterlife issues impinged on any number of broader doctrinal issues which typically are discussed (even hotly debated) with little reference to their afterlife implications. Without chasing too many rabbits, I've tried to note these anomalies as they present themselves. In Part II, I will have much more to say about how certain contrived afterlife scenarios expose the fallacies in their underlying theological assumptions. What we believe about the afterlife has an interesting way of being a litmus test for scrutinizing our core doctrinal beliefs.

Stylistically, I have found myself quoting more passages in full than I normally do. It's not simply a case of letting the Scriptures speak for themselves, which would be a worthy endeavor on its own. But the afterlife, by its very nature, is a subject which calls for careful study of the text. Because discussion of events yet to come on the "other side" is often couched in apocalyptic hyperbole and flamboyant metaphor, we are forced to make hard decisions about what is intended to be merely figurative and what is meant to be taken literally. There is the additional difficulty of having to interpret the many prophetic passages involved, and especially in distinguishing more-immediate applications from subtle overtones possibly anticipating far-distant fulfillment. And then there are the necessary word studies to be done, so that we can be confident we're not confusing linguistic apples and oranges.

Perhaps the greatest difficulty we have with the language in this study is that, for the most part, it is orientally oriented! The Jews' "eastern" way of thinking could not be farther removed from our own Aristotelian logic or Lockean rationality. For centuries, the Jews lived comfortably with embellished, apocalyptic imagery, and the simultaneous (seemingly inconsistent) language of "delay" and "nearness." And so, we are forced to use our logical "western" minds to understand that what we are reading may never have been intended to be strictly logical!

Of course, the difference between "eastern" and "western" thinking pales by comparison with the difference between human, earthly thinking and divine, spiritual thinking. Try as we might, it is almost impossible to understand a realm of which we are not yet fully a part.

Above all, there is the constant battle to insure that we adhere to the first rule of exegesis: context, context, context! Miss (or avoid) the context, and we can jump to just about any conclusion we want to reach. Get the context right, on the other hand, and we begin to see familiar passages in a whole new light—sometimes in a quite-shocking, unexpected light. And, of course, there is that other important context to consider: the wholeness and unity of Scripture. It's as if we were assembling a puzzle into which all the pieces must fit together comfortably. And not just all the pieces pertaining to the afterlife (which itself is difficult enough), but all the pieces of any tangential doctrines which interface with afterlife issues. A tall order, indeed!

But (to change the metaphor), if we believe that God's complete Truth is an interwoven tapestry of multiple truths, how can we settle for anything less than total harmony of God's revelation? Should any single thread threaten to make the whole fabric unravel, we must carefully (and courageously) examine where we've gone wrong.

This possibility—that we may have been mistaken in some of our fundamental assumptions—suggests yet another reason why I've chosen to include so many scriptures in full. Orthodoxy tends to be orthodox for the very reason that it has withstood the test of time and criticism. Therefore, one challenges orthodox understandings at one's peril, and never without the full backing of God's own word on the matter. So, how can we know "God's own word" on any given issue? A good start is to read again his very words—in their original context, and in harmony with all his other words on the subject. (From time to time I have italicized words in the cited scriptures to focus attention on their special relevance to the point being made.)

I must tell you up front that what you are about to read is not always orthodox thinking about the afterlife, particularly with regard to the traditional understanding that human mortality is the result of the Fall; nor the often-assumed ascent of the saved immediately into heaven; nor the consciousness (or lack of it) in the intermediate state of the dead; nor, finally, the nature of hell's fire. While I have presented the strongest case I can muster based upon my personal study of the Scriptures, I accept that, in the end, all of our best efforts to penetrate the unseen world of the dead must remain tentative. Surely, there will be many surprises when we reach the world beyond. On the other hand, it behooves us not to knowingly harbor unbiblical notions about matters which God clearly has entrusted to our understanding through his Word. And that is what this textual study is all about: clarifying what can be known, while avoiding speculation about that which simply hasn't been revealed.

May God richly bless us, then, as together we attempt to catch a glimpse of eternity through the doorway of death.

—F. LaGard Smith

PREFACE

It is said that there are two things of which we can be certain: death and taxes. But if death itself is certain, what follows after death appears to be far from certain. Indeed, there is great confusion, even among believers, as to just what the Bible teaches regarding the destiny which awaits us beyond the grave. Toward the goal of achieving greater clarity on the subject, this book brings to the table a fresh study of the Scriptures regarding death, sheol, hades, resurrection, judgment, heaven, and hell.

The conclusions reached in this work do not necessarily align with any well-delineated pattern of traditional afterlife assumptions. Its basic premises are as follows:

◆ That human mortality is not the result of sin, but is reflective of man's having been created "of dust" and "made a little lower than the angels."

◆ That, before the beginning of time, God envisioned an eternal relationship with humankind in his own heavenly realm, never intending that man would live forever on the earth.

◆ That by creative design, therefore, death is the "birth canal" leading from the "womb" of life on earth to an immortal life in heaven.

◆ That man's sin brought about his spiritual death, putting in jeopardy the eternal life which God desires with every person.

◆ That, just as spiritual death entered the world through Adam, spiritual life has been made possible by the atoning death of Jesus Christ.

◆ That when physical death occurs, the earthly human body disintegrates forever, never to be reconstituted from the dust to which it returns.

◆ That, upon death, man's innermost essence—known variously in Scripture as soul or spirit—rests in the "waiting room" of hades (sheol) until the simultaneous resurrection of both the righteous and the wicked.

• That hades (sheol) is a state of passive inactivity in which the soul is not conscious, but is said to be "sleeping;" and that, as with sleep, the moment one "awakes" at the resurrection will be as if no time whatsoever has passed since "falling asleep."

• That on the day of Christ's appearing, the dead will be raised, the present heavens and earth will be utterly destroyed, and Christ will sit in judgment on all who have ever lived.

• That the saved will be arrayed in immortal bodies fit for life with God in the heavenly realm; and that "eternal life" is not about length of time, but about the nature and quality of a life lived in intimacy with God.

• That the lost will be punished in hell, not with ongoing torment, but with everlasting destruction of the soul; and that this "second death" is the death of the soul which was the subject of God's many warnings, from the Garden to Jesus, and from Paul's epistles to John's Revelation.

• That there is no biblical support for the idea of purgatory within either hades or hell.

• That the popular notion of rapture is a fiction arising from a relatively recent misunderstanding of apocalyptic texts.

While, obviously, we won't know all the mysteries of life on the other side until we actually experience it, the central thesis of this book is that God has revealed much that we can understand; and that, even now, this perception can imbue our temporal life with a measure of the eternal.

PART I
Peering Over the Edge of Eternity

Can you fathom the mysteries of God?
Can you probe the limits of the Almighty?
They are higher than the heavens—what can you do?
They are deeper than the depths of the grave—
What can you know?

–Job 11:7-8

Anchor Verse - Matthew 25:34

"Come, you who are blessed by my Father; take your inheritance,
the kingdom prepared for you since the creation of the world."

Chapter Preview

If eternal life in heaven was *always* the idea, then we were never
meant to live forever on this tiny globe in a distant corner of the universe. Of one thing we can be sure: our physical, earthly bodies were
never intended for heaven, else why were they made of dust, "a little
lower than the angels"? Far from being a curse, our present mortality
is simply God's chosen way of taking us home to an eternal inheritance in heaven.

What results from sin is spiritual, not physical, death. As with
Adam and Eve, your sin and mine would forever slam shut the door to
our eternal home were it not for the grace of God in Christ by which
eternal life for even the sinful soul is made possible.

1

FRAIL CHILDREN OF DUST, MADE FOR ETERNITY

If I find in myself a desire which no experience in this world can satisfy, the most probable explanation is that I was made for another world.

–C. S. Lewis

Perhaps you've heard of the young boy who had been particularly impressed with what he had learned from his Sunday School lesson the previous week–that man had come from dust and would also return to dust. Calling his mother to his room, he pointed at the unswept floor under his bed with an air of excitement, saying, "I don't know whether he's coming or going, but there's someone hiding under there!"

The young man may have missed the point somewhat, but it is all too easy for those of us who are older to forget that, in our human, physical bodies, we are essentially *dust*: "Frail children of dust," as William Crofts penned the phrase in his great anthem. Composed entirely of chemical elements which are of the earth, our natural bodies eventually will decompose, with every ounce of flesh and subatomic particles being recycled back into the lower elements. From earth to earth, dust to dust. Simple as that.

Although Paul reminds us (in 2 Corinthians 4:16) that even now "outwardly we are wasting away," it is only at the point of death that our rapid and complete disintegration will occur, whether the flesh itself deteriorates in a grave or whether the body's cremated ashes become indistinguishable from the dirt into which they fall. If this somehow seems an inglorious end for the physical body which we have grown to love, and in which we find reassuring personal identity, the fact remains that the fleshly part of us is destined to an ignominious desecration. (If you dare, think grub worms....) As often noted but rarely fully appreciated, our ultimate physical end is truly "the way of all flesh." Or as God put it to Adam (whose very name sounds like, and may be related to, *adamah*, the Hebrew word for *ground*): "By the sweat of your brow you will eat your food until you return to the ground, since from it you were taken" (Genesis 3:19).

If dust, what are the implications?

All of which leads to the compelling question of this chapter: Was physical, biological death a curse cast upon man as a consequence of Adam's sin, or was the process of "dust to dust" a part of God's plan from the very beginning? As undoubtedly you are aware, centuries of theological consensus has held that man's mortality is a result of the Fall. How much clearer could it be, for instance, than when God says to Adam: "You must not eat from the tree of the knowledge of good and evil, for when you eat of it you will surely die"? And, of course, Eve confirms that warning when she's talking to the serpent. Moreover, when Adam and Eve finally eat of the forbidden fruit, we all know that they are banished from the garden so that, among other reasons, they can't continue to eat of the tree of life and live forever. Besides all that, doesn't Paul say that death entered the world through Adam? And isn't death an enemy? And doesn't Satan have the power over death which Christ one day will overcome by throwing death and Hades into the lake of fire?

It's all there, plain as the nose on your face. How could anyone possibly take issue with this time-honored understanding of sin and death? And indeed, it *may very well be true*. Nothing is necessarily lost doctrinally if it *is* true. At the very least, virtually everyone agrees that sin brings about *spiritual* death, and also that, short of the Lord's coming while we are still alive, we are all going to die physically. So there is no disputing that both biological death and spiritual death are life-threatening realities, and if there is a biblically-supported nexus between the two kinds of death, who's to say otherwise?

The possibility remains, however, that there is an alternative way of biblically understanding biological death and spiritual death which could greatly enhance our appreciation of what ultimately is at stake. Are we really so sure that what we've always believed presents the strongest possible case for *why* we die? Are there any textual or practical difficulties raised by our traditional understanding? Might we have a deeper and fuller understanding of the significance of even biological death when we examine it more closely through unfamiliar lenses? Have we looked carefully enough at the pertinent texts, or perhaps even overlooked other scriptures which might point to the contrary?

It need hardly be said, of course, that to challenge any consensus of this magnitude is to engage in an enterprise in which one can only think aloud and beg the scrutiny of others. If the case is not made, what most of us have always believed at least will be better understood. If, on the other hand, the case is convincing, then our understanding will be all the better for having conformed more closely to the Word.

Although the rest of this book does not necessarily hinge upon the conclusions reached in this chapter, the potential for an enhanced understanding of the whole range of afterlife issues is well worth the present discussion. So think of it as tentative. Just consider it. Allow yourself to sit back and ask: What if? If, in the end, you remain more comfortable with the obvious rather than the inferred, then by all means stick with it. Without any question, the traditional view is certainly more obvious.

God obviously had options

When you think about it, *immortality* has meaning only with reference to *mortality*. But what does it mean to be "mortal"? Is dying necessarily part of being "mortal"? It is not outside the realm of possibility that God initially might have intended to "translate" every human being out of this *mortal* world at some point into the heavenly, *immortal* realm (just as he did with Enoch and Elijah); and that, instead, biological death was introduced as a penalty for man's sin, bringing with it both pain and fear, and a brevity of life never originally contemplated. Yet if, indeed, death was meant as a necessary penalty for sin, then it hardly seems likely that either Enoch or Elijah would have been "translated," since presumably neither of them was sinless.

It is also conceivable that God knew in advance we would sin, and determined even before Creation that he would impose on us the penalty of biological death, intending all along that he would then redeem us from physical death to bring us into a glorified state with him in heaven. But that hypothesis doesn't speak particularly well of a God who would make any part of his plan for transporting us into the eternal realm dependent upon the contingency of our own sinfulness.

So from this point forward, when we speak of man's "mortality," we are not talking merely about some outer limitation on man's earthly experience before entering into an eternal realm, but specifically about the physical, biological death which all of us will experience should the Lord tarry. The crucial question remains: Do we die in the flesh because of sin, or is death simply part of God's original plan to bring us into a fuller, more intimate relationship with himself? Naturally, the clearer understanding we have of death itself, the greater our appreciation will be for that which lies beyond.

Where did we get the idea of death as punishment?

Support for the traditional understanding of death's origin and meaning is partially drawn from what appears to be the penalty clause of Genesis, Chapter 3: "for dust you are and to dust you will return." Given the extraordinary nature of Adam and Eve's existence in the Garden (Who today has conversations with serpents?), any uncorroborated understanding we might gain from their experience must surely be conditional. But the context of that statement certainly appears to be concerned with manly sweat and menial labor, not death: "Cursed is the ground because of you; through painful toil you will eat of it all the days of your life" (Genesis 3:17). If anything, those closing words—*all the days of your life*"—would suggest that man's life on earth was intended from the very beginning to have natural, temporal limitations. That man's days on earth are numbered appears in this verse merely to be assumed as a matter of fact.

The same assumption also seems to be reflected in the parallel structure of verse eighteen: "By the sweat of your brow you will eat your food [penalty] until you return to the ground [simply indicating the *duration* of the penalty], for dust you are and to dust you will return [recognizing Adam's natural mortality]."

Also note in this regard what is said when Adam is finally sent into exile: "So the LORD God banished him from the Garden of

Eden to work the ground from which he had been taken" (Genesis 3:23). Not a word about death. Instead, the emphasis once again is on Adam's having to earn his living. No longer does he have the luxury of simply reaching out and eating from the tree of life. The grand irony is that, in order to sustain his life until he once again becomes "dust," Adam is forced to engage in the sweaty work of breaking up the very clods of dirt out of which he himself has been created.

Where penalty seems not to be a factor

Reaching beyond the Creation account itself, in what way, if any, is the "dust to dust" phraseology in Genesis qualitatively different from the quite matter-of-fact usage which we find in the "prayer of Moses" (Psalm 90)?

> *Before the mountains were born*
> *Or you brought forth the earth and the world,*
> *From everlasting to everlasting you are God....*
>
> *You turn men back to dust,*
> *saying, "Return to dust, O sons of men."*
> *For a thousand years in your sight*
> *are like a day that has just gone by,*
> *or like a watch in the night.*
> *You sweep men away in the sleep of death;*
> *they are like the new grass of the morning–*
> *though in the morning it springs up new,*
> *by evening it is dry and withered....*
>
> *The length of our days is seventy years–*
> *or eighty, if we have strength....*
>
> *Teach us to number our days aright,*
> *that we may gain a heart of wisdom....*

In the sentiments of this moving psalm, man's return to the dust is but an assumed feature of the brevity of man's life in contrast to the Ancient of Days. Granted, this text is no "smoking gun" providing irrefutable proof that life's brevity was not a matter of punishment.

But there's simply no hint here that our physical death is a curse for sin; if anything, that it was God himself who determined our life on earth would be as fleeting as "the new grass of the morning."

Should anyone still insist that the "dust to dust" clause is not merely *descriptive* of what happens naturally but *prescriptive* of what would happen in the future because of sin, there is yet another question to be asked. Is it not incredibly strange that there is no comparable penalty of death imposed on Eve, who was, after all, the first to eat the forbidden fruit? Yet her "sentencing," if you will, consists of increased pain in childbirth, not death; and of conjugal submission, not capital punishment.

Overtime, not sudden death

Which brings us back to the first of two primary proof texts in favor of the traditional view, the warning itself which God gave to Adam: "You must not eat from the tree of the knowledge of good and evil, for when you eat of it you will surely die" (Genesis 2:17). As several translations indicate, the original text implies an even greater immediacy of punishment, saying "*in the day you eat thereof,* you will surely die." Taken literally, of course, that never happened. Unlike Ananias and Sapphira (Acts 5), neither Adam nor Eve dropped dead on the day of their sin, or anytime soon thereafter. In fact, Adam lived to the ripe old age of 930.

It can be argued quite legitimately, of course, that Adam's *eventual* demise is the "death" which never would have happened but for his sin in the Garden–that the penalty attached at the moment of sin, but the execution of that penalty followed in time. (1 Corinthians 1:18 suggests an intriguing parallel with spiritual death, where Paul uses the word *perishing* in an ongoing, continuing sense, as if to remind us that, just as salvation remains an ongoing process for those who are already saved, death too is a process.) However, the first objection surely has to be that, with each passing year of additional life, the "sting" of death was further and further mitigated. For those of us living in the era of "threescore and ten," Adam's prolonged life span seems generous indeed–hardly resembling anything like punishment.

Do plants and animals die because of sin?

Then there is the problem of relating human death to the natural deaths experienced by all the other living creatures–deaths which obviously are unassociated with sin. Are we to believe that, but for Adam's sin, cats and dogs and fish and fowl would have lived forever on the planet? Are we to believe that death in both the plant and animal kingdoms is a result of the Fall? Given God's expressed grief over having made man, one does begin to wonder. For it was not animals, but man, whose thoughts were continually evil (Genesis 6:5). Yet surprisingly we read about a mystifying linkage made between sinful man and unsinful lower animals when God contemplated wiping the slate of creation clean with the Flood. Said the Lord in his anger: "I will wipe mankind, whom I have created, from the face of the earth–men and animals, and creatures that move along the ground, and birds of the air–for I am grieved that I have made them" (Genesis 6:7).

Them? Does God mean that he's grieved at having made all the other living creatures as well as morally-rebellious humans? If perhaps there is much more we might like to know about why, in Noah's day, God chose virtual extinction for more than the single offending species, two things are crystal clear: 1) the Flood wasn't the fault of any insect, bird, or beast; and 2) neither faith nor righteous living had anything to do with the fact that a particular boatload of animals happened to survive. There being no apparent link between death and sin in the animal kingdom, the human process of dying cannot automatically be considered as inconsistent with man's created nature prior to Adam's sin. If animals die without sinning, what reason is there to believe that man's sin was necessarily the cause of human death?

The writer of Ecclesiastes confirms the obvious, that in terms of sheer mortality, "Man's fate is like that of the animals; the same fate awaits them both: As one dies, so dies the other. All have the same breath; man has no advantage over the animal....All go to the same place; all come from dust, and to dust all return" (Ecclesiastes 3:19-20).[1] Do you not find it striking that the same "dust-to-dust" language which we've always associated with Adam's death penalty is here applied to both man *and animals?* If we are to take the words "to dust you shall return" as a judicial sentencing for sin, does this mean that

---

1 Using Ecclesiastes for doctrinal support on any issue is always problematic, as is also true of the book of Job. In each case, the writer is struggling with what he should believe about some of life's greatest questions. In Ecclesiastes the meaning of life is at issue. In Job, the question has to do with why the righteous suffer. Unlike other genre of biblical literature, one cannot always be completely certain whether any given statement is intended to state a doctrinal truth as opposed to merely expressing a quite natural human doubt. What may be said safely is that, unless the context is plainly contrary, statements in Ecclesiastes and Job at times can be corroborative of more straightforward texts and thus provide significant pieces of the puzzle which ultimately informs our doctrinal understanding of the afterlife.

animals are also sinful; or perhaps that animals were destined to dust all along, but man ended up there only because of sin? To the contrary, does it not seem that our working hypothesis is further confirmed here–that returning to dust has nothing to do with sin, either for animals *or man*; and that biological death in both the animal kingdom and in the family of man was part of God's plan all along?

Naturally, if we had nothing else to go on apart from our own human observation, we could be excused for asking, as did the writer of Ecclesiastes: "Who knows if the spirit of man rises upward and if the spirit of the animal goes down into the earth?" (3:21). By revelation, of course, we know that, unlike animals, man is not just a *mortal* being but also a *moral* being with a spirit created in the image of God which will indeed rise upward from the earth. Yet Ecclesiastes surely is right in noting man's common mortality with animals, wholly apart from the issue of sin.

If we listen carefully to Job, there is no hint of only the unrighteous dying, but *everyone*. "I know you will bring me down to death," Job says to God, "*to the place appointed for all the living*" (Job 30:22). Even considering the two well-known exceptions to that rule, Enoch and Elijah, we see again that sin and physical death are not always invariably bonded together. Are we to believe that Enoch and Elijah were sinless? Yet neither one tasted death, being supernaturally translated out of this world for having (as specifically noted in Enoch's case) "walked with God"–which was also said regarding Noah, who died nevertheless. Thus, even the exceptions prove the rule. Unlike horse and carriage, love and marriage, there is no necessary pairing between man's sin and the physical corruption of his fleshly body.

Where physical death is, in fact, the punishment

Before leaving Noah and the Flood behind, it should be noted that, without question, the tens of thousands of those who died in the deluge were being put to death for sin. In this case, of course, the hastening of mortality for those who drowned was a judicial penalty, no less than that imposed on all those who were stoned to death under the Law of Moses. But we mustn't forget that even the righteous Noah was a man of sin, yet death by drowning did not come to him as a penalty for sin. Were someone to insist that Noah the righteous sinner was saved by the grace of God (which is true), he nevertheless eventually died of old age, all of which suggests that neither sin nor salvation was a factor in his mortality...or in ours. Whereas sin can result in a person's being put to death prematurely as a penalty hastening the inevitable, the inevitable itself (biological death) may well not be a penalty for sin.

Crucially, the new perspective under consideration here would go a long way toward explaining Jesus' own death on the cross. Are we to believe that the Son of Man never would have died of old age had he not been crucified–that, because he was without sin, he would have lived forever on this earth? The Hebrew writer (Hebrews 2:14) tells us that, since we are of flesh and blood–which is to say *mortal*–Jesus shared in every aspect of our humanity, from being born of a woman to suffering the pangs of death. No matter how it might have happened–whether by accident, disease or old age–we have no reason to believe other than that even the sinless Jesus eventually would have died, both to identify with us in that common human experience and to show us by a subsequent resurrection that death is not the end. (Indeed, to *ensure* that death was not the end!)

But when Jesus' crucifixion on Golgotha hastened his inevitable death, that cruel, man-imposed, yet God-purposed sacrifice made it possible for Jesus' blood to atone for your sins and mine. The prospect that Jesus quite probably would have died in any event does not in the least detract from the enormity of his personal sacrifice in giving up his physical life on the cross so that the sin which separates us from God in spiritual death might be taken away.

A time to die

Whatever else it may be, death is as natural as dust. Whether for man or for animals; whether for ancient giant redwoods or for the fragile lilies of the field–the story is the same for all living creatures: There's "a time to be born and a time to die." The writer of Ecclesiastes was not mistaken when he wrote: "There is a time for everything, and a season for every activity under heaven" (Ecclesiastes 3:1-2, 11)–the operative words being *under heaven*. Can we begin to accept that, *under heaven*, "He made everything beautiful [or "appropriate" NASV] in its time"...including death?

Beautiful Perhaps this idea is what Paul had in mind when he observed that "while we are in this tent, we groan and are burdened, because we do not wish to be unclothed but to be clothed with our heavenly dwelling, so that what is mortal may be swallowed up by life" (2 Corinthians 5:4). *Under heaven*, there cannot be unending life, only mortality. It's not a question of *man's* nature, but of *heaven's*. Anything less than heaven has built-in limitations. Because immortality is a unique characteristic of heaven, that which is associated with earth has no option but to be mortal. Therefore, it is as a gateway to the immortal realm that death on earth becomes "beautiful" or "appropriate," or at least begins to make more sense. Qualified only by what we said earlier about God's theoretical option to "translate" us into heaven, the fact remains that, without mortality on earth, the immortality of heaven could never be experienced. So it is that the psalmist could write with serenity, "Precious in the sight of the Lord is the death of his saints" (Psalm 116:15). Viewing death's effectual role from the perspective of heaven, God has a far more positive outlook on funerals, cemeteries, and graves than do we.   Heb. 2:14+15

When death our friend becomes death our enemy

It is, of course, a truism that most folks want to go to heaven, but who among us is eager to die? It's the sting of death which prompts our schizophrenia. As that illustrious theologian, Woody Allen, put it: "I'm not afraid to die. I just don't want to be there when it happens!" And, of course, even our Lord prayed that, if it were possible, he would rather not partake of the agonizing cup of death which he faced.

If death can be our trusted friend ushering us into the realm of the imperishable, death can also be an implacable enemy. For the unsaved, of course, death is not a bridge to joyous immortality with God, but a grim and final barrier beyond which all hope is lost. Nor is death our friend when we think of the often-excruciating pain, horrible separation, and earthly sorrow which accompany it. That's a part of death in which Satan takes special delight–the part which tempts us to think that no loving God could permit the pain of death, or to believe that God *doesn't care* when our loved ones are suddenly and violently taken from us. But most of all, Satan loves our *fear* of dying. He knows how that fear immobilizes us. How it puts us in denial. How we frenetically busy ourselves with empty earthly pursuits, as if in so doing we could block out death's eventuality.

24

Jesus was under no illusions about death as an enemy. Even knowing that he was about to bring his friend Lazarus back to life, Jesus wept. In a far more profound way, Jesus acknowledged human mortality seriously by his willingness to personally experience death. If "God wrapped in human flesh" was ever to be anything more than a meaningless charade, the incarnate Christ had to identify with us in every way, including both the experience of death itself and sharing in our fearful anticipation of death. The Hebrew writer assures us that Jesus tasted of death in both senses: "Since the children have flesh and blood, he too shared in their humanity so that by his death he might destroy him who holds the power of death–that is, the devil–and free those who all their lives were held in slavery by their fear of death" (Hebrews 2:14,15).

Note, here, that man's death is specifically tied to our "having flesh and blood"–not to our having a sinful nature or to personal sins which we have committed. Without question, Jesus' blood was necessary as an atonement for our sins. But it is equally true that he died simply to share in our mortality, and to help us overcome our fear of that very mortality.

By his death on the cross, and even more so by his resurrection from the grave, Christ forever unclenched Satan's death grip on our fear of death's finality. Whereas, in the Garden of Eden, Satan's cunning lie was that sinful man would never die, his new tack was the equally cunning lie–still believed by many–that nothing of man survives death...that when we die–like the proverbial dog, Rover–we're dead all over.

Such a hopeless death, of course, could hardly be anything but fearful. Nor could it ever be thought of as "beautiful" or "appropriate," as suggested in Ecclesiastes. But death as an open door to eternal life takes on a wonderful new meaning. And so Ecclesiastes does not leave us simply with the morbid reminder that there is "a time to die," but speaks positively of a Creator who "has also set eternity in the hearts of men...." (Ecclesiastes 3:12).

The idea here is not necessarily that God has put a little bit of eternity in all of us to make us long for heaven while we are in this world, but perhaps simply that (as the NRSV puts it) "he has put a sense of past and future" into our minds. Even so, the history of most cultures, replete with their elaborate death rituals anticipating the afterlife, stands as ongoing testimony to man's irrepressible belief that something of the human experience must live on even after death.

Death in God's eternal plan

If, indeed, there is life beyond the grave, nevertheless it's first things first. *Under heaven*, death's indispensable role in relation to eternity becomes crucial. Since "flesh and blood cannot inherit the kingdom of God" (1 Corinthians 15:50), our earthly bodies must of necessity be laid aside to make way for our full entry into that heavenly kingdom. Of one thing we can be sure: our physical, earthly bodies were never intended for heaven, else why were they made of dust? Not some glorified "angel dust" or stardust, mind you. Simply dust. Closer to the kind of dust the young man spied with wonder under his bed. As Paul pointedly reminds us, that which is perishable by nature was never meant to inherit an imperishable heaven (1 Corinthians 15:54).

Perhaps we've rushed too quickly over Paul's introduction in his letter to Titus, where he speaks of "a faith and knowledge resting on the hope of eternal life, which God, who does not lie, *promised before the beginning of time....*" (Titus 1:2). Long before the Fall, in the eternal realm of heaven when mankind was but a gleam in God's eye and time on earth had not yet begun, God promised (to whom but himself?) that one day man would share the bliss of eternal existence. So why did he not create us as heavenly beings to begin with? We simply aren't told. Why planet Earth? Why dust? Why three-score-and-ten *here* first instead of a timeless eternity *there* now? God alone knows.

All we know is what has been revealed: that before we can experience that which is but a wishful hope of eternity embedded deep within our hearts, our earth-bound mortality must take leave of its senses and be tossed forever into oblivion. That this was the plan from the very beginning–long before man was created, much less sinned–we have on the highest authority, from Jesus' own lips. Describing the Great Judgment scene when the Son of Man will sit on his throne in heavenly glory and divide the sheep from the goats, Jesus tells us that the King will say to those on his right: "Come, you who are blessed by my Father; take your inheritance, *the kingdom prepared for you since the creation of the world*" (Matthew 25:34).

If eternal life on earth were ever the idea, there would have been no need for heaven. By contrast, if eternal life in heaven was *always* the idea, then man was never meant to live forever on this tiny globe in a distant corner of the universe. Far from being a curse, our present mortality is simply God's chosen way of taking us home to our eternal inheritance in heaven. How could it be any plainer? "Now it is God who has made us for this very purpose" (2 Corinthians 5:5).

Lower than the angels

Surely it is not without significance that David refers to man's being made "a little lower than the angels" (Psalm 8:5). In fact, a footnote to Hebrews 2:7 in the NIV (which quotes Psalm 8:5) suggests the intriguing alternative: "You made him *for a little while* lower than the angels." Was the writer speaking only of Jesus, the Son of Man, or of all humankind? Given the reference to Psalm 8, the suggestion is that, unlike the angels, who do not experience death within the timelessness of heaven's eternity, man was never intended to live forever in his earthly environment. *For a little while*, man was to experience a mortality unknown to heavenly beings. The obvious implication is that man's mortality was not at all a judicial penalty for sin. Rather, it was God's intent all along that man's existence on earth would be but a temporary prelude to our ultimate destiny in the life to come, when, along with the angels, we too will be immortally arrayed.

Have you ever considered that Christ's incarnation was an exact reversal of our own destiny, in which the One who was immortal, for our sakes became mortal? Little wonder the Hebrew writer tells us that "surely it is not angels he helps" by his having appeared in flesh and blood, "but Abraham's descendants" (Hebrews 2:16). Like the temporal, mortal descendants of Abraham, the Son of Man was also made a little lower than the angels, so that he might be crowned with glory and honor "*in the world to come*" (Hebrews 2:5-8).

What could be clearer? From the dawn of creation, there have been two parallel worlds...worlds apart: a heavenly world of the eternal; and an earthly world enmeshed in time. There's the heavenly world, both immortal and imperishable; and the earthly world, where mortality reigns and all nature is prone to perish. Paul pointedly contrasts those parallel worlds when he urges the Colossians: "Set your minds on things above, not on earthly things" (Colossians 3:2). There is, he says, an earthly nature and a heavenly nature. Things pertaining to the one are temporal and passing; things of the other are eternal.

And how can we ignore Paul's contrast between Christ and Adam? "The first man was of the dust of the earth," says Paul, "the second man from heaven" (1 Corinthians 15:47). Before Adam ever took his first furtive glance at the forbidden fruit, he was a qualitatively different person than any heavenly being. Heaven is an immortal realm. By contrast, dust is...well...*dust!* There's nothing immortal about it. So in order for mortality to put on immortality, there must be *some means* of being transported from dust to glory, a function which biological death suitably provides.

Even the universe is in a death spiral

Indeed, it is not only man who groans for an end to his earthly existence and eagerly looks forward to being clothed in immortality. Our decaying universe itself longs to shrug off the diminishing force of its own entropy and, as it were, to share in the fulfillment of all things in heaven. In one of Paul's most intriguing and enigmatic passages ever, we are told that "the creation waits in eager expectation for the sons of God to be revealed. For the creation was subjected to frustration, not by its own choice, but by the will of the one who subjected it, in hope that the creation itself will be liberated from its bondage to decay and brought into the glorious freedom of the children of God" (Romans 8:19-21).

What Paul appears to be telling us is that God made the cosmos itself to be as temporal as man—that, as we know even from science, the universe is growing old, getting tired, slowing down. Not only is there "change and decay in all around I see..." as William Monk penned it, but we know that "the earth will wear out like a garment" (Isaiah 51:6); and that—finally, dramatically, and cataclysmically—in the day of the Lord, "the heavens will disappear with a roar; the elements will be destroyed by fire, and the earth and everything in it will be laid bare" (2 Peter 3:10). Thus, even the natural universe itself anticipates that Great Day when our human bondage to death and decay finds freedom and fulfillment in a spiritual universe beyond.

There is, then, *this world*–in which both man and the Son of Man have operated on a level of human activity lower than that of the heavenly beings–and there is *the world to come*, in which immortally-arrayed man, like the ascended Son of Man, will know nothing of "dust," but only glory! That, and not the eating of forbidden fruit, seems to be a better, stronger explanation of why "death is the destiny of every man" (Ecclesiastes 7:2).

We're homeward bound!

Rather than being the result of sin, our earthly mortality has to do with where we are headed, which is *home!* After describing in detail the inexorable process of our growing old, Ecclesiastes concludes by saying: "Then man goes to his eternal home and mourners go about the streets" (Ecclesiastes 12:5). Whatever the writer may have understood (or misunderstood) about the nature of man's "eternal home," on this side of the cross we have a hope made certain of an eternal, heavenly abode. So it is that we joyfully sing: "This world is not my home; I'm just a-passing through."

If our working hypothesis is correct, death is not a consequence, but a sequence; for it is both the end of life on earth and the beginning of a life beyond. More to be anticipated, it's the very mode by which, in God's divine plan, we are borne away to our heavenly home. Our true home. The eternal home which God had in mind for us from before the dawn of creation.

Don't forget the other tree

Much has been made of Adam and Eve's having eaten from the tree of the knowledge of good and evil. But what about the *other* tree in the middle of the Garden–the tree of life–from which, presumably, Adam and Eve were eating life-sustaining fruit? Although the tree of life had never been put off-limits, apparently alarm bells sounded all around the heavenly Throne when the tree that *was* off-limits became the object of man's desire. Once man had presumed to know (by eating of the first tree) what only God could know, God said of man: "He must not be allowed to reach out his hand and take also from the tree of life and eat, and live forever." Evidently, man's sin only confirmed to God that man was not yet ready for the eternal life which God had contemplated for man. But (as later scriptures clearly signal) it still begs the question of *where* God had intended man's eternal existence to be, whether on the earth or in heaven.

There is also possibly something more to be read between the lines. After all, what makes God *God*? Is it not timeless existence and ultimate moral wisdom–the two quintessential hallmarks of divinity put at risk when God dared to create man in his own image? So it is that, on earth (*under heaven*), man was never meant to have the kind of eternal nature characteristic of God himself. Both by definition and declaration, God alone is from everlasting to everlasting, without either beginning or end. In stark contrast, humankind was created finite, temporal, and mortal. Which is to say, subject to death. If future immortality of man's soul was the ultimate goal, it would be on God's terms, not man's; in God's timing, not within man's own grasp. In the meantime, death would be as integral a part of man's existence as immortality is an integral part of God's.

What death are we talking about?

If earthly mortality was not an intended punishment for our sin, but rather a natural, necessary part of our earthly human existence, what are we to make of Eve's conversation with the serpent? As we all know, the wily serpent had the temerity to ask, "Did God really say, 'You must not eat from any tree in the garden'?" To which Eve replied, "We may eat fruit from the trees in the garden, but God did say, 'You must not eat fruit from the tree that is in the middle of the garden, and you must not touch it, or you will die.'" Whereupon the serpent hissed out the most cunning of lies–"You will *not* surely die"–and Eve fell for it, bringing on herself God's judgment (Genesis 3:1-5).

As previously noted, Eve did not drop dead the moment she succumbed to temptation. Nor did Adam. So, if the hypothesis presented in this chapter is correct–that not even their eventual deaths were the consequence of sin–what are we possibly to make of this conversation? Was the serpent right after all, or is the problem, perhaps, that we have misunderstood the nature of the "dying" which God promised and which the serpent denied? Is it possible that we've jumped wrongly to the conclusion that the "dying" in dispute refers to the physical body's biological demise, when, with far greater consequences, it has reference to death of the soul?

Assuming for a moment that it's *death of the soul* we're talking about, what exactly does that mean? Did Eve's soul die the moment she sinned? In a sense, yes. Just as death is a separation of the soul from the body, spiritual death is a separation between ourselves and God. In that sense, you and I and everyone who has ever sinned have all died spiritually. No less life-threatening than a critical-care patient being taken off life-support, we have disconnected ourselves from the only source of spiritual life that can sustain our inmost essence. When that happens, it is only by reconnecting to God through Christ that any of us have hope of renewed spiritual life.

However, as we shall see more and more clearly throughout this study, there is yet another, more literal sense in which we must understand "death of the soul." When a person refuses to reconnect to God, what is at risk is not simply temporary spiritual alienation, but ultimate, total, and terminal destruction of one's personhood. *That* irreversible, eternal "death of the soul" is the potential of all who sin and fall short of God's glory. It is *that* complete, once-and-for-all separation from God's presence which every one of us would experience but for the grace of God through Christ.

The ancients themselves, of course, did not have a fully articulated understanding of "spiritual death," much less the ultimate, final "death of the soul." (It's even hard to imagine that Adam and Eve would have had any initial appreciation for death of any kind, whether physical or spiritual, without God explaining it to them further. Did they see animals devouring one another in the Garden, or dying perhaps for other reasons?) But the ancients must have known *something* of the distinction between physical and spiritual death.

Everybody dies, but not everyone dies!

Consider in this regard the compelling text of Ezekiel, Chapter 18, where we find the familiar words which (more often in times past) have made their way onto any number of billboards and hand-scrawled road signs: "The soul that sins, it shall die." While the point of the chapter has more to do with personal responsibility for sin ("The son will not share the guilt of the father, nor will the father share the guilt of the son"), one can hardly miss the obvious link between sin and death. Referring to three generations within the same family, the text tells us first of "a righteous man who does what is just and right." After listing all his many virtues, the passage concludes, saying: "That man is righteous; he will surely live."

But it seems our righteous man has a violent son who wickedly does just the opposite of his father. "Will such a man live?" Ezekiel asks rhetorically. "He will not! Because he has done all these detestable things, he will surely be put to death and his blood will be on his own head."

The good news is that this wicked man himself has a son who, despite witnessing all the sins of his father, does not follow in his father's evil footsteps, but is righteous instead. No prizes for guessing that "he will not die for his father's sin; he will surely live."

Beyond the issue of personal accountability, what we learn from Ezekiel's three hypotheticals is that death is inextricably related to sin. Yet, once again the question is begged: What kind of death are we talking about—*physical* or *spiritual?*

Under the Mosaic Law, of course, numerous listed sins warranted literal bodily death by stoning. And at first sight it looks as if the unrighteous father in our family trilogy is one such example. (When he is *put to death*, his *blood* is to be on his own head.) Further along, however, the text speaks about the "wicked man who turns away from all the sins he has committed...and does what is just and right." Of that penitent man, Ezekiel says, "he will surely live; he will not die." It is obvious, then, that we're not dealing here with those who were literally stoned to death for their sins under the Law, else what opportunity would they have had to change their wicked ways? Clearly, Ezekiel has to be talking about something far more profound.

When we go back to basics, the one thing we know for sure is that *everybody dies*—the righteous and the wicked alike. But it is only the wicked of whom it is said, "The soul who sins is the one who will die." So the crucial question is: *In what way will the unrighteous "die" that the righteous won't?* Since we know that the unrighteous do not simply drop dead because of their sin, we are left with only one conclusion: that Ezekiel is pointing us to an obvious causal connection between sin and *spiritual* death—indeed, eventually, even *eternal* death, the ultimate destruction of the unredeemed soul at some point following Judgment.

Death of the soul

For the moment, listen closely as Jesus says: "I tell you the truth, if anyone keeps my word, he will never see death" (John 8:51). Is it even remotely likely that Jesus is talking here about physical, biological death? If not, in what way are his words any different from God's warning to Eve about dying? In fact, put the two statements back to back, and what you have is merely two sides of the same coin: a) If you eat of the prohibited fruit, you will die; b) If you keep my word, you will not die. In the same way that Jesus paired sin with spiritual death, surely it was also spiritual death of which God spoke in his caution to Adam and Eve. Rather than contemplating mere death of the body, God's warning was about death of the soul—the very distinction which Jesus made when he warned his disciples: "Do not be afraid of those who kill the body but cannot kill the soul" (Matthew 10:28).

What results from sin, therefore, is the death—either temporary or eternal—of that part of us which will survive the complete deterioration of our bodies. As with Adam and Eve, your sin and mine separates us from God and slams shut the door to our prepared eternal home. Their own banishment from the Garden is a graphic picture of our being denied entrance into what ought to be our heavenly abode. Because of sin, immortality with God is put at risk. And because of sin, we have every reason to fear the finality of death. For when the body dies, the soul lives on; but if soul dies, there is nothing left to live.

Praise God, of course, that spiritual death having the potential for ultimate, eternal death of the soul is not the end of the story. As even the youngsters among us know by heart: "God so loved the world that he gave his one and only Son, that whoever believes in him shall not perish but have eternal life." Through the overflowing grace of God in Christ, eternal life for even the sinful soul is made possible. We who are saved, therefore, need not fear either the physical death of the body, as if it were ushering us into oblivion, nor spiritual death of the soul, which could indeed cast us irretrievably into oblivion. And so, together with saved sinners from Adam to Abraham, and David to Daniel, all the faithful righteous on this side of the cross shout in anticipated triumph, "'Where, O death, is your victory? Where, O death, is your sting?' The sting of death is sin, and the power of sin is the law. But thanks be to God! He gives us the victory through our Lord Jesus Christ" (1 Corinthians 15:55-57).

Death for all through Adam?

The second set of traditional proof texts–from Paul's letters to the Romans and the Corinthians–also appears to speak of physical death in relation to Adam's sin. But, on closer inspection, what first meets the eye may be misleading. Certainly, it is tempting to second Peter's motion regarding Paul's writing–that "his letters contain some things that are hard to understand" (2 Peter 3:16). However, the blame for Paul's seeming obscurity on the issue at hand may fall more at our feet than his. Since the word *death* can mean either physical or spiritual death, the particular meaning we take away from Paul's discussion of the subject is likely to be whichever definition we ourselves bring to the table. The challenge, therefore, is to take a fresh and honest look at all-too-familiar text–or, indeed, at all-too-often-ignored context.

In Romans, Chapter 5, the following words literally seem to jump out at us: "Therefore... sin entered the world through one man, and death through sin, and in this way death came to all men, because all sinned...." (Romans 5:12). Taken without further reflection, this verse could easily lead one to believe that physical, biological death became the fate of every man and woman as a result of Adam's sin. But first we must investigate what precedes the pivotal word, *Therefore,* which comes at the beginning of verse 12. What is it that Paul has been talking about which leads him to this point of summary and conclusion?

The letter to the Romans begins with Paul's bold declaration that he is not ashamed of the gospel, "because it is the power of God for the salvation of everyone who believes: first for the Jew, then for the Gentile. For in the gospel a righteousness from God is revealed, a righteousness that is by faith from first to last." All of which is not-too-subtle code signaling that, even with their venerated Laws of Moses, the Jews are no more acceptable to God than are Gentiles. Whether Jew or Gentile, all are sinners in need of a Savior.

After listing the sins of idolatry and homosexuality (which first-century Jews considered as heinous *Gentile* sins), Paul suddenly turns the tables and extends the list of sins to include those of which even the Jews would have to admit being guilty, such as greed, envy, malice, and arrogance. Since none of those particular sins would warrant the death penalty under the Laws of Moses, Paul's point takes on added significance. "Although they know God's righteous decree that those who do such things *deserve death*," says Paul, "they not only continue to do these very things but also approve of those who practice them" (1:32).

Why do they *deserve death*? Because "there is no one righteous, not even one" (3:19); "for all have sinned and fall short of the glory of God" (3:23). Yet, the good news is that all is not lost. There is hope for every sinner. Although Jews and Gentiles alike *deserve death*, "God 'will give to each person according to what he has done.' To those who by persistence in doing good seek glory, honor and immortality, he will give eternal life. But for those who...are evil, there will be wrath and anger" (2:6-8). Whereas even the righteous are sinners, and thus *deserve* death, by the grace of God they will be gifted with life eternal. By contrast, the unrighteous will get exactly what they deserve, which is death!...spiritual separation from God in this life and eternal, irreversible destruction of the soul following the Judgment to come.

But if sin—even the sin of the righteous—brings spiritual separation from God, how can anyone be saved? The simple, if profound, answer is that "while we were still sinners, Christ died for us" (5:8). While we were still God's enemies, "we were reconciled to him through the death of his son," and having been reconciled, we were "saved through his life!" (5:10).

Drum roll for the conclusion

With this glorious thought, we are brought full circle to chapter 5, verse 12, and that crucial word *Therefore*. Can there be any question at this point that Paul is addressing the issue of spiritual death and how we are saved from it? It was not physical, bodily death that entered the world through Adam's sin, and continues even now because of your sin and mine. Were that the case, then—by contrast—Christ's saving death would have brought an immediate end to all physical, biological death.

Note carefully the parallelism Paul presents between the two prototypes: Adam, representing death; and Christ, representing life. "For if by the trespass of the one man, death reigned through that one man, how much more will those who receive God's abundant provision of grace and of the gift of righteousness reign in life through the one man, Jesus Christ" (5:17). If the "death" which Adam represents were meant to be physical death, then, by the same token, the "life" which Christ represents would be merely physical life.

Had this been what Paul intended to say, then all physical death would have been done away with in Christ (or, at the very least, those who put their faith in Christ would never taste of death on earth). Since we know this isn't the case, we are left with but one conclusion: that the "death" of which Paul is speaking is spiritual separation from God's life-giving power, not the natural demise of the human body.

Should there be any remaining doubts about that, surely verse 19 puts them to rest. "For just as through the disobedience of the one man the many were made sinners, so also through the obedience of the one man the many will be made righteous." From beginning to end, Paul's argument presents a contrast between sin (together with the spiritual deadness which it brings) and salvation (together with the spiritual life it brings). The wonderful irony is that not even Adam, the first man to sin and thus the first to die spiritually, is outside the bounds of God's grace as made manifest through Christ.

Naturally, care must be taken not to extend Paul's parallelism beyond its intended bounds. We know that not all sinners who deserve ultimate destruction of the soul will be made righteous through Christ. Christ is simply the Door through which those who put their faith in him pass from spiritual death into spiritual life. Likewise, not all who sin were condemned to death by Adam's sin. Adam was simply the door through which sin entered the world, and thus the one who first brought condemnation raining down on man. In our theme passage (5:12), Paul is quick to remind us that each of us deserves death because of our *own* sin (*"because all sinned"*).

How to die before dying

As Paul's argument continues into Chapter 7, he simply can't quit talking about sin and its relation to spiritual death. "Once I was alive apart from the law," he says, "but when the commandment came, sin sprang to life and I died" (7:9) And again he laments, "For sin...put me to death" (7:11). Obviously, Paul is not telling us that he has already died physically. Rather, he's candidly describing his own life and death struggle with sin, which he shares with us in that well-known passage about not doing what he knows he should, and doing precisely what he knows he shouldn't. One gets the sense that, for Paul, sin and death are not just abstract theology, but a daily, personal battle. "What a wretched man I am!" he finally wails in desperation, "Who will rescue me from this body of death?" (7:24).

But Paul leaves neither himself nor us in despair, hastening on to say, "There is now no condemnation for those who are in Christ Jesus, because through Christ Jesus the law of the Spirit of life set me free from the law of sin and death" (8:1-2). Even so, Paul urges us soberly not to take that freedom for granted, but rather to live a life controlled by the Spirit. For if "the mind of sinful man is death, the mind controlled by the Spirit is life...." (8:6). According to Paul, sin and death are in a cosmic struggle, not just for our physical bodies, in and through which we sin, but for that part of us which is more closely related to the mind and the spirit.

Beginning to suffer from Pauline overload? Wish you had a neat, concise summary of Paul's understanding of the relationship between sin and death? Then look no further than Romans 6:23. "For the wages of sin is death; but the gift of God is eternal life through Jesus Christ our Lord." In the context of Chapter 6 ("offer yourselves to God, as those who have been brought from death to life...."), what Paul is saying, first of all, is that God has gifted us with a measure of his power which makes possible our living life to the fullest in the here and the now, as compared to the bleak, vacuous, meaningless existence of those who are spiritually dead. More than that, instead of paying us the wages of *eternal death* which we have earned for ourselves because of sin, God has graciously bestowed both the future promise and present empowerment of *eternal life.*

That Paul is not talking about human mortality when he uses the word "death" here is clear from the fact that, in Christ, we "have been brought from death to life" *even before we die!* So what other "death" could Paul possibly be addressing if not *spiritual* death–the same spiritual death that entered the world when Adam first sinned; and the same spiritual death for which God has mercifully given (to true believers) eternal life in exchange?

A case of mixed signals?

So are we home free at last on the issue of sin's not being related to physical, bodily death? Well, not quite. Just when we thought there were no more loose ends to deal with, Paul appears to pull one more from the fabric of the text. "If Christ is in you," he begins, "your *body* is dead because of sin, yet your spirit is alive because of righteousness. And if the Spirit of him who raised Jesus from the dead is living in you, he who raised Christ from the dead will also give life to your *mortal bodies* through his Spirit who lives in you" (8:10-11). Dead bodies? Mortal bodies? It certainly *sounds* like physical death, doesn't it?

Yet Paul just gave us a clue as to how this seeming conflict is resolved, when he asked: "Who will rescue me from this *body of death*?" Paul's body may well have been a "body of death" in a spiritual sense, but he was very much alive and well when he wrote those words! What, then, can he mean, but that his physical, earthly body is the *agency* through which spiritual death takes place? Surely, this is the very point of his admonition: "Therefore do not let sin reign in your mortal body so that you obey its evil desires. Do not offer the parts of your body to sin, as instruments of wickedness, but rather offer yourselves to God, as those who have been brought from death to life...." (6:12-13).

To say that, as Christians, we have been "brought from death to life" is not to say, of course, that our mortal bodies have now become immortal bodies. Our mortal bodies are still going to die. Paul is simply referring to that inmost spiritual part of ourselves which *deserves* to die, but is saved from eternal destruction because of God's grace working in us.

On the other hand, it is not as if our physical bodies have nothing whatsoever to do with the spiritual consequences of sin. To the contrary, because we have been imbued with spiritual life in Christ even while we remain in our mortal bodies, we therefore have a greater obligation than ever not to live according to the desires which emanate from those same bodies (8:12).

The special case where Paul speaks of physical death

That said, there remains one important sense in which Paul does indeed make a connection between Adam and physical death. It comes in 1 Corinthians, Chapter 15, where Paul is specifically responding to some who have rejected the very notion of resurrection. The context is crucial. Unlike all the other passages we have examined, including particularly Paul's Roman letter, here Paul unquestionably is contrasting physical, biological death (as represented by the first mortal, Adam) with bodily resurrection from the dead (as represented by Christ). "Christ has indeed been raised from the dead," Paul affirms, "the firstfruits of those who have fallen asleep. For since death came through a man, the resurrection of the dead comes also through a man. For as in Adam all die, so in Christ all will be made alive" (1 Corinthians 15:20-22).

In this passage, Paul is not addressing the *cause* of man's mortality, only the *fact* of it. Nor is he making any spiritual judgment about those who are raised–only the certainty that, one day, every person who has ever lived and died on earth will be brought back to life. Using a parallelism similar to that which we saw earlier in Romans, Paul is simply saying that, just as the first man, Adam, experienced physical death, so will we all; but, more importantly, that just as Christ experienced life after death, so too will we all. Christ's dramatic resurrection is proof that death is not the inescapable end of our existence–that there is life yet to come beyond the grave.

What happens to the righteous and the wicked following resurrection is the subject of later discussion. Suffice it to say for the moment that neither man's physical death nor his bodily resurrection has anything to do with the state of his spiritual relationship with God. It was God's intent all along that death and corruption of the body would be man's common fate; but also that each soul would survive to see yet another day.

A choice to make for all eternity

The writer of Ecclesiastes most probably was referring only to the *breath* or *life-force* of a man when he wrote: "Remember your Creator in the days of your youth...before the silver cord is severed...and the dust returns to the ground it came from, and the *spirit* returns to God who gave it" (Ecclesiastes 12:1-7). But if that's all that happens, why concern ourselves with remembering our Creator in the days of our youth? Whatever ambivalence Ecclesiastes may express about man's eternal destiny, from Christ's resurrection onward all doubt has been removed. As surely as our breath returns to God who gave it, so too our soul.

In his heart of hearts, of course, God's desire was for a timeless, loving relationship in the heavenly realm with every man and every woman created in his image. But, as we have been painfully reminded, our sin has made that potentially-blissful relationship problematic. In one way or another, we all have rejected God's gracious overtures of love. Nevertheless, "as a father has compassion on his children, so the LORD has compassion on those who fear him; for he knows how we are formed, he remembers that we are dust" (Psalm 103:13-14).

Wow! Is there a more reassuring passage in all of Scripture? *God hasn't forgotten that we are dust!* Indeed, "Not wanting anyone to perish, but everyone to come to repentance" (2 Peter 3:9), God offers us the same choice which Moses put before ancient Israel. "I have set before you life and death, blessings and curses," said Moses. "Now choose life, so that you and your children may live and that you may love the LORD your God" (Deuteronomy 30:19-20).

As if in a time machine, we are all taken back to the Garden and to the forbidden fruit. Which shall we choose: life or death? As for our fleshly bodies returning to dust, we have no option. Death is an open grave awaiting us all. But how we respond to sin and its eternal consequences is very much within our own hands.

Hands of dust...created for glory!

Anchor Verse - John 5:28-29

"...a time is coming when all who are in their graves will hear his voice and come out–those who have done good will rise to live, and those who have done evil will rise to be condemned."

Chapter Preview

Although the ancients did not have a clear picture of all that would happen in the afterlife, even in the Old Testament we find numerous intimations regarding resurrection. Certainly, belief in resurrection was alive and well during Jesus' day, despite the misgivings of the Sadducees. Paul, of course, speaks confidently of our being raised.

No proof of resurrection could be more compelling than Jesus' own empty tomb and his appearance before many witnesses. His resurrection is the very linchpin of a Christian's faith and hope. Any life lived in hope of heaven is a cruel joke if we are dead wrong about Jesus' resurrection, and–through him–our own.

2

THAT GREAT GETTIN'-UP MORNING

What reason have atheists for saying that we cannot rise again?
Which is the more difficult, to be born, or to rise again? That what has
never been, should be, or that what has been, should be again?

–Blaise Pascal
Pensées, XXIV

The very thought of living again after we die seems too fantastic to grasp. Indeed, it seems more fantasy than fact. As for the *fact* of resurrection, we have Jesus' own words: "Do not be amazed at this [yet we cannot help but be!], for a time is coming when all who are in their graves will hear his voice and come out–those who have done good will rise to live, and those who have done evil will rise to be condemned" (John 5:28-29). But accepting something academically, or theoretically, or doctrinally, is still a far cry from coming to grips with its reality. Why, if we are so certain of resurrection, do we live our lives in practical denial of it? Why, for instance, do we fear death as we do? And why are we so focused on living in the "here and now," as if there were no eternal tomorrow?

Maybe the reason is that the moment of death is so undeniably real to us, but beyond that–who *really* knows? As much as we might wish it (and, for weeks afterwards, still kind of expect it to happen), we know that our departed father or mother, or husband or wife, or child or best friend, isn't ever going to walk through the door again. Sure, we may be able to think of them on that ship crossing the ocean beyond the far horizon, and believe that, even though we will never see them again in this life, they're still alive as they approach that distant shore. And we can fervently believe that, one day, we will join them in that "great reunion in the skies." However, the certainty of their not walking through the door is a cruelly more tangible reality than the quite-lovely prospect of that which we believe in theory. And so, as life goes on and the memory of their death fades, we find ourselves once again living mostly in the present...and thinking only rarely and vaguely about our own death and resurrection.

In fact, with but the slightest bit of cynicism, it would be easy to believe that all the funeral emphasis on resurrection is only a saccharin palliative for those who mourn...simply words of well-meant comfort as the casket is lowered into the ground as the "final resting place" of our loved one. So, should we ever find ourselves truly beginning to wonder, it's time to seek again the assurance of God's promise that death is not the end. That resurrection is not a fantasy. That what we hope in our inmost being is actually and factually true.

Resurrection in the Old Testament

As we read through the Old Testament searching for what the ancients understood regarding death and afterlife, we are struck by the virtual absence of any well-defined afterlife teaching. Certainly, there is nothing like heaven's "pearly gates" and "streets of gold," nor anything specifically about hell, although the destruction of sinners is an oft-repeated theme. Yet surprisingly in the midst of all this uncertainty, we find numerous straightforward references to resurrection, as well as any number of indirect intimations.

To begin with, God is seen as having the *power* to bring about a resurrection. In Hannah's prayer of dedication for Samuel, she says of God: "The Lord brings death and makes alive; he brings down to the grave and raises up" (1 Samuel 2:6). Having personally experienced that God could bring forth life from the barrenness of her womb, for Hannah it wouldn't have been a great leap of logic that God could also bring life from the seeming hopelessness of a tomb.

The psalmist (in Psalm 71:20) echoes that sentiment, saying:

Though you have made me see troubles, many and bitter,
you will restore my life again;
from the depths of the earth
you will again bring me up.

But in Psalm 49, we get mixed signals. The psalmist first tells us not to envy the rich, because, like all other men (and animals alike), death and bodily decay are their final destiny:

But man, despite his riches, does not endure;
he is like the beasts that perish....

Like sheep, they are destined for the grave,
and death will feed on them...
their forms will decay in the grave....

Yet, for himself, the psalmist sees hope:

But God will redeem my life from the grave;
he will surely take me to himself....

We must exercise care regarding a number of Old Testament passages which seem to speak of resurrection, when, in fact, the intent is probably nothing more than being saved from the grave on *this side* of death. One such passage is Psalm 9:13-14. "Have mercy and lift me up from the gates of death, that I may declare your praises." Rather than referring to resurrection, it sounds more like the prayer of everyone who has ever bargained with God in the midst of the storm, vowing in desperation: "If you'll just get me out of this dire situation, I'll be the most righteous person you've ever seen!"

Another good example is found in Psalm 116, where the psalmist says, "For you, O LORD, have delivered my soul from death," making us wonder whether he is possibly contemplating resurrection. But a closer look reveals that he is talking about having knocked on death's door, yet lived to tell the tale. By God's grace, he can once again "walk before the Lord in the land of the living." While the "anguish of the grave [*sheol*]" momentarily stared him in the face, he never entered *sheol* to be resurrected from it.

Yet, there can be no mistaking the explicit language of resurrection in Psalm 16:10. Indeed, it is a messianic psalm having specific overtones regarding Christ: "You will not abandon me to the grave, nor will you let your Holy One see decay." And there is also the unforgettable imagery of Jonah and the "whale," about which every

Sunday School child has been told. Christ himself compared his death, burial, and resurrection to the extraordinary episode of Jonah who, while still in the belly of the great fish, prayed: "From the depths of the grave I called for help, and you listened to my cry....You brought my life up from the pit" (Jonah 2:2,6). Even if Jonah was rescued from a premature death, what, if not resurrection, is the picture we who are Christians read back into Jonah's being swallowed, as if in death, only to be brought back to life?

Children's eyes brighten, not only at the story of the whale-sized fish, but also at Ezekiel's vision of dry bones rattling back to life in the valley of the bones (Ezekiel 37:1-14). Although the vision is principally a prophecy of the new life Israel will have when God restores her spiritual dryness to spiritual life, the imagery of resurrection once again resonates throughout. "Son of man, can these bones live?" the Lord asks Ezekiel, reminiscent of Job's oft-quoted question about whether man will live again. God then answers his own question, saying to the bones, "I will make breath enter you, and you will come to life....Come from the four winds, O breath, and breathe into these slain, that they may live."

If you didn't know the historical context of Ezekiel's vision, you could be forgiven for thinking that the words which follow are from one of Paul's epistles, specifically addressing the Resurrection: "O my people, I am going to open your graves and bring you up from them....Then you, my people, will know that I am the LORD." And the imagery extends even to heaven itself when God promises, "I will put my Spirit in you and you will live, and I will settle you in your own land." As Israel was to be restored to her promised land, so we, too, will rise from the grave to dwell in ours.

Then there is that powerful passage from Hosea 13:14 which Paul later cites:

I will ransom them from the power of the grave;
I will redeem them from death.
Where, O death, are your plagues?
Where, O grave, is your destruction?

That Paul should conclude his treatise on resurrection (in 1 Corinthians 15) with this quotation from Hosea leaves no doubt about what this passage was meant to portend. Resurrection was not an afterthought to man's relationship with God as recorded in the Old Testament. It was what God had in mind for us all along.

Insights from the Book of Job

The uniqueness of the story of Job never leaves us completely comfortable about its intent. Sometimes what is said is simply devil's-advocate argumentation. So when Job asks (in 14:7-15) "If a man dies, will he live again?" we're not altogether sure whether the question is rhetorical, doubtful, factual, or simply wishful:

At least there is hope for a tree:
If it is cut down, it will sprout again,
and its new shoots will not fail....

But man dies and is laid low;
he breathes his last and is no more....

so man lies down and does not rise;
till the heavens are no more, men will not awake
or be roused from their sleep....

If only you would set me a time
and then remember me!
If a man dies, will he live again...?

You will call and I will answer you;
you will long for the creature your hands have made.

In the end, at least, there does seem to be hope. Indeed, it is Job who also gives us the opening words of that great hymn of encouragement (Job 19:25-26):

I know that my Redeemer lives,
and that in the end he will stand upon the earth [or upon my grave].
And after my skin has been destroyed,
Yet in my flesh [or apart from my flesh] I will see God;
I will see him with my own eyes—

I, and not another.
How my heart yearns within me!

Since Job specifies that he's talking about what will happen *after* his body has decayed, this is a particularly significant resurrection passage.[1] For Job, life after death is as certain as knowing that his Redeemer lives! Not necessarily, of course, meaning Christ our Redeemer, of whom Job would have had no knowledge.

Some scholars (as far back as John Chrysostom) believe this passage is more of a Christian-influenced "commentary" rather than a pure translation, seen especially in Jerome's Latin Vulgate. Given Job's seeming despair and hopelessness, David Clines (*Word Biblical Commentary*) renders the verse: "But I know that my champion lives and that he will rise last [to speak for me] on earth, even after my skin has thus been stripped from me. Yet, to behold God while still in my flesh–[that is my desire,] to see him for myself, with my own eyes, not as a stranger. My inmost being is consumed with longing."

As presented by the New English translation (revised), the picture is of a courtroom scene in which the defender has the final word: "But I know that my vindicator lives and that he will rise last to speak in court." Even if this breezy translation is truer to the text than Jerome's Vulgate (or even Handel's *Messiah*), the irony is that what Job hopes for comes to fruition in the person of Jesus Christ, our "advocate with the Father" (1 John 2:1). It is the resurrected Christ whom every eye will see as he speaks the final words at the last Judgment!

How could anyone miss it?

Given the texts we've just examined (as well as some inter-testamental writings which expanded on the resurrection motif), it seems curious that any Jew in the time of Christ could have had doubts about a future resurrection. We do know that belief in resurrection was alive and well during Jesus day, as evidenced, for example, by Jesus' conversation with Martha upon the death of Lazarus (John 11:23-26):

---

1 Given the "destruction of his skin," the NIV's alternative translation-apart from my flesh-best seems to capture the intended meaning. And how can the reference to his "eyes" be anything but metaphorical, emphasizing the personal nature of his own resurrection?

> *Jesus said to her, "Your brother will rise again."*
> *Martha answered, "I know he will rise again in the*
> *resurrection at the last day."*

Yet we also know that the sect of the Sadducees–constituting a respectable segment of the Jewish religious establishment–denied that very possibility. When Paul made his defense before the Roman governor Felix, he said to him: "I have the same hope in God as these men, that there will be a resurrection of both the righteous and the wicked" (Acts 24:15-21). "These men," to whom Paul referred, were resurrection-believing Pharisees, including the High Priest and some elders who had gone from Jerusalem to Caesarea to testify against Paul. However, as Paul went on to explain, what had landed him in trouble a few days earlier was the incident before the Sanhedrin where he had shouted out: "It is concerning the resurrection of the dead that I am on trial before you today." At that point, "a dispute broke out between the Pharisees and the Sadducees, and the assembly was divided" (Acts 23:6-8).

As the text goes on to explain, the Sadducees–unlike the Pharisees–did not believe in resurrection, nor in angels or spirits. Since the Sadducees had largely denied the world of the supernatural, any prospect of a metaphysical life following death would not have resonated well with their world view. Their attempt to hold hands with a supernatural God while remaining skeptical about the realm of the miraculous mirrors the perplexing schizophrenia of many theologians and religious leaders even today.

Earlier, of course, the Sadducees had challenged Jesus with their debate-portfolio hypothetical of the woman with the seven deceased husbands (Matthew 22:22-33)–asking whose wife she would be in heaven. Jesus dumbfounded them, saying their problem was not just being ignorant of the Scriptures (How could they have missed those passages which alluded to resurrection?), but also having a naturalistic worldview which automatically excluded virtually anything supernatural or miraculous. ("You do not know the power of God.")

Jews though they were, they might just as well have been the idolatrous Greeks whom Paul addressed on Mars Hill. According to Luke's record: "When they heard about the resurrection of the dead, some of them sneered" (Acts 17:32). Many in the halls of academia and elsewhere today are still sneering. One can hardly believe in resurrection when he has accepted, *a priori*, a purely naturalistic view of man's origin. "Natural selection" leaves no room for the supernatural, and "survival of the fittest" precludes any notion of survival of the soul. If man descended from apes, he has no soul.

Paul's defense of the resurrection

In his day, Paul took up the challenge of the skeptics who denied Jesus' resurrection, including, quite incredibly, even some in Corinth who were converted believers in Christ! How, possibly, could they have missed the whole point–"that Christ died for our sins according to the Scriptures, that he was buried, that he was raised on the third day according to the Scriptures....," and that in the days which followed he had appeared, not only to the apostles, but to more than five hundred of the brothers at the same time (1 Corinthians 15:1-7)?

Using a series of "if-then" arguments, Paul proceeds to show how Christ's resurrection is the very linchpin of a Christian's faith and hope. "If there is no resurrection of the dead, then not even Christ has been raised....And if Christ has not been raised, your faith is futile....If only for this life we have hope in Christ, we are to be pitied more than all men" (1 Corinthians 15:12-19).

One must never underestimate the importance of this fundamental Christian premise. If the story of Jesus' resurrection is nothing more than fanciful fiction dreamed up by his followers to justify their fanaticism, then our hope of living after death is equally fanciful. But if *in fact* Jesus was raised from the dead, never again to die, then the basis for our hope of immortality is real.

Not just an academic discussion

What so few seem to fully appreciate is that all the cards are on the table. It's either one way or the other; there's no middle ground. Life itself is defined by which answer we give to the question of resurrection. As Paul pointed out, "If the dead are not raised, then we might as well eat, drink, and be merry, for tomorrow we die" (1 Corinthians 15:32). If life on earth is a dead-end street, then there's nothing to be gained by being righteous, and no compelling incentive for being morally upright. Take away resurrection and eternal judgment, and the conscience-seared gang member is given the green light to kill his rivals. On what basis can anyone tell him otherwise? And if there is no life beyond death, then Hitler is not to be scorned for his "Final Solution" for the Jews. Without the prospect of resurrection, death would be the final solution for everyone.

That millions of people since the time of Christ have lived and died in hope of resurrection is not, in itself, irrefutable proof of its reality. After all, for at least four millennia longer, many millions more have been offering vain sacrifices to heathen gods and man-made idols. What can be said, however, is that–if resurrection is as much a false rumor as is pagan idolatry–then all the heroic acts of faith done in hope of resurrection are pointless.

In that regard, Paul mentions in passing the practice of some, apparently in Corinth, who (like some religious folks still today) were being baptized on behalf of unimmersed relatives and friends, in the hope that they too could be saved at the Day of Resurrection (1 Corinthians 15:29). What they didn't understand, of course, is that baptism apart from faith is a meaningless ritual–that faith (and thus baptism) must be personal, not vicarious. While Paul's purpose in this text was not to address their misguided, if well-intentioned, acts, he does point out how absolutely misguided they would be if, in fact, there were no resurrection. The lesson for the rest of us is that any life lived in hope of heaven is a cruel joke if we are dead wrong about Jesus' resurrection, and–through him–our own.

Resurrection in the Gospels

With so much at stake, it is no wonder we see such great attention given in the Gospels to Jesus' resurrection. Not once, but repeatedly, Jesus explicitly predicted that he would be raised after his death. To the Jews he said, "Destroy this temple, and I will raise it again in three days....The temple he had spoken of was his body" (John 2:19-22). To his disciples, Jesus began early on to explain that he must go to Jerusalem, "and that he must be killed and on the third day be raised to life" (Matthew 16:21-22). In Galilee, he once again said virtually the same thing to them, and they were so confused by it "they were afraid to ask him" (Mark 9:30-32). Finally, while they were approaching Jerusalem for the last time, Jesus tells them yet again that the Son of Man will be betrayed, killed, and then, "three days later, he will rise." Only slightly less amazing than Jesus' eventual fulfillment of all these predictions is the disciples' slowness to believe what had happened when they first learned of the empty tomb.

But, wonder of wonders, what Jesus had predicted all along is exactly what happens! When the women come rushing to the tomb expecting to anoint Jesus' body, they are amazed instead to hear the angels saying to them: "Why do you look for the living among the dead? He is not here; he has risen! Remember how he told you...?" (Luke 24:4-8). And, indeed, they did remember!

Resurrection in the early church

It may have taken Jesus' upper-room appearance to finally convince the apostles, themselves–especially Thomas–but their eyewitness account of the risen Lord quickly becomes the centerpiece of their preaching. On Pentecost, Peter proclaims with boldness: "God has raised this Jesus to life, and we are all witnesses of the fact" (Acts 2:32). And to the Jews in Solomon's Colonnade, he puts it even more pointedly: "You killed the author of life, but God raised him from the dead. We are witnesses of this." (Acts 3:15). Everywhere they went, "with great power the apostles continued to testify to the resurrection of the Lord Jesus...." (Acts 4:33).

What can possibly be more stirring than Jesus' appearance to an aging apostle John on the island of Patmos, when he declared to his trembling servant: "Do not be afraid. I am the First and Last. I am the Living One; I was dead, and behold I am alive for ever and ever!" (Revelation 1:17-18). Could there be any better news? Actually...yes. It's Jesus' next words that mean even more to the rest of us: "And I hold the keys of death and Hades." For all of us inching our way closer and closer into the pit of death, the best news of all is that the risen Lord has proven he has the power to make us alive along with him for ever and ever!

Resuscitation, revival, and resurrection

To say that Jesus is the "firstfruits" of resurrection is not to say, of course, that he is the first person ever to have been brought back to life. The history of God's people is replete with accounts of the dead being raised. The long list includes the widow's son whom Elijah revived (1 Kings 17:17-24); the Shunammite's son whom Elisha restored to life (2 Kings 4:18-37); that wonderfully funny incident in which the dead man hurriedly thrown into Elisha's tomb literally bounced back to life when his body touched the prophet's bones (2 Kings 13:20-21); the widow of Nain's son whom Jesus raised up from his coffin (Luke 7:11-17); Jairus' precious twelve-year-old daughter (Mark 5:35-43); and, of course, Jesus' good friend Lazarus (John 11:38-44). When Jesus called to him in a loud voice: "Lazarus, come out!", Lazarus walked right out of the tomb, undoubtedly hobbling with his feet still bound with strips of linen and with a burial cloth still hanging around his face. What a strange, ghoulish sight he must have been!

Just what number of people were involved we aren't told, but at the moment of Jesus' death, "the tombs broke open and the bodies of many holy people who had died were raised to life. They came out of the tombs, and after Jesus' resurrection they went into the holy city and appeared to many people" (Matthew 27:51-53). Who were these "holy people"? And how long had they been dead? We are given no clues. What's clear is that, one moment, they were in the tomb, and the next moment they were walking the streets of Jerusalem, undoubtedly to the complete astonishment of their family and friends.

Even during Jesus' ministry, he had commissioned the apostles to heal the sick and "raise the dead" (Matthew 10:5-15). Although we have no record of their bringing anyone back to life while Jesus was still on the earth, following his ascension into heaven we begin to see just that. In Joppa, Peter takes Tabitha (Dorcas) by her hand and raises her from her bed of death (Acts 9:36-43). And after putting Eutychus to sleep with his long-winded preaching, Paul rushes down to where the man has fallen from the third-story window and brings him back to life (Acts 20:7-12). Along with the prophets before them, the apostles were actually doing what Abraham believed in faith that God could do, if necessary, if he obeyed God and sacrificed Isaac. For "Abraham reasoned that God could raise the dead, and figuratively speaking, he did receive Isaac back from death" (Hebrews 11:19). What Abraham had believed *in theory* was actually happening *in fact*.

"Near-death," or after death?

Which raises the first of at least two important questions: What, *in fact*, was happening in these instances of the dead being revived? In a modern world of medical marvels, it has become almost commonplace even for Christians to say that they were "clinically dead" before being revived by the doctors. You are probably familiar with the many "near-death" stories where people are said to have entered into "tunnels," are "embraced by the light," hear voices, and see their loved ones. There is no end of people claiming even to have seen themselves lying dead on the operating table while hovering above it. Indeed, an entire industry has been built around such stories, and one expresses doubts about their veracity only at his peril.

Whatever else might explain these intriguing phenomena, they can't compete with the biblical accounts of people who were verifiably dead and, in some instances, even in tombs when they were brought back to life. "Near-death" is *not* death. No one doubts that people can be brought back from the very threshold of death, or even that someone on the verge of slipping into eternity might experience light and sounds and familiar faces. But the difference between "clinically dead" and "dead and buried" is huge. In fact, let's talk the stench of decay.

Of course, not everyone miraculously raised in the Scriptures was dead long enough to have rotting flesh (certainly not Eutychus); however, surely there is good reason for our being told in Lazarus' case about Martha's concern when Jesus ordered the stone to be removed from the entrance to the cave. "'But Lord,' said Martha...'by this time there is a bad odor, for he has been there four days'" (John 11:38-39). Know of any "near-death" experiences which can match that? Or so-called "clinical deaths"?

What we learn first, therefore, is that undeniably dead people were being brought back to life. No heroic "medical miracles." No last-minute resuscitations. No check-out-counter headlines of bodies in the morgue mysteriously beginning to breathe again.

What we learn secondly (despite its being only an implied assumption) is that each one of those who were brought back to life eventually died again. There's simply no evidence—nor even the slightest allegation by anyone—that they are still alive. Which both raises and answers the next obvious question: In what way, if any, was Jesus' emerging from the tomb any different from Lazarus being raised, or Tabitha, or any of the others? The amazing answer is that, unlike all these, Jesus never again experienced death. He was raised from the grave immortal, ascended into heaven, and even now still lives!

That is the crucial difference between *revival* and *resurrection*–the very difference which makes Jesus "the firstfruits" of the Great Resurrection; and the same difference which gives Christ alone power over death and the grave. Hear him again, as if for the first time: "I am the resurrection and the life. He who believes in me will live, even though he dies; and whoever lives and believes in me will never die" (John 11:25).

What an awesome possibility! What a hope! To die without dying. To live on when the mourners have gone. And then, one day, some day–Lord come quickly!–to meet him face to face.

"I declare to you, brothers, that flesh and blood cannot
inherit the kingdom of God, nor does the perishable
inherit the imperishable."

Chapter Preview

If in this life man's body and soul are a "package deal," nevertheless, it is the body which is the "package." In his inmost essence,
man is a soul (spirit) which will survive the decay of the body at
death and then be re-embodied eternally at the Resurrection.

We have no reason to believe that at the Resurrection God will
somehow "vacuum up" our deteriorated flesh and bones and re-
assemble our bodies just as they were before we died, only with
"new and improved," immortal qualities. There will be little or no
recognizable relation between the physical body "planted" in the
grave, and the new resurrection body. Nor will our resurrection bodies bear any resemblance to the sometimes-fleshly, sometimes-glori-
fied body with which Jesus emerged from the tomb.

3

A MOST MYSTERIOUS METAMORPHOSIS

The Body of Benjamin Franklin, Printer, (like the cover of an old book, its contents torn out, and stript of its lettering and gilding) lies here food for worms. Yet the work itself shall not be lost; for it will (as he believed) appear once more in a new and more beautiful edition, corrected and amended by the Author.

–Epitaph on Franklin's tombstone, written by himself

Ever wonder what you will look like after resurrection? Or if those whose limbs are amputated in this life will remain amputated in their eternal bodies? Or if still-born infants and octogenarians will be as distinct on that side as they are on earth? Our natural curiosity runs amok once we begin thinking about the details of resurrection.

As if on cue, Paul turns from his defense of resurrection itself to these very details, saying, "But someone may ask, 'How are the dead raised? With what kind of body will they come?'" (1 Corinthians 15:35-53). Going straight for the jugular, Paul immediately disabuses us of any notion that our resurrected bodies will be just a restored and immortalized version of our present fleshly bodies. (Consider, for example, the disparity which would continue to exist between "the beautiful people" and the aborted, the stillborn, the deformed, and the old and wrinkly.) Aware that this is the natural starting place for most of us, Paul dismisses such thinking out of hand with a simple, forcefully-punctuated: "How foolish!"

Okay, Paul...so we're wrong to think in human terms about a non-physical body. Do you have any clues for us?

Indeed he does, all of which are drawn from that which we can easily observe in nature, but rarely relate to our own eternal destiny. Take a tiny seed, Paul begins. Any seed will do. "What you sow does not come to life unless it dies." Right? "When you sow, you do not plant the body that will be, but just a seed, perhaps of wheat or of something else. But God gives it a body as he has determined, and to each kind of seed he gives its own body."

Seems pretty elementary. Watermelon seeds quickly come to mind. Although even more of them end up in the middle of what they each turn out to be, what they turn out to be doesn't look anything like the seed that was planted in the first place. That seed is small, black, light in weight, and sort of oval; but the melon it produces is big and round, heavy, watery, and red on the inside, green on the outside. Without looking on the inside, no one would ever pick the melon out of a lineup as a relative of the seed! The same goes for that tiny mustard seed Jesus loved to talk about, which grows into a plant so big the birds fancy it for a home. Point taken, then, Paul. There will be no recognizable relation between the physical bodies we "plant" in the grave, and the resurrection bodies which are produced on the Day of Resurrection.

Yes, but not only that, Paul hastens on. Think about it. "All flesh is not the same: Men have one kind of flesh, animals have another, birds another and fish another." True? For that matter, think about how different celestial bodies are. "There are also heavenly bodies [as in outer space], and there are earthly bodies; but the splendor of the heavenly bodies is one kind, and the splendor of the earthly bodies is another." Indeed, even in the sky, "the sun has one kind of splendor, the moon another and the stars another; and star differs from star in splendor." And your point, Paul?

Well, that's how it will be with your resurrected bodies compared with your present bodies. They will be vastly different, as different as alligators are from swans, elephants from mice, the sun from the moon, and planets from asteroids. If there are any similarities at all, they will likely be overshadowed by their dissimilarities. "So will it be with the resurrection of the dead. The body that is sown is perishable, it is raised imperishable; it is sown in dishonor [remember those grub worms?], it is raised in glory; it is sown in weakness, it is raised in power; it is sown a natural body, it is raised a spiritual body."

Now that's the part that stumps us—the difference between "natural" and "spiritual." Can you give us any help there?

Sure. Look at it this way. "If there is a natural body, there is also a spiritual body. So it is written: 'The first man Adam became a living being'; the last Adam, a life-giving spirit. The spiritual did not come first, but the natural, and after that the spiritual."

Still with me? So put it all together now. "The first man was of the dust of the earth, the second man from heaven. As was the earthly man, so are those who are of the earth; and as is the man from heaven, so also are those who are of heaven. Just as we have borne the likeness of the earthly man, so shall we bear the likeness of the man from heaven." Couldn't be simpler!

Looking more closely at the resurrected Jesus

Well, actually, it could be simpler. One could have hoped that, having contrasted Christ's heavenly body with our earthly, human bodies, Paul might have addressed what seem to be some fairly obvious questions in that regard. For example, are we to understand that our *resurrected* bodies will be like Jesus' resurrected body? A lot of folks seem to think so, particularly because of a parenthetical comment that the apostle John makes in his first epistle. "Dear friends," John writes, "now we are children of God, and what we will be has not yet been made known. But we know that when he appears, we shall be like him, for we shall see him as he is" (1 John 3:2).

Reasoning from this very passage, amazingly enough, some (including no less a scholar than Thomas Aquinas) have suggested that at the Day of Resurrection we will all have 33-year-old bodies—the presumed age at which Jesus was raised and ascended into heaven! How else, they seriously ask, could everyone—including those still-born infants and octogenarians alike—see him as he is?

Of course, John's actual words were: "as he *is*," not "as he *was*." Are we to believe that, at this very moment, the ascended Christ is the same in his heavenly form as was the resurrected Jesus? Or that when he ascended, Christ kept the body he had shown to the disciples in the upper room, complete with the nail prints in his hands? The same body which ate the fish in their slack-jawed presence in order to prove that he wasn't just a ghost? Listen again carefully to what Jesus said: "Look at my hands and my feet. It is I myself! Touch me and see; a ghost does not have flesh and bones, as you see I have" (Luke 24:36-44). And for the *pièce de résistance*, he asked them, "'Do you have anything here to eat?' They gave him a piece of broiled fish, and he took it and ate it in their presence." Is it even wildly possible that we will be eating fish in heaven? Or even be capable of it? Or know hunger of any physical kind?

Actually, Paul doesn't leave us hanging on this one. As he continues his description of our resurrected bodies, he emphatically says: "I declare to you, brothers, that flesh and blood cannot inherit the kingdom of God, nor does the perishable inherit the imperishable" (1 Corinthians 15:50). What was it again that Jesus said about his resurrected body...something to do with "flesh and bones"...?

New, or just improved?

Could it be that we are so fixed to our earth-bound moorings that, when we read "we shall see him as he is," we instinctively picture a human form, no matter how glorified? In fact, is it not Jesus' glorified body which makes us think that, somehow, we too will have the exact same earthly bodies we had before we died...only *glorified*? The same product in the same package, but with a shiny new label reading "New and Improved"? The same recognizable faces and bodies we've always had, just no longer subject to pain, or illness, or decay and death? Little more than "mortal bodies" that are no longer mortal; and "perishable bodies" except that they are no longer perishable? Perhaps even our same old familiar, comfortable bodies but which, in heaven, will be able do amazing things they could never do before?

Admittedly, when we consider that Jesus not only ate the fish but also mysteriously appeared in the upper room despite a locked and bolted door, we're no longer talking about a normal human body. In his resurrected state, Jesus stood right next to Mary Magdalene in the garden without her immediately recognizing him; and, as if a total stranger, he walked virtually incognito with the two disciples on the road to Emmaus. One minute he's with the women on their way back from the tomb; the next minute he's somewhere else appearing to Peter, and then to James. In its resurrected state, Jesus' body defied all conventions, both human and divine. It was at once corporeal; at once incorporeal. At once invisible; at once tangible to the doubter's touch.

In order for the disciples to appreciate the full implications of Jesus' resurrection, it was necessary that he show them both sides of his resurrected self–at times, in the flesh, as the same person they easily recognized; at other times, in various manifestations they would not naturally expect. Beyond that, Jesus needed to wean the disciples away from his physical presence among them so that they might focus their attention, not on what can be seen with the eye, but on that which can only be seen through the eye of faith. For true faith is being convinced about things you hope for, but cannot actually see. Whatever is capable of being seen through human sight is only temporary. It is the unseen which is eternal (2 Corinthians 4:18).

Until his ascension back into heaven, therefore, Jesus had to be, as it were, the transitional "chrysalis" between "larva" and "butterfly." That is, both *flesh and blood* (complete with the wounds of his crucifixion) and *glorified* (able to function in the spirit beyond the human limitations of time and space). But as Jesus' feet lifted off this earth, and the spirit of Christ raced through clouds and planets and the most far-flung stars of the universe back to the throne of heaven, surely all traces of his borrowed humanity were left behind. No hands. No feet. No fish.[1]

To be transformed like Christ

When Christ comes again and we see him as he is, what we'll see is not the man from Galilee–as pictured by the artists–majestically arrayed in a flowing white robe and gleaming gold halo. Nor, surely, any "man" at all. When he comes again, the Son of Man's appearance will not be like anything ever before seen by human eyes, nor dreamt of in our wildest imagination. And if that is how *he* is, then it also is how *we* will be! For "our citizenship is in heaven...and we eagerly await a Savior from there...who...will transform our lowly bodies so that they will be like his glorious body" (Philippians 3:20-21).[2]

How, precisely, will our *flesh and blood*, earthly bodies be "transformed"? First and foremost by no longer being *flesh and blood*! For all the mystery surrounding our resurrected bodies, the one thing of

---

1 Passages which speak of Christ *standing* at the right hand of God, or *seated* on the throne, must not be taken as anything more than anthropomorphic, attributing to God human shapes and characteristics. Long before Jesus' incarnation (when God was wrapped in human flesh including face, and feet, and hands), there were any number of anthropomorphic references to God in the Old Testament. For example, God–who is spirit (John 4:24)–was said to have a *face* (Exodus 33:20); *feet* (Exodus 24:10); and *hands* (Job 19:21).

2 For those who believe that John's *Apocalypse* should be interpreted literally, the returning Christ will have eyes like blazing fire, and a sharp sword coming out of his mouth (Revelation 19:11-16). Are we to believe that this is the model of our resurrection bodies?

which we can be certain is that "flesh and blood cannot inherit the kingdom of God." (Lest we forget, that is Paul's concluding line when he's describing what our heavenly bodies will be like.) Although it might be thought that the natural sense of "transformed" would suggest that the original would be available for alterations, Paul has already discounted that idea in his analogy of seeds and their fruit. While there is continuity in essence between the "sown" earthly body and its "fruit" (the resurrection body), the radical transformation between the two will be as dramatic as watermelon seeds and watermelons.

So to think that our resurrection bodies will bear any resemblance to the body with which Jesus emerged from the tomb is to miss the transcendence of our resurrection. It's to think still in earthly, not heavenly, terms. It's to be bound inextricably by the natural, not freed by the spiritual. It's to believe in Jesus' resurrection, but to forget his ascension.[3]

Body, mind, soul, and spirit

There is, incidentally, that other part of Jesus' death and resurrection that wasn't quite the same as ours–the fact that, as the psalmist prophesied and Paul confirmed, Jesus' body "did not see decay" (Psalm 16:10; Acts 13:34-37). Unless we are blessed to be alive at the Lord's coming, the inescapable reality is that one day we will die and our bodies will irretrievably decompose. Are we given any reason in Scripture to believe that at the resurrection God will somehow "vacuum up" our deteriorated flesh and bones and re-assemble our bodies just as they were before we died, only with superhuman, immortal qualities? Isn't that precisely what Paul is telling us will *not* happen–that we're not going to get a *renewed* body, but a *new* body?[4] ("You do not plant the body that *will* be....")

---

3 Christ having now ascended to the heavenly realms, he has an altogether different kind of body in a spiritual sense. "God has placed all things under his feet and appointed him to be head over everything for the church, *which is his body*...." (Ephesians 1:22-23). Beyond the anthropomorphism of "his feet," Christ's flesh-and-blood body on earth has been replaced with a spiritual body on earth, the church. We are now his "hands" to serve and "feet" to spread the good news of salvation.

4 This says nothing about God's *power* to "vacuum and re-assemble," if that were his intent. As strange as it may seem, God possibly might have done that very thing in the extraordinary resuscitation of the holy people who came out of their tombs at the time of Jesus' death on the cross (Matthew 27:52-53). Unlike all the other resuscitations (Lazarus' four days entombment being the longest period of death), these holy ones may have been deceased long enough for their bodies to have deteriorated. If so, then something like "vacuum and re-assemble" would have been required. Of course, even if that were the case, their restored earthly bodies apparently died again, which distinguishes them from the radically different, immortal bodies which we will all receive at the resurrection.

How is it, then, that Paul speaks of eagerly awaiting our "adoption as sons, the redemption of our *bodies*" (Romans 8:23)? Given what Paul tells us about our resurrection bodies, surely he can only mean the redemption of our *sinful* bodies, which points to the salvation of something other than flesh and blood. In Jesus' case, there was still a body to redeem–a body miraculously kept from decay. Not so with us. But that's not all. In Jesus' case, more importantly, there was also a *sinless* body which had no need of redemption.

Yes, of course, to speak of a "sinless body" is to speak of a "sinless soul," for it is the soul that is the arbiter of the deeds done in one's body. Or is it a man's spirit...? In Romans 8, Paul mentions "your spirit," but not "your soul."

Body? Soul? Spirit? What are we talking about that's redeemed on the Day of Resurrection? Indeed, if the body itself is fully decayed and no longer exists, what's left at all to be raised? Is there such a thing as a disembodied soul? Or disembodied spirit?

What is it that lies in the dust?

The mystery of resurrection is the mystery of man himself. How, possibly, can that which is "dust" rise from the ground to live again? All the right language is there, of course. Merely consider the imagery in Daniel's apocalyptic vision: "Multitudes who sleep in the dust of the earth will awake: some to everlasting life, other to shame and everlasting contempt" (Daniel 12:2). Isaiah, too, weighs in on the subject, saying (in 26:19):

> *Your dead will live;*
> *their bodies will rise.*
> *You who dwell in the dust,*
> *wake up and shout for joy.*
> *Your dew is like the dew of the morning;*
> *the earth will give birth to her dead.*

That Isaiah speaks metaphorically in terms of "bodies" which long since would have disintegrated does not cloud the fact that the dead will rise "from the dust." But even that phrase is clearly a euphemism, as is the idea of departed souls being called literally "from the grave." Dead souls don't live six feet under. Augustine was unquestionably correct when he observed that "the soul, which is spirit, can not dwell in the dust" (*Decretum*, IX, 32, 2). Not literally. Even Henry Wadsworth Longfellow had that part right, when he wrote: "Dust thou art, to dust returned, was not spoken of the soul." How could it be? The dust of the earth is physical, not spiritual.

Yet, closing those doors only opens still other doors. If, as the song goes, "John Brown's body lies a mould-ring in the grave," what precisely is his "soul" that "goes marching on"?[5] When every cell and atom of our flesh has decayed, what is left of us? No more eyes. No more blood-pumping heart. No more little grey cells of the brain with which to think. When all of that is gone, any remaining life force has to be...Where? ...What?

Are we soul, spirit, or both?

To say glibly that we are body, soul, and spirit raises more questions than it answers. We know, of course, what the body is, and we can recognize its animation, or lack of it. (Observe an autopsy, and you'll quickly appreciate that what may well be a perfectly normal human specimen has but the remotest correspondence to its former self.) Yet to this point, we've described nothing more than the breath of life common to all living creatures, whether on land, in the air, or in the depths of the sea. They, too, all die, but not a single scripture hints that they will be resurrected.

One could have wished for greater clarity in the Scriptures regarding the ethereal nature of humankind, and especially for a sharper distinction between the words *soul* and *spirit*. At times, their meanings seem to overlap; at other times, to differ in some qualitative sense. Whereas David speaks in the 103rd psalm of his *soul* as his "inmost being," the writer of Proverbs says that when the lamp of the LORD searches the *spirit* of a man, it too searches out "his inmost being" (Proverbs 20:27). Two separate words in the Hebrew (*neshamah* and *nephesh*) are in each instance translated the same, as "inmost being." Yet when Paul prays: "May your whole spirit, soul and body be kept blameless at the coming of our Lord Jesus Christ" (1 Thessalonians 5:23), two different words in the Greek (*pneuma* and *psuche*, respectively) are given distinct interpretations, despite lexicons providing virtually the same definitions for both. It's all an interpreter's nightmare.

---

5 "John Brown's Body," composer unknown.

Little wonder the Hebrew writer uses the two Greek words translated *soul* and *spirit* as an example of the incredible power of the Word to penetrate our lives. "For the word of God is living and active. Sharper than any double-edged sword, it penetrates even to dividing soul and spirit, joints and marrow...." (Hebrews 4:12). Indeed, the more intriguing question is how we can ever hope to distinguish either soul *or* spirit (the non-fleshly essence of man) from "flesh and bone," never mind the marrow!

Mystery of the soul

Even considering the words separately, it's difficult to get a grip on either one. Consider, for example, the multiple nuances of the word *soul* used in David's well-known 42nd psalm:

As the deer pants for streams of water,
so my soul pants for you, O God.
My soul thirsts for God, the living God....

These things I remember
as I pour out my soul....

Why are you downcast, O my soul?
why so disturbed within me?

In each case, David's "soul" seems nothing more than one's temporal emotions–panting and thirsting for God; being poured out in grief; and feeling downcast. One would be hard pressed to distinguish between this "emotional soul" and "my soul" which God restores as he leads me beside still waters in the comforting 23rd psalm.

Beyond describing the wellspring of human emotions, the word *soul* is sometimes used in conjunction with other words to express the totality of one's person. There's "heart and soul," for example (1 Samuel 14:7); and Paul's earlier pairing of "spirit, soul and body" (preceded, significantly, by the word *whole*); and, of course, Jesus' reiteration of the admonition in Deuteronomy 6:5 that we are to love God with all our "heart, soul, mind, and strength" (Matthew 22:37)–which is to say, with every fiber of our being.

Yet, quite distinct from all of these meanings, other passages appear to speak of the soul as something undeniably "tangible" (if not literally touchable) which is subject to eternal repercussions. For instance, there is that familiar proverb (23:14) regarding discipline of a child:

> *Do not withhold discipline from a child;*
> *if you punish him with the rod, he will not die.*
> *Punish him with the rod*
> *and save his soul from death.*

Especially in light of our opening chapter, note the compelling contrast between physical death (the child won't fall over dead if you discipline him) and the more consequential death from which his soul will be saved if you do. In this instance, the word *soul* bespeaks not simply one's innermost *feelings*, but one's inmost *essence*.

This appears to be the same sense in which Jesus used the word *soul* when he warned his disciples that they should fear him who can destroy body and soul in hell (Matthew 10:28). Jesus doesn't appear to be referring specifically to the resurrection body, which the wicked will have on the day of Judgment, but rather to the *complete person*. As elsewhere, "body and soul" here denotes man's *wholeness*, as if to say that in hell's destruction *nothing whatsoever* will remain. Hell will completely wipe out even the inmost essence of one's earthly personality. "What good is it," then, asks Jesus, "for a man to gain the whole world, yet forfeit his soul? Or what can a man give in exchange for his soul?" (Matthew 16:26).

Likewise, when Micah asks rhetorically, "With what shall I come before the LORD?" (Micah 6:6-8), he pointedly distinguishes between acts of the body and that part of him which bears the weight and consequences of his acts. "Shall I offer my firstborn for my transgression, the fruit of my body for the sin of my soul?" Whether or not Micah himself understood all the implications of God's revelation through him, we know from Paul's writings, in particular, that the soul is the seat of sin within man which morally colors the ephemeral nature of that which survives. If all this seems elementary for anyone steeped in Christian doctrine, honesty compels us to say nevertheless that it is virtually impossible to isolate and define precisely what that ephemeral nature actually is.

Getting into the spirit of it

It is with equal difficulty that we understand the word *spirit*. Since both *pneuma* and *psuche* appear to have something to do with "breath," we are initially tempted to think that our *spirit* is more closely associated with the animating life force in our body than is our *soul*. For example, James seems to take us in that direction when he declares that faith without works is dead, as surely "as the body without the spirit is dead" (James 2:26).

Such also appears to be the case in Psalm 146:4, in which yet a third word, *ruwach*, is translated as *breath* in the KJV, but *spirit* in the NIV:

> *Do not put your trust in princes,*
> *in mortal men, who cannot save.*
> *When their spirit departs, they return to the ground;*
> *on that very day their plans come to nothing.*

In the NIV, *breath* and *spirit* are considered virtually one and the same when Isaiah records God saying, "I will not accuse forever, nor will I always be angry, for then the *spirit* of man would grow faint before me—the *breath* of man that I have created" (Isaiah 57:16). However, a check of the original words reveals that they are used exactly opposite from how they are translated in other contexts, and the KJV even throws in the word *soul* at that point, despite elsewhere translating the same root word as *spirit*. Linguistic confusion is the order of the day!

One of the more interesting usages of the word *spirit* is found in Ecclesiastes, where (in 3:21) we first see the writer asking: "Who knows if the spirit of man rises upward and if the spirit of the animal goes down into the earth?" Then we discover that (using the same Hebrew word in 12:7), the writer says of man—not animals—"and the dust returns to the ground it came from, and the spirit returns to God who gave it." Whereas *spirit* in the first passage might be (for animals) only the animating breath of life, countless funeral sermons have referenced the latter passage as confirming the resurrection of man's inmost essence, which animals neither have nor experience. Yet, considering the writer's use of the identical root word (meaning *breath* or *life-force*), is it possible that all those funeral sermons are relying on a suspect proof text?

The intrigue is only heightened when, using the same root word as we saw in Ecclesiastes, Isaiah draws altogether fascinating distinctions (in 31:3), saying: "But the Egyptians are men and not God; their horses are flesh and not spirit." If horses, which are flesh, *have* "spirit" (in the sense of animating breath), there is some sense in which they are *not* "spirit" as compared with either man or God.

What do we learn from Jesus' "spirit"?

This, of course, raises a far more significant question: What was "his spirit" which Jesus himself gave up on the cross immediately after quoting Psalm 31:5–"Father, into your hands I commit my spirit"? The strongest clue comes from Luke's gospel. When quoting Jesus' words from the psalm, Luke uses *pneuma*, one of the three root words translated variously as "breath" or "spirit." Given his prayer of entrustment, it is hardly likely that Jesus would bother to say, "Father, into your hands I commit my breath." Surely, what he is committing to God is his inmost self, his very soul. And in that sense, his *spirit*.

But to describe what Jesus thereafter "gave up," Luke introduces a completely new root word–*ekpneo*. Whereas the other root words are more ambiguous, *ekpneo's* meaning seems tightly focused on "breathing out," as in breathing out one's last breath. If, like many of us, you've always assumed that "the ghost" which Jesus gave up (according to the KJV) was his inmost essence, there may be reason for reassessment. Though at the point of death Jesus undoubtedly did experience a separation of the metaphysical part of his nature from his physical body, it may be that what's being recorded here (by Luke *the physician*) is simply our Lord's last, dying breath.

Staying with Jesus a moment longer, one simply has to love his upper-room encounter with the astonished disciples, when he "breathed on them and said, 'Receive the Holy Spirit'" (John 20:22). It is remarkable enough that Jesus literally breathed on the disciples before talking about the Holy Spirit. (His connection between what gives life to the body and what animates the inner person can hardly be missed.) But more remarkable still is that the root word John uses at this point (*emphusao*) was used only once by the translators of the Greek version of the Old Testament (known as the LXX), and that was in Genesis 2:7, where God breathed into Adam's nostrils the "breath of life," and he became "a living being." The linkage between "breathing," "breath of life," "living being"–and then the real stretch–"Holy Spirit" is itself fairly breathtaking. To find that the Holy *Spirit* of God is taken from the same root word (*pneuma*) as is man's spirit, could easily bring chill bumps to anyone who appreciates word studies. At the very least, it gives wonderful new meaning to our being created in the image of God...lowly dust that we are in our mortal bodies.

One also can't help but wonder if the close connection between God (who we know is spirit) and the inmost essence of man helps explain the witch of Endor's gasp when she sees Samuel's ghostly presence coming out of the ground (1 Samuel 28:13). Her first reaction was to describe his appearance as "godlike," using a word normally associated with God himself (*elohiym*). That the NIV translates *elohiym* as *spirit* in this context is undoubtedly insightful, given that the nature of God's spirit is so closely associated with man's.

Being filled with God's spirit

Knowing that God breathed his own spirit into Adam, who thereby became, not only an animated, breathing "living being," but a living being *in God's image*, we begin to understand the profound implications when God says through Ezekiel, "I will sprinkle clean water on you, and you will be clean....I will give you a new heart and put a new spirit in you....I will put *my Spirit* in you...." (Ezekiel 36:25-27). When God created Adam, he made him special by breathing into him, not only the "breath of life," but also something of his own Spirit. Even now, when God re-creates man spiritually, he instills something of his own Spirit into man's inner being.

Listen again to what we hear from Peter on the day of Pentecost when he answers the crowd's question about what they should do to be saved: "Repent and be baptized, every one of you, in the name of Jesus Christ for the forgiveness of your sins. And you will receive the gift of the Holy Spirit" (Acts 2:38-39). Peter was not talking merely about miraculous gifts *from* the Holy Spirit, but–imagine it!–the gift *of* the Holy Spirit within one's own inmost essence.

If, therefore, God's spirit is intermingled with our spirit, we're not talking about simply the breath that goes in and out of the body to keep it alive on this earth. God is not promising us *new breath*, but *new life*! He's not merely filling our lungs. He is interacting with that part of us which will still be alive when our lungs no longer even exist, much less breathe. For, as Peter tells us, even if by man's cruel judgment our bodies were put to death in this life, we have the same hope as those long since dead, who, even now, "live according to God in regard to the spirit" (1 Peter 4:6).

Mystery of mysteries

Although precisely what part of our human personality will survive death defies present description, we do know that the spirit within us is somehow distinguishable even from the mind. ("I will pray with my spirit, but I will also pray with my mind; I will sing with my spirit, but I will also sing with my mind"–1 Corinthians 14:15). And also that the spirit can be "willing" even when the body is weak (Matthew 26:41). And that, in the same way as the body–but entirely on its own–the spirit, too, can be contaminated (2 Corinthians 7:1).

Most importantly, it is our inmost essence which becomes the "spirit saved on the day of the Lord"...or *not saved*, if we have morally rebelled against our Maker (1 Corinthians 5:5).

Finally, then, we are brought full-circle to our point of divergence from the companion word *soul*. After all this wordplay (a necessary exercise, if not wholly satisfying), we find ourselves somewhat in the shoes of Justice Potter Stewart, who is remembered for having said of hard-core pornography (in the 1964 *Jacobellis* decision) that, although he could never intelligently succeed in defining such pornography, "I know it when I see it."

Although we will always remain at a loss to define precisely the nature of our soul or spirit, what we can easily understand from Scripture is that we are more than the sum of our minds and our animated, breathing bodies. Whereas here on earth we are simultaneously body and soul, one day we will find ourselves standing before the Throne, a resurrected, re-embodied spirit in the presence of the Almighty. Until that day when all mysteries will be revealed, the gossamer interface between the body and our inmost essence must remain a great mystery. As Algernon Charles Swinburne put it so deftly, "Body and spirit are twins: God only knows which is which."

The duality debate

Anyone familiar with the discussions about the nature of man will know that there is a great debate over whether man *has* a soul or *is* a soul. Plato, as well as his student, Socrates, launched the debate in their own day saying that each person *has* a soul which is immortal and can never die. Of course, the idea that man has a soul which lives apart from God puts man very nearly in the position of God himself, with neither beginning nor end. From such a notion can easily come the belief in reincarnation or in the transmigration of souls. According to such teaching, never-dying souls find themselves trapped in a series of human bodies while working their way—in Hindu thinking, for example—to some nebulous Nirvana.[6]

In reaction to this fundamental misconception of man's created nature, many have adamantly insisted that man doesn't *have* a soul, but *is* a soul. They vehemently deny any duality in man's nature, and cannot conceive of any possibility of personhood where a soul is disembodied. This, in turn, leads to the position of some that when a person dies and his body decays, no trace of the soul remains except perhaps in the memory of God. Following on from that premise, these proponents deny any intermediate state of the dead prior to resurrection, at which point they believe God re-creates the former soul, complete with its new resurrection body (or perhaps even *former* body, simply glorified).

Unfortunately, it may be a case where one badly mistaken extreme fosters another extreme equally lacking merit. Biblically, it is clear that the truth lies somewhere in the middle: that in his very essence, man *is* a soul, but a soul with a body which will be laid aside at death, and

---

6 New Age claims that Jesus taught reincarnation must be dismissed out of hand. When Jesus pointed to John the Baptist as "the Elijah who was to come" (Matthew 11:13-14; 17:11-13), there is an identification of mission, not person. The angel said to John's parents: "...he will go on before the Lord, *in the spirit and power* of Elijah" (Luke 1:13, 17)–not *he will be Elijah reincarnated*. When John was specifically asked whether he was Elijah, he ended the matter, saying: "I am not" (John 1:19-21).

In John 9:1-2, Jesus is asked by his disciples about a man blind from birth: Was it because of his parents' sin or his own? How could it possibly be his own sin unless he either sinned in the womb or in a previous life? But Jesus dispels any notion whatsoever of a karmic, cause-and-effect relationship between the man's blindness and sin, saying that it had nothing to do with anyone's sin.

Nor did Jesus teach reincarnation's companion notion of karma when he said, "As a man sows, so shall he reap," as New Agers often tell us. In fact, Jesus didn't say those words at all. It was *Paul* (in Galatians 6:7-10), and the context has nothing to do with the afterlife.

The definitive biblical response to alleged reincarnation teaching in Scripture is Hebrews 9:27, where the Hebrew writer says that "a man is destined to die *once*, and after that to face judgment."

then re-embodied eternally at the Resurrection. Call that "duality" if you wish, but it is far from the duality of Plato and Socrates.

The kind of duality known to Scripture is seen, for example, in John's third epistle, when he writes to his friend Gaius. "Dear friend," says John, "I pray that you may enjoy good health and that all may go well with you, even as your soul is getting along well" (3 John 2). Here, John distinguishes between Gaius' physical and spiritual health; between his body and his soul.

A case study of man's dual nature

It's worthy of a whole chapter, but suffice it to say that Paul's meaty (and mysterious) discussion of sexual purity in 1 Corinthians 6:12-20 has us running breathlessly in and out of man's duality. Just when we think he is talking only about the body, he is really talking about the spirit. And just when we think he is talking about the spirit, he is talking about the body. That there are two separate entities–body and spirit–which constantly interact with each other is clear. And that the Holy Spirit himself dwells within that same human body is equally clear, if also rather mind-boggling. ("Do you not know that your body is a temple of the Holy Spirit, who is in you, whom you have received from God?")

What Paul seems to be telling us is that sexual relations (whether in or outside of marriage) are not just the obvious physical interaction of two bodies, but the literal intermingling of two inner spirits–so much so that, if one were blue and the other red, they each would come away from that experience with a tinge of purple! And because that is also true of our intimacy with Christ ("...he who unites himself with the Lord is one with him in spirit...."), what we do in our bodies directly affects our relationship with God. "Therefore honor God with your body."

If in this life man's body and soul are a "package deal," nevertheless, it is the body which is the "package." At the point of death, that "package" is unwrapped, revealing the "prize" within. In his Corinthian letter, Paul is warning against abusing the "package," because any staining of the outer container inevitably seeps through and stains the contents.

What Christ tells us about body and soul

Jesus, too, is quick to make a distinction between the body (which lasts only temporarily) and the soul (which faces eternal consequences). "If your hand causes you to sin, cut it off. It is better for you to enter life maimed than with two hands to go into hell, where the fire never goes out" (Mark 9:43). The importance of our mortal body is a distant second to the importance of our soul's ultimate destiny. How can there not be a significant duality given that distinction?

Of course, Jesus addresses both matters in issue (man's duality and the immortality of the soul) in the passage we referred to earlier: "Do not be afraid of those who kill the body but cannot kill the soul. Rather, be afraid of the one who can destroy both soul and body in hell" (Matthew 10:28). Does man have a dual nature? Clearly, yes. Someone might put to death the "package" in which the soul presently exists, but only God has power of life and death over the soul itself which, in this world, resides in that "package." However, it is equally obvious that man's soul has no natural, inherent immortality over which God has no control, for God can destroy man's soul (and resurrection body) in hell forever. That Plato and Socrates never factored God's righteous judgment into the equation of man's potential for immortality was the Achilles' heel of their understanding.

Framing the issue more precisely

In the war of words over this issue, there does not seem to be a clear demarcation between different usages of the word *immortal*. As a result, when the question is posed–"Is the soul immortal?"–we end up talking past each other. Compared to our mortal, biological bodies which die and deteriorate forevermore, our surviving souls are *not* mortal, but rather "immortal." But the fact that we are "immortal" in this sense doesn't address the quite separate question of whether the soul is so inherently "immortal" that it can never be extinguished in any way. On that question, when Plato, Socrates, and even a fair number of believers claim that the soul is "immortal," they are saying that the soul can *never* be destroyed–a position which flies in the face of Jesus' warning about the soul's destruction.

Troubling implications regarding Jesus' death

A final thought, here, about continuity of the soul after death. If it were true that man's soul is so inextricably entwined with his body that it does not separately survive physical death, then Jesus' death itself becomes extremely problematic. What, exactly, of God-wrapped-in-human-flesh existed for the three days and nights our Lord was in the tomb? Although, uniquely, his body did not experience decay as will ours, are we to believe that the God-man, Jesus Christ, was virtually extinct during his entombment? Did God re-create a wholly non-existent Jesus (Son of God!) on the third day? Without denying God's *power* to do that, there is simply no correlation between such a concept and what we know otherwise about Jesus' death and resurrection.

To insist that man's soul cannot exist in a disembodied state not only raises any number of insurmountable practical and textual problems, but also places a primacy on the fleshly part of man which God never intended. That man in this life is not complete without his body says nothing about our ongoing continuity on the other side of death prior to our being resurrected and re-embodied. Perhaps the most that can be said is that the root word typically used regarding the dead is *rephaim*, which connotes something less than a whole person. (See Job 26:5; Psalm 88:10-11; Proverbs 2:18; 9:18; 21:16; Isaiah 14:9) As we shall see shortly, the dead do indeed exist in a shadowy realm far removed from human experience on earth.

A modern picture for an ancient conundrum

How then should we understand the continuity of the soul between its discarded human form and its resurrected spiritual form? Given our limited perspective, resorting to analogy is about all one can do. For example, in computer terms, just because one might dispose of the floppy disk containing this very chapter, it doesn't mean that these words no longer exist. Nor are they simply still resonating in the author's mind so that at some future point the chapter could be re-created if necessary. (If you've never "lost" an entire chapter at the end of a long night of writing and quickly had to re-write it, perhaps your appreciation of this analogy is not as keen as it might be!)

The fact is, words from the floppy disk exist on the screen at this very moment and will soon lie peacefully in latent storage on the hard disk, awaiting the time when once again they will be "pulled up" and stored on a new form. The good news is that, this time, it won't be on the same square-sided, easily-corruptible floppy disk initially inserted into the computer and now discarded, but on a round, shiny-new CD with a capacity never dreamed of on the old floppy! There remains, of course, the option of pulling up the words again and then, at some point, completely deleting them from memory—even dumping them from the Recycle Bin forever!

Mirror image of the Godhead

As the discussion about the state of Jesus' soul in the tomb suggests, the mystery of resurrection is not only the mystery of man but the mystery of the tripartite Godhead—Father, Son, and Holy Spirit. If we are at pains to understand the nature of man, it is nothing to be compared with our inability to fully grasp how there could be one God relating to us in three different personalities, sometimes simultaneously (as at Jesus' baptism). And yet, the very fact that the One God himself can have a three-part complexity to his nature should tell us something about ourselves—that we, too, may be but a mirror image of that complexity in our body, mind, and soul. As with most mysteries and paradoxes, the usual quick-fix is found through the avenue of analogy, despite its inevitable limitations. Hence, Paul speaks of our earthly bodies as "tents" and our heavenly bodies as "eternal houses." And Jesus speaks of the righteous and the wicked as "sheep" and "goats."

Could it be that the analogies we use with reference to the manifestations of God might be helpful in understanding our own humanity? There is, for example, the analogy of water, which can be either fluid (as in a river or faucet), or frozen (as solid ice), or vaporous (as steam)—the same essential elements manifested in recognizably different forms. Perhaps some have stretched the analogy too far, suggesting that God is the fluid water permeating the universe; that the incarnate, bodily Christ is like the solid ice; and that the Holy Spirit is not unlike vaporous steam. But if we believe that God in his wisdom has created a correspondence between all nature and the realm of the spiritual (upon which Jesus draws freely in his many parables), then maybe such natural analogies help us to explain the inexplicable.

As applied to humankind, the water analogy would suggest that we are *body* (obviously the "solid" part of us), *soul, or spirit* (the vaporous, potentially-immortal part of us), and *mind* (a fluidity of mental thought and moral consciousness which permeates both body and soul). Certainly, Paul seems to be expressing something similar to this in Romans, Chapter 8, when he talks at one and the same time about "the *mind* of sinful man;" "the misdeeds of the *body*;" and "your *spirit*" being alive because of righteousness.

The crunch, of course, comes at the moment of death, when the body, including the mind (or at least that part of the mind associated with the brain) begins its process of rapid and irreversible deterioration. What part, if any, of our "mind" survives beyond the brain itself? And if there is a disembodied human personality, as there appears to be, how are we to think of it? What is the nature of the soul which awaits its resurrection?

Did we mention the word *mystery*? When all analogies fail, we see even the apostle Paul resorting to the word; but beyond the indescribable, thankfully, comes something of profound certainty. "Listen," says Paul eagerly, "I tell you a mystery: We will not all sleep, but we will all be changed–in a flash, in the twinkling of an eye, at the last trumpet. For the trumpet will sound, the dead will be raised imperishable, and we will be changed. For the perishable must clothe itself with the imperishable, and the mortal with immortality" (1 Corinthians 15:51-53).

As for our curiosity about the details, Paul might well have said, "Watch this space." In the meantime, don't forget about watermelons.

Anchor Verse - John 3:13; 2 Corinthians 5:10

"No one has ever gone into heaven except the one who came from heaven–the Son of Man."

"For we must all appear before the judgment seat of Christ, that each one may receive what is due him for the things done while in the body, whether good or bad."

Chapter Preview

The dead in Christ do not immediately ascend to heaven. Not until the Lord comes to claim his own will any saved person rise to receive his eternal reward. Both the righteous and the wicked have an appointment with Christ the Judge. Until that day, nobody is going anywhere.

One looks in vain for any clue that Jesus ascended to heaven during the three days his body was in the grave. So, if Jesus didn't go into heaven when he died, neither did the thief on the cross. Nor did any of those, like Lazarus, who were raised temporarily from the dead–none of whom had anything to say about a place to which they'd not yet been.

4

IT'S ALL IN THE TIMING

"Heaven Can Wait"

–Film Title (1943, 1978)

How many times have you heard someone say, typically at funerals, that we can take comfort in knowing our deceased loved one is in heaven with the Lord? Or that the angels in heaven are rejoicing at the arrival of a new soul? Or that our beloved mother or father, husband or wife, is looking down at us from heaven this very moment? And what else are we going to tell the crying young child, but that "Daddy's in heaven with Jesus"?

Certainly, it's what we'd all like to think. And, for most people, it's what we've always believed–that when you die you go to heaven. Even folks who aren't particularly religious believe that. But is it true?

Ignoring for the moment the minor detail of allowing God to decide who will enter heaven and who will not, there is a critical matter of timing of which most of us seem to be oblivious. How can anyone be in heaven–or hell–before the Day of Judgment? And how can judgment take place before the Day of Resurrection? And how can the Resurrection occur until the Lord appears in his glory? In short, aren't we jumping the gun just a bit in our rush for comfort and certitude?

That both the wicked and the righteous dead await resurrection is a fundamental fact of Scripture. We have already heard Jesus himself say: "A time is coming when all who are in their graves will hear his voice and come out–those who have done good will rise to live, and those who have done evil will rise to be condemned" (John 5:28-29). But if the righteous immediately go to heaven when they die, how could they be called from some other place? (Since neither body nor soul would literally be in the grave at that point, Jesus' reference to "grave" must surely be metaphorical.)

Texts which point to a time of waiting

What Daniel told us earlier is also worth repeating–that "multitudes who sleep in the dust of the earth will awake: some to everlasting life, others to shame and everlasting contempt" (Daniel 12:2). In fact, it's only a few verses further when God says to Daniel himself: "As for you, go your way till the end. You will rest, and then at the end of the days you will rise to receive your allotted inheritance" (Daniel 12:13). Dare we attempt to make the case that Daniel went straight to heaven when he died?

And what of David, the man after God's own heart? In his sermon on Pentecost, Peter uses David's nearby tomb as proof that, unlike David, Jesus of Nazareth had risen from the grave and ascended to the right hand of God. By contrast, "*David did not ascend to heaven....*" (Acts 2:29-35). Not yet. Not till it's time. And when is that time? If we can put any weight at all on what Job said to us earlier, "man lies down and does not rise"–not, at least, "till the heavens are no more...." (Job 14:12).

Speaking specifically of the faithful dead, the Hebrew writer focuses on Christ's coming as the pivotal point in time for the culmination of their eternal hope: "He will appear a second time...to bring salvation to those who are *waiting* for him" (Hebrews 9:28).

In his Ephesian letter, Paul presents us with an intriguing paradox in which we both must wait and, in a sense, are already in heaven before we die! "God raised us up with Christ," says Paul, "and *seated us with him in the heavenly realms* in Christ Jesus, in order that *in the coming ages* he might show the incomparable riches of his grace, expressed in his kindness to us in Christ Jesus" (Ephesians 2:6-7). One absolutely has to love this passage. The bus won't pick us up for some time now, but we're already riding on it!

Peter, too, joins the chorus, with a wondrous passage of expectation for Christians. "In his great mercy he has given us new birth into a living hope through the resurrection of Jesus Christ from the dead, and into an inheritance that can never perish, spoil or fade–*kept in heaven for you* who through faith are shielded by God's power *until the coming* of the salvation that is ready to be revealed *in the last time*" (1 Peter 1:3-5). We need not fear. Our salvation is a secure inheritance kept in heaven until Christ comes again at the end of time! This was the reassuring message of John's *Apocalypse* to first-century martyrs, when in his vision he wrote: "I saw under the altar the souls of those who had been slain because of the word of God and the testimony they had maintained" (Revelation 6:9). What safer hiding place could the souls of dead martyrs have than being kept beneath the altar of God?

But until Christ comes, both they and we must wait for our heavenly crowns—just as Paul, who wrote with confident expectation: "Now there is in store for me the crown of righteousness, which the Lord, the righteous Judge, will award to me on that day—and not only to me, but also to all who have longed for his appearing" (2 Timothy 4:8). If you carefully tease out every nuance, Paul is telling us: 1) that he'll receive his crown from the Judge; 2) on "that day"—unquestionably the Day of Judgment; and 3) not until all the other righteous saints of God get their crowns as well. Or to put it in more familiar terms, all the courses may have been completed and every academic requirement met, but no one's going to get his diploma until the day of Commencement when all the graduates file across the stage together.

But didn't Paul say...?

Paul's own words here serve as a forceful corrective to those who cite him in support of our immediate ascendancy into heaven at the point of death. In his letter to the Philippians, Paul shared with them his struggle about remaining in this world when, really, his fervent preference was to be with Christ. "Yet what shall I choose? I do not know! I am torn between the two: I desire to depart and be with Christ, which is better by far; but it is more necessary for you that I remain in the body" (Philippians 1:22-24).

If we didn't already know what Paul wrote to Timothy about when he would get his crown, it would not be particularly unreasonable to conclude from these words alone that, if Paul did depart from his body, he immediately would be with Christ. On the other hand, even in everyday conversation, if someone were to tell us he couldn't wait to leave the States and be in England, none of us would assume his plane landed at Heathrow the very moment it took off from Chicago's O'Hare. "Simultaneous" is not a word we normally associate with departures and arrivals.

The difference in Paul's case, obviously, is that the spiritual realm is not subject to temporal limitations. And if Paul thought he'd have to wait until Judgment to get his crown, then what's the rush to depart from his body here on earth? It would only be the military's classic complaint: Hurry up and wait!

But, surely, we are missing the point of Paul's agonizing "dilemma" about whether to go or to stay. After all, short of committing suicide, Paul didn't have much choice in the matter. In point of fact, Paul was writing this letter to the Philippians while enchained in a Roman prison, facing the quite real possibility he would be put to death. Surely then, all he is saying is that, in light of such daunting circumstances, he is happy to stay alive if he can serve the Lord further on earth, but equally content to die a martyr's death. Should martyrdom be his fate, he joyfully anticipates he would be just that one step closer to the Lord.

Preferring to be with Christ doesn't make it so

To his credit, Paul was mentally prepared all along for such an eventuality. Some five years before his imprisonment, he expressed virtually the same sentiments to the saints in Corinth. Referring even then to persecution and threats against his life (2 Corinthians 4:7-11), Paul wrote that, nevertheless, "we are always confident and know that as long as we are at home in the body we are away from the Lord....We are confident, I say, and would prefer to be away from the body and at home with the Lord" (2 Corinthians 5:6-10). As Yogi Berra classically put it, "It's déjà vu all over again"–except that, this time, Paul ends up exactly where he began in his letter to Timothy...waiting for Judgment! "So we make it our goal to please him," says Paul, "whether we are at home in the body or away from it. *For we must all appear before the judgment seat of Christ,* that each one may receive what is due him for the things done while in the body, whether good or bad."

Could Paul's point possibly be clearer? Both the righteous and the wicked have an appointment with Christ the Judge. Until that day, nobody is going anywhere. We can yearn to be released from our earthly bodies and to experience the joy of being in Christ's company forever. But our departure from this life and our arrival in the presence of the Lord is like a night flight over the Atlantic. Even if we were to sleep the whole way and be unaware of the time, we won't get there until we get there. Indeed, until *everybody* gets there!

An orderly resurrection

That there should ever have been any confusion about when the saved get to heaven is mystifying. Responding to what apparently are specific questions from the disciples in Thessalonica about the fate of their departed brothers and sisters in Christ, Paul provides a play-by-play commentary on the events to come. "Brothers," Paul begins, "we do not want you to be ignorant about those who fall asleep, or to grieve like the rest of men, who have no hope. We believe that Jesus died and rose again and so we believe that God will bring with Jesus those who have fallen asleep in him" (1 Thessalonians 4:13-14).

When you say, "he'll bring them with Jesus," do you mean this has already happened, Paul? Or do you mean that it will take place when Christ comes again? Has God already received the saved into heaven just as he received the risen Christ himself? And what if we happen to still be living when the Lord appears–will we enter heaven before our departed brothers and sisters?

The answers are not only quick in coming, but preceded by an unusually weighty preface: "*According to the Lord's own word*, we tell you that we who are still alive, who are left till the coming of the Lord, will certainly not precede those who have fallen asleep. For the Lord himself will come down from heaven, with a loud command, with the voice of the archangel and with the trumpet call of God, and the dead in Christ will rise first. After that, we who are still alive and are left will be caught up together with them in the clouds to meet the Lord in the air. And so we will be with the Lord forever" (1 Thessalonians 4:15-17).

Anyone who can follow an Order of Worship on the Lord's Day should be able to follow Paul's Order of Resurrection for the saved:

• The Lord will come down from heaven. (Accompanied by loud command, voice of archangel, and trumpet call)
• Those in Christ who have long since died will be brought back to life.

♦ Those in Christ who are still living on earth will be caught up in the clouds.

♦ Together, all of them will meet the Lord in the air to live with him forever.

Because Paul is specifically addressing questions regarding the fate of those who have died in Christ relative to those who are still alive, there is no reason here for Paul's mentioning either the simultaneous resurrection of the wicked, or the Judgment–the formal ceremony, if you will, when the saved will receive their eternal inheritance. In other contexts, Paul has been explicit about both of those aspects of that same action-packed Day of the Lord.

The point for the moment is that nothing could be more certain: the dead in Christ do not immediately ascend to heaven. Not until the Lord comes to claim his own will any saved person rise to receive his eternal reward. All we need to know in the meantime is that "He died for us so that, whether we are awake or asleep, we may live together with him" (1 Thessalonians 5:10).

While Luke tells us that, just before being stoned to death by the mob, Stephen the martyr was given a Moses-like sneak preview of the heavenly Promised Land (he "looked up to heaven and saw the glory of God, and Jesus standing at the right hand of God"–Acts 7:55), let there be no mistake. Before the Day of Resurrection, no one–not even the faithful Steven–will be admitted in advance. Nor, for that matter, will anyone–whether righteous or wicked–ever be left behind.

What about the thief?

In case you are wondering, yes, we need to think about the thief on the cross, to whom Jesus famously said: "I tell you the truth, today you will be with me in paradise" (Luke 23:43). Apart from unconvincing quibbles about where the comma should appear in the sentence, there's no disputing that, whatever Jesus is talking about, there's a sense of immediacy attached to it. Today! This very day! But what, in fact, is Jesus talking about?

Immediately, one is struck by Jesus' choice of words. For whatever reason, he did not say "Today you will be with me in *heaven*," as he well could have. Naturally, if *heaven*–meaning the eternal realm of the saved–is what the Lord actually intended, then there would have been no confusion about the matter. And certainly it would have been within Jesus' divine prerogative to grant the thief immediate entrance into eternal life as an exception to the rule of resurrection. But, as we shall see, there is no compelling reason to believe that the thief was to be such an exception.

The word *paradise* which Jesus did use is found only three times in Scripture: here in Jesus' assurance to the thief; then in 2 Corinthians 12:1-6, where Paul said he was "caught up to the third heaven...to paradise;" and finally in Revelation 2:7, where we're told that those who overcome will "eat of the tree of life which is in the paradise of God."

Although further definition of *paradise* is lacking in Scripture, it is possible to speculate from various extrabiblical texts what the understanding of first century Jews might have been. For example, 2 Enoch 8 (and 42) seemingly equates both *paradise* and *the third heaven* with the eternal abode of the saved. There is also 2 Baruch 51:11; and 2 Esdras 8:52, which mentions the tree of life; and 2 Esdras 7:36, which, by contrasting *paradise* with *gehenna* (the root word for hell), once again suggests a correspondence between paradise and heaven.

On this evidence, one would certainly be tempted to conclude that Jesus was ushering the thief into heaven on that very day. Certainly, that would not have been outside the bounds of possibility, especially given Paul's mysterious experience with the paradise which he called "the third heaven." Unfortunately, Paul sheds virtually no further light on "paradise," having heard "inexpressible things, things that man is not permitted to tell."

With mystery and uncertainty abounding, the most probable key to Jesus' reference to paradise is found in our third passage, Revelation 2:7, where Christ says to John: "To him who overcomes, I will give the right to eat from the tree of life, which is in the paradise of God." If, as seems to be the case here, *paradise* refers to heaven, nevertheless the emphasis clearly is on Christ giving *the right* to participate in that eternal realm, not necessarily promising immediate entrance. Despite what appears to be the obvious temporal (and even "geographical") import of "Today you will be with me in paradise," at least consider for a moment the possibility that what Jesus is really saying to the thief is not unlike what Christ revealed to John many years following the events which transpired on Golgotha.

Listen again to the conversation at the cross, and particularly to the thief's request: "Jesus, remember me when you come into your kingdom." What he's asking for is not a *place* but a *relationship*. In his own non-theological way, he's asking for salvation. And it is that salvation, surely, which Jesus is granting him: "*the right* to eat of the tree of life in the paradise of God." That day–"today"–was the day of his salvation! Or as someone has put it: "The day of salvation has dawned on you!"

Where was Jesus going to be that day?

To insist that the plain meaning of Jesus' words indicates that the thief was immediately going to be *in paradise*–and thus *in heaven*–would certainly be reasonable enough were it not for one major problem. By that interpretation, Jesus, too, would have gone straight to heaven at the point of his death, since we know that wherever one was going so was the other. The crucial question, then, is not whether the *thief* went to heaven (paradise) that day, but whether *Jesus* did!

It would be easy to point to Jesus' final words on the cross–"Father, into your hands I commit my spirit"–as proof that Jesus' spirit entered into heaven as he breathed his last breath. However, Jesus' words may have expressed merely an attitude of entrustment, as seems also to be the case when Stephen prayed virtually the same words: "Lord Jesus, receive my spirit." Who, but God, would we want to be the caretaker of our spirits when we die? Yet, whether God *imme-diately* opens the gates of eternal life to our departing spirits remains a separate matter–which, from all of the topic-specific scriptures we have examined thus far, simply cannot be the case.

Nor would it have been anything but a mockery of the idea of Jesus being raised from the dead on the third day, if in the meantime he had already appeared in heaven. Repeatedly, we are reminded of Christ's death, burial, and resurrection, but never once are we given any intimation that there was a heavenly interlude.

In the gospel accounts themselves, one looks in vain for any clue that Jesus' soul was transported to heaven (paradise) during the three days his body was in the grave. Quite to the contrary, what we find is

Jesus' own unmistakable repudiation of such a notion. To Mary Magdalene he said: "Do not hold on to me, for *I have not yet returned to the Father.* Go instead to my brothers and tell them, 'I *am returning* to my Father and your Father, to my God and your God'" (John 20:17). Can any doubt possibly remain? Surely, those words alone put to rest any thought of Jesus being in heaven during his entombment.[1]

So it is that we are faced with the rather compelling conclusion that, if Jesus didn't go into heaven (paradise) when he died, neither did the thief. (Momentarily, we'll suggest a rather different sense in which it could be said that the thief would be in Jesus' heavenly presence almost immediately–but certainly not within the time-frame of this temporal realm.)

Did Christ lead dead "captives" into heaven?

Perhaps our problem is that we've attached too little importance all along to Jesus' ascension. It is on that occasion, and not before, that Jesus returned to his Father and the fullness of the Godhead in the eternal realm. That is, to heaven. Of course, mere mention of Jesus' ascension has some people asking about Ephesians 4:7-13, and especially Paul's reference to Psalm 68:18–

> *"When he ascended on high,*
> *he led captives in his train*
> *and gave gifts to men."*

Launching out from this passage, it is suggested that, when Jesus ascended into heaven (whether during his entombment, as some believe, or later in the presence of his disciples), he took with him all those who were bound in death as "prisoners" in hades. So much is wrong about this notion, it's hard to know where to start.

To begin with, as always it's context, context, context. What Paul is talking about in this section of Ephesians is the gracious bestowal of gifts upon each Christian for the overall good of the kingdom of God on earth. In the more familiar part of the passage, Paul tells us that it was Christ "who gave some to be apostles, some to be

---

1 Most versions render the passage: "I have not yet ascended...." Some have suggested that ascension may connote the idea of the whole person-body as well as soul-being taken up; and that, therefore, Jesus did not necessarily rule out his having gone up into paradise (heaven) as a disembodied spirit during the three days prior to his resurrection. The problem is that, either way, Jesus claims not to have been in the presence of his Father, which surely rules out any sort of appearance in heaven.

prophets, some to be evangelists, and some to be pastors and teachers, to prepare God's people for works of service, so that the body of Christ may be built up...." (Ephesians 4:11-12).

But the force of Paul's argument is set up back in verse seven, where Paul begins: "To each one of us grace has been given as Christ apportioned it. This is why it says...." and there follows the "quotation" in question in which Christ gave gifts to men when he ascended on high. What's surprising about the "quotation" is that it is, in fact, a *misquotation*–or, more precisely, a power-packed subtle shift in emphasis. Whereas here Paul's focus is on gifts which Christ himself gives to us, in the psalm the picture (of God marching victoriously into his sanctuary) is just the opposite:

> *When you ascended on high,*
> *you led captives in your train;*
> *you received gifts from men,*
> *even from the rebellious–*
> *that you, O LORD God, might dwell there.*

What David is describing in his psalm is the typical victory procession where the conquering king returns triumphantly to the seat of his power, with a long train of captives following in his wake, and bearing gifts from the kings who have been conquered. In earthly terms, such processions were all about the display of kingly power. But Paul turns that picture on its head, proclaiming that our King, the ascended Christ, *gives* gifts instead of *receiving* them.

Where all the confusion lies

Ironically, the confusion regarding this passage arises when Paul tries to explain further what he is talking about regarding Christ's ascension. Speaking parenthetically, Paul says: "(What does 'he ascended' mean except that he also descended to the lower, earthly regions? He who descended is the very one who ascended higher than all the heavens, in order to fill the whole universe.)"–Ephesians 4:9-10.

Paul's meaning is obvious: that Christ descended to earth in his incarnation as Jesus of Nazareth (and even further into the "depths of the earth" when he died and was buried), and then ascended back into heaven following his resurrection. Therefore, because he was

God to begin with, and even now is God, Christ has both the power and prerogative to give whatever gifts are needed for his kingdom.

Any misunderstanding about this passage undoubtedly stems from the phrase in verse nine, which the King James Version and others translate as: "to the lower parts of the earth." Drawing from passages such as Psalm 63:9, where similar language points beyond the grave to the place of the dead, some have surmised that it was the "captive dead" in *sheol* whom Jesus led in his train when he ascended to heaven. Such an application not only ignores the obvious context of Ephesians 4, but also packs far more into the bag than it was ever intended to hold. In neither Psalm 68 nor Ephesians 4 is deliverance from *sheol* the subject at hand.

We see this best by comparing Psalm 68 with a strikingly similar passage in Isaiah 61:1-3, which, of course, is the very passage Jesus later applies to himself just before being run out of his hometown of Nazareth (Luke 4:16-30). Through the eyes of both Isaiah and Jesus, we can see all the more clearly that Psalm 68 is talking, not simply about the historical restoration of Israel from captivity, but in a broader sense the spiritual restoration of the fatherless and widows, the lonely, the poor, and those who find themselves either literally in prison or perhaps, figuratively, in "prisons" of blindness. It wasn't for predicting his descent into *sheol* to raise the pious dead that Jesus was booted out of town, but for daring to suggest that he had descended to earth to meet the spiritual needs of every person ever born—Jew and non-Jew alike!

From the vantage point of both the obvious context and these parallel passages, the speculative theory drawn from Ephesians 4 simply won't withstand close scrutiny. Even if we were to conclude that the saved are indeed the "captives" to sin whom Christ has already led into his eternal kingdom, it is a bridge too far to suggest that, either during his entombment or at his ascension, Jesus gathered up the righteous dead in *sheol* and carried them with him into heaven.

If there is any question at all about what Paul writes in Ephesians 4, surely there can be no question about what he means in 1 Corinthians 15 when he tells us straight out: "In Christ all will be made alive. But each in his own turn: Christ, the firstfruits; then, *when he comes*, those who belong to him" (1 Corinthians 15:22-23).

And, of course, we are not left simply with Paul's teaching on the matter. Even after Jesus' death on the cross and his ascension back into heaven, what Jesus earlier said to Nicodemus remains true to this very day, that "no one has ever gone into heaven except the one who came from heaven–the Son of Man" (John 3:13).

Testimony from the dead

Suppose for a moment that you are Martha or Mary, or any of Lazarus' closest friends who've just seen him walk out of the tomb after being dead for four days. What is the first question you're going to ask him? Don't you just have to believe that his family and friends simply couldn't wait to ask the intriguing question of all time: "Hey, Lazarus–what's it like when you're dead?" And from the end of the first century till today, that question undoubtedly would be followed quickly by a second: "What's *heaven* like?"–reflecting the almost universal belief that you go to heaven when you die. Inquiring minds want to know! And who better to ask than someone who has been on the other side?

Yet, what do we learn about heaven from Lazarus? Or from the three young boys who were brought back to life by Elijah, Elisha, and Jesus? Or from Jairus' daughter? Or the "holy people" raised from their tombs at the moment of Jesus' death? Or from Tabitha, or Eutychus? The answer, of course, is not a single word! Interrogate these former residents of death as we might, and there is nothing but silence about heaven. Whatever they said to family and friends fueled no rumors, nor found its way into either history books or folklore. Is that not a story in itself?

Sure, it's possible that, like Paul's "third-heaven" vision, they were not permitted to tell what they experienced. However, unlike Paul, there is no record of any of them having demurred on that basis or any other from telling what they knew. Granted, the silence of a potential witness is never as trustworthy as actual testimony. Even so, given man's inveterate curiosity regarding the nature of heaven, the silence of these "dead witnesses" is deafening! How could they possibly tell anyone about a place to which (as Scripture plainly confirms) they'd not yet been?

Which, for the next chapter, raises an altogether more interesting question: What does their silence tell us about the place to which, unquestionably, they *had* been—in the "waiting room" of the dead?

Anchor Verse - Luke 20:37-38; Job 14:12

""He is not the God of the dead, but of the living,
for to him all are alive."

"So man lies down and does not rise; till the heavens are no more,
men will not awake or be roused from their sleep."

Chapter Preview

What can we expect from the moment we die until the moment
we are resurrected? The two biblical terms for the intermediate
"waiting room" of the dead, *sheol* and *hades*, indicate not so much a
place of the dead, as the *state* of the dead. In that state, there is darkness, inactivity, and unconsciousness–most often referred to as
"sleep." Yet, as with any sleep, time will pass unnoticed until our
awakening at the Lord's appearing.

There is no compelling evidence of punishment, licking flames,
or gnashing of teeth for the wicked in the intermediate state of the
dead. The story of the rich man and Lazarus, correctly understood
in its context, was never meant to be a realistic picture of *sheol* or
hades (nor–more certain still–a preview of hell).

5

FALLING ASLEEP IN THE WAITING ROOM

One short sleep past, we wake eternally,
And death shall be no more; death, thou shalt die.

–John Donne
Holy Sonnets, no. 10

Knowing what we know at this point, we are left with a matter of simple deduction. If our souls survive the disintegration of our physical bodies, but will neither be raised nor re-clothed with their spiritual bodies until the Day of Resurrection–then we can only conclude that the souls of the dead exist, disembodied, in some intermediate state.

That's the easy part.

From that point forward, the questions seem endless. Just where, exactly, are the souls of the dead? Are they all in the same place, or is there a separation between the righteous and the wicked? Are they conscious or unconscious? Do they feel either comfort or discomfort? Is there memory? Can they perceive current events on earth, or perhaps communicate with the living?

That we have few direct answers given to us in Scripture should be obvious from the wide disparity of opinions evidenced throughout the centuries. And it should also be self-evident that there are many things about which we will never be certain until we, ourselves, reach the other side. But, until then, it behooves us to make a serious effort to assemble the scriptural puzzle with as few pieces missing as possible. Hopefully, even with no missing pieces.

Rightly dividing the words

The first and most important step in building the outer edges of our puzzle is to practice precision regarding the root words which are used in Scripture to denote the "waiting room" of the dead. Much of our frustration and misunderstanding derives directly from the seemingly-whimsical translations of four key words: *sheol, hades, tartarus,* and *gehenna.* If each of those words simply had been left intact and untranslated, most of our confusion would be non-existent. Toward the goal of greater clarity, the original root words will be indicated in italics throughout this chapter.

The Old Testament's "sheol"

Sheol is the single Hebrew word found in the Old Testament referring to the realm of the dead–or, literally, to that which lies "beyond." It occurs 65 times. In the King James Version we see *sheol* translated as "hell" in 31 places; as "grave" 31 times; and as "pit" 3 times. In fact, every appearance of the word "hell" in the (KJV) Old Testament, is a substitute for *sheol.* Because the connotations associated with "hell" are more properly linked with *gehenna,* its use in the place of *sheol* has been the single most contributing factor to the widespread misunderstanding which now exists.

Although *sheol* is often translated as "grave," it must be carefully distinguished from the literal hole in the ground, or sepulcher, or tomb, where dead bodies are buried. That specific word in Hebrew is *qeber,* and–unlike *sheol*–can be used in the plural (as in "graves"), or even refer to a burial site that can be owned, or borrowed. By contrast, *sheol* invariably refers to that which lies beyond the grave. Beyond death. Beyond life under the sun.

The New Testament's "hades"

The word most closely identifying with *sheol* in the New Testament is the Greek word *hades,* which means that which is unseen, or unseeable. It occurs 11 times. In the King James Version, *hades* is rendered as "hell" 10 times and once (in 1 Corinthians 15:55) as "grave." The New International Version translates *hades* as "hell" only once (in Luke 16:23–the story of the rich man and Lazarus); twice as "grave" (Acts 2:27,31); once as "death" (1 Corinthians 15:55); twice as "the depths" (Matthew 11:23; Luke

10:15); and in the remaining five times the NIV simply capitalizes "Hades"–usually in conjunction with "death," as in Revelation's "death and Hades."

The common identity between the Hebrew *sheol* and the Greek *hades* is best seen in Psalm 16:10 (where David says: "you will not abandon me to *sheol*") and in Acts 2:27 (where Peter quotes that very psalm, saying, "you will not abandon me to *hades*"). So whatever is true of *sheol* is also true of *hades*.

A mystery realm–"tartarus"

Our third root word, *tartarus*, is used only once in the entire Bible (in 2 Peter 2:4), and is translated in both the KJV and the NIV as "hell." The meaning of *tartarus* is obscure, but is thought to refer to a distinct part of *hades* which the Greeks apparently associated with the wicked. Its unique use may stem from its application, not to humans, but to the rebellious angels, about which we will have more to say momentarily.

The "gehenna" of "hell"

Finally, we have the Greek word *gehenna,* which–significantly–never appears in the Old Testament, and occurs only 12 times in the New Testament. In each instance (both in the KJV and the NIV), *gehenna* is rendered as "hell." *Gehenna* itself is a Greek derivative from the Hebrew *Ge-Hinnom*, or Valley of Hinnom, historically related to the ravine under the southwest wall of Jerusalem where children were "passed through the fire." As Jeremiah records that most despicable era in Israel's history, "They built high places for Baal in the Valley of ben Hinnom to sacrifice their sons and daughters to Molech...." (Jeremiah 32:35).

Less certain in detail, but undoubtedly true in substance, this same valley eventually became Jerusalem's garbage dump into which rubbish, offal, dead animal carcasses, and even the bodies of criminals were unceremoniously cast. The vivid imagery of preying worms, and fires that were kept burning both to consume the rubbish and to prevent stench and pestilence from wafting into the streets of Jerusalem, perfectly prefigured the final doom of the lost. So it is that *gehenna* is the word used by Jesus himself to denote the "hell" in which the souls of the wicked are destroyed (Matthew 10:28).

That both the final doom of the wicked in *gehenna* and Revelation's figurative portraits of heaven are conspicuously absent before the time of Christ must surely speak volumes about why the ancients seemed to know so little of either realm. And the fact that it was Jesus himself–the Judge of the living and the dead–who tells us most about what we know of *gehenna* cannot be inconsequential. Whereas *sheol* and *hades* unquestionably refer to the resting place of both the righteous and the wicked, *gehenna* is exclusively associated with the wicked and their eternal damnation.

The distinction, then, between *gehenna*, on the one hand, and *sheol* and *hades*, on the other, is of crucial importance. While *sheol* is sometimes spoken of as the fitting destiny of the wicked (they deserve to die!), never once does the context of any passage using the word *sheol* insinuate any kind of punishment. In the Old Testament, certainly, there is no sense in which *sheol* contemplates either the torture of wicked souls, or their total destruction. As the righteous "live" on in the world beyond the grave, so too the wicked.

How the ancients viewed death

Lacking God's full revelation, the ancients viewed death and the afterlife even more opaquely than ourselves. While there was an innate hope of an afterlife (even among the pagans, as evidenced in both Greek and Roman society, and especially in the Egyptian cult of the dead), the earliest language of Scripture speaks only vaguely of the soul's continuity. For example, God promises Abram: "You will go to your fathers in peace and be buried in a good old age" (Genesis 15:15). And when Abraham finally breathed his last, the text confirms that "he was gathered to his people" (Genesis 25:8). At the deaths of Ishmael, Isaac, and Israel, as well as Moses and Aaron–in each instance we read again that "he was gathered to his people." Indeed, we see that a generation grew up not knowing the LORD after a "whole generation had been gathered to their fathers" (Judges 2:10).

In a slight variation on theme, it was said of David that he "rested with his fathers" (1 Kings 2:10). By the same token, he must also have rested with the son born of his adultery with Bathsheba, upon whose death David lamented, "I will go to him, but he will not return to me" (2 Samuel 12:23). That David likely had in mind what all of the Old Testament writers referred to as *sheol* is seen in the parallel passage where Jacob is told by the lying older brothers that Joseph has been torn to pieces by ferocious animals. Refusing to be comforted, Jacob says defiantly, "In mourning will I go down to *sheol* to my son" (Genesis 37:35). However dim his understanding, Jacob seems to believe that Joseph is still existent in another realm.

The geography of "sheol"

Undoubtedly, the ancients had as much difficulty as we do, staring down into a freshly-dug grave and wondering how any part of the person lowered into it could possibly survive. No surprise, then, that there is so much talk about the earth itself, and what's *in* the earth, or *under* the earth, relative to death. For example, David says of his enemies: "They who seek my life will be destroyed; they will go down to the depths of the earth" (Psalm 63:9).

Nor is it surprising that the word "pit" would be a favorite metaphor for death's dungeon (wholly apart from any mistranslations of *sheol*). In his judgment against the ancient city of Tyre, God warns: "When I bring the ocean depths over you and its vast waters cover you, then I will bring you down with those who go down to the pit, to the people of long ago. I will make you dwell in the earth below, as in ancient ruins, with those who go down to the pit, and you will not return or take your place in the land of the living. I will bring you to a horrible end and you will be no more" (Ezekiel 26:19-21). That they would "be no more" does not rule out the continuity of their souls; only that they would no longer be in the land of the living on earth.

In a particularly insightful passage, God speaks to Ezekiel about the destruction of Israel's enemies, saying: "Son of man, wail for the hordes of Egypt and *consign to the earth below* both her and the daughters of mighty nations, with those who go down to the pit" (Ezekiel 32:18). And so it happened that, "All who had spread terror in the land of the living went down uncircumcised *to the earth below*" (Ezekiel 32:24).

Yet, even if the earth or some inner part of it provides the euphemism, there is no doubt but that it was *sheol* the ancients had in mind. "From within *sheol*," the passage continues with envisioned personification, "the mighty leaders will say of Egypt and her allies, 'They have *come down* and they lie with the uncircumcised, with those killed by the sword'" (Ezekiel 32:21). If *sheol* had a compass point for the ancients, it would not be north, south, east, or west–but *down!*

All this talk of "the pit," or "dwelling in the earth below," seems terribly out of fashion with our contemporary scientific knowledge of what lies beneath the surface of the earth. If perhaps we have trouble coming to grips with what lies merely "six feet under," even so, we no longer assign the location of the dead to some mysterious subterranean realm. But can we say that our modern sophistication has provided us with any *better* sense of where the souls of the dead reside?

The wicked in *sheol*

The passage we've just seen from Ezekiel, Chapter 32, is also a good introduction to the way in which *sheol* was linked with the punishment of God's enemies without necessarily contemplating the eternal damnation of the soul. It was said of the heathen warriors lying in their graves: "The punishment for their sins rested on their bones...." (Ezekiel 32:27). In other words, the fact that their bodies are now nothing but bones is evidence that they got what was coming to them! (Which, from our vantage point, doesn't seem all that punitive, given that the bodies of the righteous dead are also nothing but bones.)

In this linkage between *sheol* and the fate of God's enemies, we see the roots of a curious ambivalence among the Jews about the role of death. In a rather perverse way, their sense of death's finality helps explain the invectives uttered towards one's enemies, hoping that they will quickly experience all that is encompassed within the gloom of the grave. When so used, *sheol* has the familiar ring of a curse (as in, "Go to *sheol!*"), and not even David was above expressing such feelings. "Let death take my enemies by surprise," he fairly shouts, "let them go down alive to *sheol*...." (Psalm 55:15)! Perhaps David had in mind the fate of Korah and the other rebels, who went down "alive into *sheol*" when the earth literally opened up and swallowed them (Numbers 16:27-34).

In somewhat cooler blood, Job observes matter-of-factly that, despite their many sins, ultimately the wicked will face death like everyone else. "As heat and drought snatch away the melted snow, so *sheol* snatches away those who have sinned" (Job 24:19). And yet, for Job, the irony is that death really isn't good enough for the wicked, who often not only prosper in life but may also have easy deaths. Says Job with chagrin: "They spend their years in prosperity and go down to *sheol* in peace" (Job 21:13). Probably for that very reason, among David's last words of advice to Solomon came the admonition (regarding Joab): "Do not let his gray head go down to *sheol* in peace" (1 Samuel 2:6). In other words, kill him!

Thus, even as an invective against one's enemies, "sending them to *sheol*" never had quite the same punch as "sending someone to hell." It's more like angrily saying to someone, "Drop dead!" One might wish that his enemies and all evildoers would pass through death's portals *prematurely* or perhaps even *painfully*, but *sheol*–being also the destiny of the righteous–promised no greater punishment than death itself. To give us a more contemporary sense–when Hitler put a bullet into his brain, he went to *sheol* (and we may be glad), but so did Mother Theresa.

If destruction, perhaps, still not final doom

Of course, there are many allusions to the wicked's being destroyed. However, such destruction is never directly associated with *sheol*. For example, when Zophar insists to Job that God eventually will "get" the wicked, he says: "A fire unfanned will consume him and devour what is left in his tent....A flood will carry off his house, rushing waters on the day of God's wrath. Such is the fate God allots the wicked, the heritage appointed for them by God" (Job 20:26-29).

If perhaps the language of destruction used here and elsewhere presages the final doom of the wicked, there is no indication that it actually occurs in *sheol*. In fact, it is entirely possible here that the words "tent" and "house" (as in Paul's later writings) refer metaphorically to nothing more than the wicked man's dead body, which is consumed in fire or washed away by floods. Hardly eternal damnation of the man's soul!

Although Jesus appears to make stronger use of the companion word *hades* in upbraiding faithless Capernaum, he does so uniquely in the context of the final judgment. As with the cities of Korazin and Bethsaida (of which Jesus said: "It will be more bearable for Tyre and Sidon *at the judgment* than for you"), Jesus asks: "And you, Capernaum, will you be lifted up to the skies? No, you will go down to the depths *[hades]*" (Luke 10:14-15). For the unbelievers in Capernaum, the penalty of certain death awaited them (commensurate with the language of Psalm 63:9, a *non-sheol* passage having a similar ring to it).

That strange reference to "tartarus"

With that thought in mind, we arrive, appropriately, at 2 Peter 2:4-9–the only text in which *tartarus* is ever used, apparently depicting an especially deep or dark part of *hades*. Using the word "hell" instead of *tartarus*, the NIV renders the passage: "For if God did not spare angels when they sinned, but sent them to hell, putting them into gloomy dungeons to be held for judgment...then the LORD knows how to rescue godly men from trials and to hold the unrighteous for the day of judgment, *while continuing their punishment*."

Use of the word "hell" in conjunction with "continuing punishment" could certainly give us the idea that *tartarus*–and thus *hades*, and thus *sheol*–all have a hell-like nature for the unrighteous even before the Day of Judgment. But, especially in light of quite the opposite teaching from the many *sheol* passages we've already noted, such an interpretation gives far too much weight to the single use of a root word whose meaning is already obscure.

In fact, the NIV footnote to verse nine renders the text: The LORD knows how to *hold the unrighteous for punishment until the day of judgment*. This is in line with the KJV's rendering: "The Lord knoweth how to...reserve the unjust unto the day of judgment to be punished." As we have seen repeatedly and consistently, that is what the Bible teaches from cover to cover about the state of the wicked after death. Whether rebellious angels or disobedient humans, they are all waiting for the Judge to arrive and pronounce sentence on them. Until that Day, punishment for the wicked is held in quiet abeyance...as is also the eternal reward of the righteous. Lest we forget after this bright focus on the state of the wicked following death, *sheol* is the resting place of *all the dead*–the righteous and the wicked alike–and therefore should never be thought of as a place of punishment.

The stillness of *sheol*

It might be thought that "in quiet abeyance" is not a phrase to be used with reference to *sheol* or *hades*. Is the realm of the dead really that *quiet*? After all, there is that exciting passage where Isaiah is describing Babylon's Satan-like fall into the abyss. "*Sheol* below is all astir to meet you at your coming...." says Isaiah of the king of Babylon (Isaiah 14:3-11)—

> *...it rouses the spirits of the departed to greet you—*
> *all those who were leaders in the world;*
> *it makes them rise from their thrones—*
> *all those who were kings over the nations.*
> *They will all respond, they will say to you,*
> *'You also have become weak, as we are;*
> *you have become like us.'*
> *All your pomp has been brought down to the grave,*
> *along with the noise of your harps;*
> *maggots are spread out beneath you*
> *and worms cover you.*

Not only does it appear that there is animation in *sheol*, but conversation as well! Or is there...? Surely, one has to take these supposed conversations with a grain of salt, as simply another case of literary license, like we saw earlier in Ezekiel 32:21. That we aren't meant to interpret this passage with wooden literalness is obvious from the immediately preceding verses, where Isaiah has even trees talking!

> *Even the pine trees and the cedars of Lebanon*
> *exult over you and say,*
> *"Now that you have been laid low,*
> *no woodsman comes to cut us down."*

Only when trees begin to talk will departed spirits be heard to talk! If anything, this passage tells us something about life as normal in *sheol*. In order for the fictional conversations to take place, the departed kings first had to be *roused*. As if from sleep, not activity. What comes immediately to mind is Samuel's question when he suddenly appeared with King Saul and the witch of Endor and had a real, live conversation back on earth. "Why," asked Samuel, "have you disturbed me by bringing me up?"(1 Samuel 28:15). *Disturbed?* Again, is it not as if from sleep?

You may wish, incidentally, to make a mental note for future reference. Despite the obvious fact that his *very presence* in *sheol* (instead of still being alive and wielding his once-great power on earth) is a kind of preliminary punishment for the king of Babylon's wickedness, there is no hint in this fictional scene of anything like punishment *within sheol*. No fire. No licking flames. No gnashing of teeth. Solely a reference to the maggots and worms which would have eaten away at the king's earthly body. But never fear...the king's *ultimate punishment* is yet to come in the fiery destruction of hell.

As we turn to examine other passages pertaining to *sheol*, we must view with caution questions raised by the living about the state of the dead, knowing that their own answers may be more relative to what happens here on earth than to what actually happens in *sheol*. That said, the psalmist (in Psalm 88:10-12) asks God the questions we'd all like to ask:

> *Do you show your wonders to the dead?*
> *Do those who are dead rise up and praise you?*
> *Is your love declared in sheol?*
> *your faithfulness in Destruction?*
> *Are your wonders known in the place of darkness,*
> *or your righteous deeds in the land of oblivion?*

The question for us is: Was the psalmist merely curious, or were his questions knowingly rhetorical? If the former, inactivity after death remains only a natural assumption. But if the latter, then *sheol* is indeed a place of stillness, darkness, and deathly quiet. Or as the psalmist puts it (in Psalm 115:17)—"It is not the dead who praise the LORD," which is to say, "those who go down *to silence*...." Heaven and earth may bring praises to God, but those who live in death are as silent as the grave itself.

The question of consciousness

We asked earlier in one of our opening questions whether the dead are aware of what happens to those who are still alive. A tentative answer is found in Job's lament as he contemplates the threshold of death: "You overpower [man] once for all, and he is gone; you change his countenance and send him away. If his sons are honored, he does not know it; if they are brought low, he does not see it. He feels but the pain of his own body and mourns only for himself" (Job 14:20-22).

That the "suffering Job" should speak of the pain in one's body (which would no longer exist, and could never be in *sheol*) suggests that Job may be projecting a more earthly understanding of *sheol* than having any actual insight. Still, there is nothing anywhere in Scripture to suggest that Job is wrong about death being a complete separation from the land of the living.

Nowhere is this more pointedly expressed than in Ecclesiastes. Again, the writer may be doing nothing more than stating the obvious about what ceases "under the sun" when one is dead. However, we can't wholly dismiss his working assumption that what pertains to the land of the living find its opposite in *sheol*, the land of the dead.

Note, for instance, the writer's observation (in Ecclesiastes 9:5-6) that

> ...*the living know that they will die,*
> *but the dead know nothing;*
> ...*never again will they have a part*
> *in anything that happens under the sun.*

If we take it as a "given" that the dead will have nothing more to do with life "under the sun," there remains the question of what happens in the darkness of *sheol* itself. Without further evidence, we can only assume that whatever is true of life's normal activities is likely not at all a part of *sheol*, as is suggested in Ecclesiastes' admonition: "Whatever your hand finds to do, do it with all your might, for in *sheol*, where you are going, there is neither working nor planning nor knowledge nor wisdom" (Ecclesiastes 9:10).

Perhaps this explains something of why God forbade the practice of consulting the spirits of the dead. There being neither knowledge nor wisdom in *sheol*, any claim of special spiritual insight coming from the dead has to be bogus! Listen again to Isaiah's warning (in Isaiah 8:19-22): "When men tell you to consult mediums and spiritists, who whisper and mutter, should not a people inquire of their God? Why consult the dead on behalf of the living? To the law and to the testimony! If they do not speak according to this word, they have no light of dawn."[1]

And what is the destiny of those who pretend to consult the dead? Ironically, "they will be thrust into utter darkness"–the very darkness of *sheol* where they will know no more than the departed spirits they claimed to consult! (The possibility that there may yet be an even greater "thrusting into utter darkness" at the Judgment likely would have been lost on the ancients.)

If, therefore, *sheol* is as dark and quiet and still as all these passages indicate, then we begin to sense that the next question–about consciousness in *sheol*–is virtually answered. There being nothing in *sheol* either to know or to do, consciousness quickly becomes problematic. So do we have any further clues?

Night of the living dead

Of all the words used in Scripture regarding death, the single word used most frequently is *sleep*. Of course, that's what it *looks like* when people die–that they are asleep–so it is no surprise that we should encounter the language of sleep. Even so, the connection between *sleep* and *sheol* seems not to be simply a matter of imagery, as we begin to see, for example, in David's life and death. When praying for rescue from his enemies, David called out to God, begging, "Look on me and answer, O LORD my God. Give light to my eyes, or I will sleep in death...." (Psalm 13:3). And as he considers the wonder of God's intimacy in every part of his life (in Psalm 139:7-8), David once again uses the language of sleep when he refers to *sheol*:

> *Where can I go from your Spirit?*
> *Where can I flee from your presence?*
> *If I go up to the heavens, you are there;*
> *if I make my bed in sheol, you are there.*

Then, of David's own death, Peter later says: "When David had served God's purpose in his own generation, he fell asleep" (Acts 13:36). Is "sleeping in death," and "making my bed," and "falling

---

1 God's wholesale condemnation of the occult suggests, not that there aren't active spirit beings on the other side, but indeed that there *are* such spirits whose mission it is to deceive. It would be to our peril, therefore, to seek them out. But Isaiah does not seem to be addressing that particular concern in his warning; rather, that trusting any perceived source of spiritual insight other than God is a certain road to disaster.

asleep," mere euphemism? Maybe. But the choice of words is interesting, since Peter simply could have said, "he died," plain and simple.

In its mere repetition, the language of sleep begs close scrutiny. Maybe it's only indicating the obvious–that when people die they *look* like they're sleeping. But maybe also we are being told something more about the nature of death. Speaking of the righteous who perish, for example, Isaiah says: "Those who walk uprightly enter into peace; they find rest as they lie in death" (Isaiah 57:2). And it's worth repeating Job's words (Job 14:12): "So man lies down and does not rise; till the heavens are no more, men will not awake or be roused from their sleep." (There's that word "roused" again, which we saw in Isaiah 14; and note the implied continuity of sleeping until the heavens are no more.) So what does it *appear* the dead are doing in *sheol*? It sure looks like they're *sleeping!*

Is that not the picture Job paints for us in vivid technicolor (Job 3:13-17)?

> *For now I would be lying down in peace;*
> *I would be asleep and at rest....*
>
> *There the wicked cease from turmoil,*
> *and there the weary are at rest.*

And how can we forget Isaiah's own descriptive preview of resurrection (Isaiah 26:19)?

> *But your dead will live;*
> *their bodies will rise.*
> *You who dwell in the dust,*
> *wake up and shout for joy.*
> *Your dew is like the dews of the morning;*
> *the earth will give birth to her dead.*

There's no question but that metaphor here is being mixed together in a linguistic soup with factual reality. Would spirits of the dead literally be lying in the dust of the earth? Of course, not. But this is no different from Jesus talking about the dead being called *from the grave* at the Resurrection. Apart from what skeletons still exist, will there be anything at all left in the grave at the Resurrection? Again, no. So when there is talk about "sleep," the fact that it is obviously a metaphor does not preclude an underlying reality.

Paul's references to the sleeping dead

If you're looking for metaphor, you'll not find it anywhere more prolific than in Paul's reference to the language of sleep in the two passages in all of Scripture (1 Thessalonians 4-5, and 1 Corinthians 15) which teach us most explicitly about the afterlife. "Brothers, we do not want you to be ignorant about those who *fall asleep*...." And again: "We believe that God will bring with Jesus those who have *fallen asleep* in him." And again, "Then [if Christ wasn't raised] those also who have *fallen asleep* in Christ are lost." And again, "Christ,...the firstfruits of those who have *fallen asleep*." And yet again, "We will not all *sleep*, but we will all be changed...."

Granted, all these might be nothing more than multiple uses of the same euphemism for what happens when we die. But is there not, here, a sense in which these many references seem to move beyond *mere* euphemism? That seems especially true of Paul's assurance that "He died for us so that, *whether we are awake or asleep*, we may live together with him." Maybe it's a stretch, but throughout these references—individually and collectively—the sleep of death appears to be both *continuous* and *present*. Those who have "fallen asleep in Christ" are *still asleep*! Right now. Wherever they are. Which is in *sheol*. Which is also to say, in *hades*.

What does Jesus tell us?

Nothing, of course, could be more significant than the fact that "sleep" was the word of choice for Jesus himself—not simply as a common metaphor for death, but as a powerful, purposeful teaching point. As Jesus entered Jairus' house, for example, he drew derisive laughter from the mourners, when he said to them, "The child is not dead but asleep" (Mark 5:39). Why should Jesus say such an outrageous thing when both he and everyone else knew for a fact that the little girl was dead, unless to make the point that death is not cessation of the "whole person" but only of the body? If "the whole person" is dead, why didn't Jesus just say, "I realize she's dead, but look what I can do about it"? Instead, he says, in effect, "Sure, her body is dead, but her soul is very much alive...alive and 'sleeping.'"

There is also that poignant passage (John 11:11-14) where Jesus told his disciples:

> *"Our friend Lazarus has fallen asleep; but I am going there to wake him up."*
> *His disciples replied, "Lord, if he sleeps, he will get better."*
> *Jesus had been speaking of his death, but his disciples thought he meant natural sleep.*
> *So then he told them plainly, "Lazarus is dead...."*

So why didn't Jesus just say that in the first place? If *sleep* is merely a euphemism, why did Jesus insist on using it at all, unless to some higher purpose? Unless to help us understand the great mystery of man's mortality–that the "dead" are still very much "*alive!*" What else could Jesus have meant when he insisted that God was *still* the God of Abraham, Isaac, and Jacob? "He is not the God of the dead, but of the living, for to him *all are alive*" (Luke 20:37-38). Not "Dead *or* Alive" as in the Wild West wanted posters, but simultaneously dead *and* alive! Dead in body, yet alive in spirit.

Alive, but as we have seen, "sleeping." No, not *natural sleep*, as the disciples mistakenly believed, but sleep of the only surviving constituent part of the dead which *could be* sleeping: the soul.

Does it really make a difference?

Forget the metaphor for a minute, and take a hard look at the options. Viewing what happens at the point of death, we're faced with some tightly-limited, clear-cut, non-negotiable choices. Either the "whole person," body and soul, ceases altogether to exist and there is not a trace of the former personality anywhere within the farthest reaches of God's own existence; or somewhere, somehow, some way the essential soul of every person who has ever died lives on. Which is it? If we say it's total extinction, then 1) we risk having reduced man to animal status; 2) we have the daunting task of explaining any number of scriptures (like Luke 20:37-38) which seem to suggest that some vital part of man survives death; and 3) we make it necessary at "the Resurrection" for God to wholly re-create each former soul from memory, which, if that is the process, would make "resurrection" little more than an empty euphemism.

On the other hand, if we believe that the soul lives on, then it must either be in an active or passive state, either conscious or unconscious. Upon what thin thread will we hang the case for conscious, active existence? Upon the very kind of metaphors which we are trying momentarily to avoid for the sake of clarity? In the absence of any direct, explicit teaching that the dead are sentient, lively, and communicative, surely we must come down on the side of passive unconsciousness. Call that what you will. The Scriptures call it "sleep."

This brings us, at last, to the question raised at the end of the previous chapter: What does the silence of all those who were miraculously raised from the dead tell us about the nature of death's "waiting room"? What it plainly suggests, of course, is that they had nothing to tell, even about *sheol*, because they were asleep the entire time! One moment they were alive (awake); the next moment they were asleep!

And, for the dead in Christ, "asleep in Jesus, precious sleep."

Mystery on the mountain

We know, of course, that God caused Moses and Elijah to appear at Jesus' transfiguration (Matthew 17:1-8). If what the three disciples saw was not simply a vision–and the factual details suggest it was not–both Moses (who died and was buried by God) and Elijah (who was taken up from the earth in a whirlwind) were very much still "alive," wherever their souls may have been resting.[2] In the case of Moses, certainly, we know that he was "gathered to his people" in the same resting place of *sheol* as all the other ancients. So–like Samuel before him–it appears that Moses, too, would have been disturbed from his "sleep" for the momentous occasion.[3]

---

2 In Elijah's case, there is reason for caution in assuming that the "heaven" into which he was taken up was the heaven of God's eternal presence, as opposed to simply passing through the sky itself into *sheol*. The ancients of Elijah's day would not have known of "heaven" as we know it from later Scripture. And, unless Elijah and Enoch are extraordinary exceptions to the rule of resurrection, they would not have gone directly to the throne room of God.

3 Exactly what kind of bodies Moses and Elijah appeared in, we aren't told. That Jesus' body was itself "transfigured" on that occasion permits any manner of metamorphosis which God might have chosen. (The word *transfiguration* is derived from the root word for "metamorphosis.") Since we know that angels appeared in human form while acting as God's envoys on earth, it would not have been unprecedented for Moses and Elijah to have taken on some human-like form. And because the disciples would never have seen their original bodies, there is no compelling reason why Moses and Elijah should appear as they were in their earthly life. Surely, they would have been recognizable with the context of their conversation with Jesus, or perhaps by his introduction of the two venerable giants of faith.

A pivotal "parable"?

It's time to step back, then, and look at the picture which has unfolded as we've moved from the outer edges of our puzzle to the center. Despite individual pieces referring to "under the earth" and "in the depths of the earth," we have seen *sheol* and *hades* emerging, not so much as a *place* of the dead, but as the *state* of the dead. In that state, there is darkness, inactivity, unconsciousness, and "sleep." Even for the wicked, we have no indication of any present punishment. No fire. No licking flames. No gnashing of teeth. Simply the ominous gloom of death away from life under the sun.

You know what's coming, don't you?

Off to the side of our puzzle is one piece still left on the table. A piece that we've picked up any number of times, scratching our heads trying to figure out where it could possibly fit. And, so far, it simply doesn't. It's the story Jesus tells of the rich man and Lazarus (Luke 16:19-31). If taken literally, that single passage gives a completely different color and pattern to our puzzle. Its competing picture couldn't be more opposite. And so, we are at a pivotal point in our understanding of the "waiting room" of the dead. Either we must force all the pieces already in the puzzle (from across the broad spectrum of the Scriptures) to fit around this one remaining piece, or we can take one last look at this enigmatic piece and see if we've possibly missed an angle that would allow it to fit neatly into the tight puzzle we've already assembled.

The scene in Luke's gospel is set with the following story-line: "The time came when the beggar died and the angels carried him to Abraham's side. The rich man also died and was buried. In *hades*, where he was in torment, he looked up and saw Abraham far away, with Lazarus by his side. So he called to him, 'Father Abraham, have pity on me and send Lazarus to dip the tip of his finger in water and cool my tongue, because I am in agony in this fire.'"

The traditional translation of *hades* as "hell" has to be our starting point. It is from the vivid imagery in this single passage that most people's idea of the final doom of the wicked is formed. But the one thing of which we can be certain in this story is that it absolutely cannot be a picture of hell. Not only is there the obvious substitution of the word "hell" for *hades*, but also the rich man's appeal on behalf of his five brothers *who are still living on earth* tells us that the story is set before the Day of Judgment, and thus prior to the punishment of hell.

So it is *hades* or *sheol* in which the story takes place—the "waiting room" of departed souls. But just how literally are we to take this story? For instance, we immediately have a problem when the rich man asks Abraham for water to cool his tongue. What tongue? What of the rich man's physical body has survived the voracious appetite of the maggots and worms which Isaiah talked about? And what water would there be in *hades*? Are we to believe, furthermore, that in *hades* the righteous can actually look across "a great chasm" and observe the wicked in torment...and yet still have a sense of comfort (particularly if they see a loved one in agony)? If we insist on taking these events literally, surely it's not water we're begging for, but trouble!

It's a story! But, because it gives a specific name to one of the characters portrayed (and throws in Abraham, as well), we assume it somehow must be "more real" than Jesus' other parables. Indeed, some would ask why Jesus would tell such a story if it were *not* real? Or why, if it is not real, Jesus would perpetuate false ideas about *hades*?

Stepping back to get a broader perspective

Undoubtedly, as always, the key is context, context, context. Since this story is found only in Luke's gospel, the context is fairly straightforward. Going back to Chapter 13, we see someone asking Jesus, "Lord, are only a few people going to be saved?" In response, Jesus said, "Make every effort to enter through the narrow door, because many, I tell you, will try to enter and will not be able to. Once the owner of the house gets up and closes the door, you will stand outside knocking and pleading, 'Sir, open the door for us.' But he will answer, 'I don't know you or where you come from'" (Luke 13:23-25). The message is clear: Opportunities to assure one's eternal salvation are not endless. At some point, the door to eternal life will be slammed shut.

And then there is Jesus' soulful lament over Jerusalem (Luke 13:34-35). "How often I have longed to gather your children together, as a hen gathers her chicks under her wings, but you were not willing!" Have I not given you opportunity after opportunity, Jesus cries?

Then, in a series of parables, Jesus continues the theme of timely acceptance of God's grace, beginning with the parable of the great

banquet (Luke 14:15-24). When all the invited guests found excuses
why they couldn't come, the master told his servant to go out into the
highways and byways and invite the poor, the crippled, the blind, and
the lame. (People just like our poor beggar, Lazarus.) At that point, the
previously invited guests were no longer welcome. "I tell you, not one
of those men who were invited will get a taste of my banquet."

What follows is the trilogy of "the lost sheep," "the lost coin,"
and the "lost (or prodigal) son" (Luke 15:1-32). In each instance,
there is rejoicing in heaven when that which is lost is found–that is,
when the sinner takes advantage of his opportunity to repent.

And then comes the parable of the dishonest manager (Luke
16:1-13), which Jesus tells to his disciples, but more likely for the
benefit of the Pharisees, who are within earshot. Focusing on one of
the sins of which the Pharisees most needed to repent, Jesus tells a
parable specifically about handling worldly wealth. When Jesus got
to the punch line–"You cannot serve both God and money"–"the
Pharisees, who loved money, heard all this and were sneering at
Jesus" (Luke 16:14). To which Jesus gave the curious reply: "The law
and the prophets were proclaimed until John."

What he was saying, of course, was that, of all people, these
strict keepers of the law ought to have known better than to be
greedy for worldly wealth, for both their vaunted Laws of Moses and
their revered prophets of old had warned against such greed. As
God's chosen people, they had had centuries to learn that lesson,
but, even now, they were throwing away every opportunity to repent
on that score.

Where is all this leading?

Which brings us immediately to the story of (who else?) the
"rich man" and his greed for luxury that led him to ignore the desperate needs of the beggar who lay each morning by the rich man's
gate, right in front of his eyes. There follows the radical reversal of
their circumstances after death (agony versus comfort), and then
Jesus' masterful teaching point: *that our only opportunity to repent
comes on this side of death. On the other side, it's too late.*

That the story of the rich man was part of Jesus' ongoing discussion with the Pharisees–not specifically about the afterlife, but about
our values in this *present* life–is seen in the ending dialogue, in

111

which Jesus brings us full circle back to his earlier curious remark to the Pharisees. Responding to the rich man's concern for his brothers, "Abraham replied, 'They have Moses and the Prophets; let them listen to them.'" What Jesus had said directly to the Pharisees just moments earlier, he now comes back and incorporates within the story as an unmistakable exclamation mark!

Then, as if to underscore his theme that repentance is about *missed opportunities*, not *misinformation*, Jesus has the rich man saying, "No, father Abraham...but if someone from the dead goes to them, they will repent." To which Abraham replies: "If they do not listen to Moses and the Prophets, they will not be convinced even if someone rises from the dead." The allusion to how Jesus, himself, would soon be rejected by many of these same Pharisees despite his resurrection from the dead is glaring.

When Jesus' story is understood in its proper context, this last piece of the puzzle begins to fit in a way we might not initially notice simply by glancing at it out of context. Ironically, it fits because it was *never intended to fit!* It fits in the same way as the envisioned personifications of *sheol* in Isaiah 14 and Ezekiel 13–as a literary device which Jesus uses to get across his point.

As to why Jesus would use a story so out-of-keeping with the realities of *hades*, we can only speculate. But in the "best guesses" department, the basis for the story may not have originated with Jesus. A reasonable possibility is that Jesus took a popular Jewish folktale about reversal of fortunes in the afterlife and adapted it to his own purposes.[4] Nothing quite has the punch of something familiar being turned on its head. And isn't that Jesus' way–to be the teacher who (as he explained to his disciples about why he taught in parables) is like the owner of a house who brings new treasures out of old storerooms (Matthew 13:51-52)...to take us where he finds us and lead us higher?

If, perhaps, we are still uneasy about this unusual piece in the puzzle, at least there is a plausible way to make it fit without radically altering it with a penknife. The only other alternative is to begin the puzzle all over again, putting this piece down in the center of the

4 During the four hundred years between the Old and New Testaments, literature of the period, collected in what we know as the *Apocrypha*, reflects a growing consciousness about the afterlife on the part of many Jews. Given that climate, there is reason to expect that stories of this type were floating around. Passages in Enoch and 2 Esdras, for example, contain words and concepts included here in Jesus' story.

table first, then forcing the other 200-plus pieces of Scripture to match its traditional interpretation. Which seems to be precisely what we have done...penknife in hand!

What about the spirits Jesus preached to?

If you want a perfect example of where we've used the penknife, take a look at the controversy surrounding 1 Peter 3:18-20. After highlighting Paul's reputation for deep and difficult writings, Peter himself presents us with a real mind-bender. Christ, says Peter, "was put to death in the body but made alive by the Spirit, through whom also he went and preached to the spirits in prison who disobeyed long ago when God waited patiently in the days of Noah while the ark was being built."

Based on this passage, there are those who confidently affirm that, during his entombment (or between his resurrection and ascension, according to some), Jesus descended into *hades* and preached to the departed dead of ages past. We know that Jesus went into *hades* when he died, for that is the state of all the dead. But that he would have preached to the departed souls awaiting Judgment can hardly be believed.

The inherent unfairness that Jesus would have preached only to the departed dead of *Noah's generation* is usually overlooked. (When that difficulty is actually addressed, it is weakly argued that the people of that time didn't have either the Law or the Prophets, as did later generations.) Beyond that, the theory seems to raise more questions than it answers. For example, Did Jesus preach to the righteous as well as to the wicked? And was it the same gospel message Jesus commissioned his apostles to preach to all creation–"Whoever believes and is baptized will be saved, but whoever does not believe will be condemned" (Mark 16:15-16)? At the thought of baptism in *hades*, the mind boggles!

It is interesting, to say the least, that those who advocate this interpretation of Peter's passage typically also contend that the story of the rich man and Lazarus is factually and literally descriptive of *hades*. Yet it is that very story which presents the strongest possible arguments against such an interpretation. First and foremost is Jesus' primary teaching point about there being no "second chances" on the other side of death. Second, in the same way that the Jews in

Jesus' day had no excuse by reason of ignorance, neither did Noah's generation. They may not have had the Law and the Prophets, but righteousness was certainly preached to them, else how could God have condemned them for their unrighteousness? And third, Jesus was emphatic in the story that the wicked are not inclined to repent, even if someone went to them from the dead—the obvious allusion being to *himself!*

But wasn't the gospel preached to the dead?

To all of this comes the response: But since they would not have had the *gospel* preached to them, it wasn't as if they were getting a *second* chance. It would be their *first* chance. And with that we are pointed to 1 Peter 4:6, where Peter says, "For this reason the *gospel* was preached even to those who are now dead...."

It is true, of course, that the good news of the crucified, resurrected Jesus of Nazareth could not have been preached as historically factual to any generation before Christ's appearance on earth. But Scripture clearly affirms that the good news of righteousness and God's mercy has been preached to every generation.

Regarding the Jews under the law, certainly, the Hebrew writer tells us: "For we also have had the gospel preached to us, *just as they did*" (Hebrews 4:2). And again, "Those who *formerly had the gospel preached to them* did not go in [to the promised land], because of their disobedience" (Hebrews 4:6). Can this be? How could the ancient Israelites possibly have been judged according to the "gospel"? Or, more to the point, if Jesus did *not* actually preach to the departed souls in the *hades*, then what is Peter talking about?

This may seem a bit strange, but think about it. Do you believe that Jesus was "the Word," and that in the beginning he was *with* God...and *was* God? (Given the prologue to John's gospel, admittedly that's a loaded question.) And do you believe that God manifests himself variously as Father, Son, and Holy Spirit? If so, we can begin to understand what Peter likely had in mind—that Jesus, *before he was Jesus*, preached in Noah's day to a generation even now being held in the "prison" of *hades* awaiting Judgment. And how did he do that? Peter tells us explicitly. He did it *through the Spirit*—the same Spirit by whom Jesus' body was made alive.

If that line of reasoning seems contrived or convoluted, just listen to what Peter had to say in the opening chapter of his epistle. "Concerning this salvation, the prophets, who spoke of the grace that was to come to you, searched intently and with the greatest care, trying to find out the time and circumstances to which *the Spirit of Christ in them* was pointing when he predicted the sufferings of Christ and the glories that would follow. It was revealed to them that they were not serving themselves but you, when they spoke of the things that have now been told you by those who have preached the gospel to you by the Holy Spirit sent from heaven" (1 Peter 1:10-12).

The same Holy Spirit that has brought the gospel to us has appeared as the Spirit of Christ in the prophets of old, and, we can also be sure, in the preaching of Noah and the other ancients of faith. To each generation, the Spirit of God has proclaimed his will for mankind–the good news of righteousness, faith, obedience, and grace. And the sober warning of judgment for those who reject that gospel.

Don't forget the rich man and Lazarus

Do you not find it fascinating that in the verses which follow hard on the heels of the story of the rich man and Lazarus, Jesus refers specifically to Noah's generation? "Just as it was in the days of Noah," Jesus says, "so also will it be in the days of the Son of Man. People were eating, drinking, marrying and being given in marriage up to the day Noah entered the ark. Then the flood came and destroyed them all" (Luke 17:26-27). And then it was too late! Too late to respond to the gospel being preached to them by the Spirit of Christ in the righteousness of Noah. Too late to repent of their continually evil thoughts. Too late to have a second chance...either at their moment of death, or at any time later in *hades*. Even now behind the "gates of *hades*," their fate–just as the fate of the unrepentant in all generations–remains sealed.

Apart from learning the lesson of timely repentance from the story of the rich man and the poor beggar, Lazarus, our focus really ought to be on the *other* Lazarus. The one who *actually* experienced *hades*–yet returned with no exciting stories to tell about having seen Abraham; or leaping flames visible from across a wide chasm; or having had animated conversations with familiar people who were in agony there.

Now *there's* your real story! It's the story of unconscious existence. The story of darkened unawareness. The story of a quiet waiting room where all the souls are sleeping.

Yet, especially for the saved, therein lies an even greater story. The story of your own sleep last night. One moment you were still awake; the next moment, asleep. From that point forward until the moment you awoke, was it not as if *no time whatsoever* had passed? So it will be when we die. One moment we will have been alive; the next moment we will rest in the sleep of death. But whether it be a day, or a decade, or ten thousand years before we are awakened at the sound of the trumpet, our presence with the Lord will be as instantaneous as waking from a night of sleep.

In *that* sense, praise God, we can join Paul in exclaiming: To be absent from the body is to be with Christ!

Anchor Verse - Matthew 25:31-46

"When the Son of Man comes in his glory, and all the angels with him, he will sit on his throne in heavenly glory. All the nations will be gathered before him, and he will separate the people one from another as a shepherd separates the sheep from the goats. He will put the sheep on his right and the goats on the left."

Chapter Preview

Both "the Day of the Lord" and "that day" are used throughout prophecy with reference to judgment which, even then, God was bringing against the nations. Yet, in the Gospels and Epistles, those phrases focus on the final Day of Judgment—the same "that day" on which the Lord will appear, the dead will be raised, and the whole universe will be utterly destroyed.

In Matthew 24, Jesus was referring simultaneously to events to take place both in the near future in Jerusalem and also at the end of time. Not only was the destruction of Jerusalem and the temple a signal that the whole of the Jewish system was forever abrogated by the blood of Christ, but it was also a graphic picture of the complete destruction awaiting the wicked at the end of time.

6

THE DAY TO END ALL DAYS

The aged earth aghast
With terror of that blast
Shall from the surface to the center shake,
When, at the world's last session,
The dreadful Judge in middle air shall spread
His throne.

–John Milton
On the Morning of Christ's Nativity

As if on a giant screen so broad that it stretches beyond our imagination, the inspired writers picture the great day of Christ's appearing as something right out of the movies. John's Revelation (1:7) provides the dramatic opening scene:

Look, he is coming with the clouds,
and every eye will see him,
even those who pierced him;
and all the peoples on the earth will mourn because of him.
So shall it be!

That the Lord is coming to claim his own and bring judgment on all mankind is the great promise of all history. "This same Jesus who has been taken from you into heaven, will come back in the same way you have seen him go into heaven," said the two men dressed in white to the awe-struck apostles at the moment of Jesus' ascension (Acts 1:11). "He must reign in heaven until the time comes for God to restore everything," Peter told his audience in Solomon's Colonnade (Acts 3:21). But when that time comes–count on it–our Lord will appear!

It is ironic that Jesus himself tells us of his grand encore in one of the most enigmatic and controversial passages in Scripture, the so-called "Olivet Discourse." Because his words are set within a discussion which he is having with his disciples about the coming destruction of the temple (which happened when the Romans sacked Jerusalem in A.D. 70), there is wide divergence of opinion as to just exactly what Jesus was referring–whether his imminent coming in judgment against Jerusalem; the Resurrection Day itself; or perhaps still other alternatives.

As always, our study of the Scriptures must be tempered with an appreciation for the fact that figurative apocalyptic language is particularly vulnerable to speculative theorizing which–especially regarding Christ's coming–has proven to be wrong time and again throughout the history of prophetic interpretation. Nor must we forget that prophecy itself is often multi-leveled, simultaneously referring to separate events perhaps even centuries apart. (Merely consider the messianic prophecies themselves.)

With that caution in mind, hear again the words of our Lord (from Matthew 24, Mark 13, and Luke 21) expanding on the vision given to John in the Revelation. "At that time the sign of the Son of Man will appear in the sky, and all the nations of the earth will mourn. They will see the Son of Man coming on the clouds of the sky, with power and great glory. And he will send his angels with a loud trumpet call, and they will gather his elect from the four winds, from one end of the heavens to the other" (Matthew 24:30-31).

No one living at that time will miss the cosmic fireworks, because, as Jesus continues, "There will be signs in the sun, moon and stars. On the earth, nations will be in anguish and perplexity at the roaring and tossing of the sea. Men will faint from terror, apprehensive of what is coming on the world, for the heavenly bodies will be shaken. At that time they will see the Son of Man coming in a cloud with power and great glory. When these things begin to take place, stand up and lift up your heads, because your redemption is drawing near" (Luke 21:25-28).

Wow! To *be there*, or not to *be there*? That, Hamlet, is the more profound question! Few would want to miss it, but who could possibly witness it without trembling in fear!

Sound familiar?

Yet, you're probably wondering to yourself: "Haven't I already seen this movie? The plot seems terribly familiar, and I just know I've heard those lines before." And, of course, you're right. You *have* heard those lines before–right down to the clouds, the trumpet blast, and all that celestial shaking going on. As the author of life, Jesus is certainly entitled to do so, but in fact he is borrowing lines he's already spoken centuries earlier through the mouths of the prophets.

The plot, too, ought to be familiar to any student of the Old Testament. It's the age-old theme of God's bringing punishment against those who have opposed his kingdom, and long-past-due justice for the faithful remnant. Whether those on the receiving end of God's wrath were his own rebellious people, or the heathen nations who conquered Israel and enslaved her, the story was always the same: There's a day coming when God's wrath against evil will be avenged. When? On *that day*! *The Day of the Lord*! A day of clouds, and trumpets, and quaking in the cosmos.

Our "opening scene," which Jesus envisioned in Matthew 24, is not unlike the events described by Daniel in his dream of the four beasts: "In my vision at night I looked, and there before me was one like a son of man, coming with the clouds of heaven. He approached the Ancient of Days and was led into his presence. He was given authority, glory and sovereign power; all peoples, nations and men of every language worshiped him. His dominion is an everlasting dominion that will not pass away, and his kingdom is one that will never be destroyed" (Daniel 7:13-14). If for any reason this passage were thought not to be a specific reference to Christ's appearing, still, we can hardly miss the unmistakable allusions.

We see the "Day of the Lord" everywhere!

And then there are all those other prophecies which bring us such a startling sense of divine déjà vu. In judgment against Babylon, for example, Isaiah brings the warning (Isaiah 13:6-11):

Wail, for the day of the LORD is near;
it will come like destruction from the Almighty.
Because of this, all hands will go limp,
every man's heart will melt.
Terror will seize them,
pain and anguish will grip them;
they will writhe like a woman in labor.
They will look aghast at each other,
their faces aflame.

See, the day of the LORD is coming
–a cruel day, with wrath and fierce anger–
to make the land desolate
and destroy the sinners within it.
The stars of heaven and their constellations
will not show their light.
The rising sun will be darkened
and the moon will not give its light.
I will punish the world for its evil,
the wicked for their sins.

It's all there, isn't it? Apocalyptic imagery, unrelenting judgment, and fierce punishment! If Jesus' prophecy was about the future, the picture he presents is straight out of the past.

We see the same apocalyptic imagery in Zephaniah's prophecy against Judah, in which he brings a terrifying prediction of doom on the day of the Lord (Zephaniah 1:14-16, 18):

"The great day of the LORD is near–
near and coming quickly.
Listen! The cry on the day of the Lord will be bitter,
the shouting of the warrior there.
That day will be a day of wrath,
a day of distress and anguish,
a day of trouble and ruin,
a day of darkness and gloom,
a day of clouds and blackness,
a day of trumpet and battle cry....

In the fire of his jealousy
the whole world will be consumed
for he will make a sudden end
of all who live on the earth."

In the vitriolic intensity of that final verse, we begin to see how prophecy is often both figurative in style and two-dimensional in application. It is obvious that the language is not meant to be taken literally. When God brought Judah to her knees in captivity, he did not, in fact, consume the whole world in fire, nor wipe mankind off the earth. Yet that is precisely what Zephaniah vividly describes at the beginning of his prophecy (Zephaniah 1:2-3):

"I will sweep away everything
from the face of the earth,"
declares the LORD.
"I will sweep away both men and animals;
I will sweep away the birds of the air
and the fish of the sea.
The wicked will have only heaps of rubble
when I cut off man from the face of the earth,"
declares the LORD.

Given such a gigantic leap from Judah's national destruction to the extermination of all living things, we simply have to ask in the case of Zephaniah whether there is a secondary prophecy having implications extending far beyond the immediate message for Zephaniah's generation. As demonstrated so clearly in this passage, prophecy often refers concurrently to two quite distinct applications of the same fundamental idea. That Zephaniah's prophecy coincides almost verbatim with what is said later in Scripture about another Day of the Lord—the Final Judgment—surely is no coincidence. What it strongly suggests about a passage as complex as Matthew 24 is that Jesus likely was referring simultaneously to events to take place both in the near future in Jerusalem and also at the end of time.

Joel paints with primary and secondary colors

Joel's separate prophecy against Judah is also an excellent illustration of primary and secondary applications. Having brought his own warning about the coming "day of the LORD," Joel then brings words of hope for Judah's eventual restoration (Joel 2:28-32):

> *"And afterward,*
> *I will pour out my Spirit on all people.*
> *Your sons and daughters will prophesy,*
> *your old men will dream dreams,*
> *your young men will see visions.*
> *Even on my servants, both men and women,*
> *I will pour out my Spirit in those days.*
> *I will show wonders in the heavens*
> *and on the earth,*
> *blood and fire and billows of smoke.*
> *The sun will be turned to darkness*
> *and the moon to blood*
> *before the coming of the great and dreadful*
> *day of the LORD.*
> *And everyone who calls*
> *on the name of the Lord will be saved...."*

That the primary application of this prophecy concerned Judah itself is seen in the immediately following verse (Joel 3:1):

> *"In those days and at that time,*
> *when I restore the fortunes of Judah and Jerusalem,*
> *I will gather all nations*
> *and bring them down to the Valley of Jehoshaphat."*

Even though, unquestionably, it was meant for the ears of his own generation, Joel's prophecy takes on an entirely new meaning some 900 years later in Peter's sermon on Pentecost (Acts 2:14-21), in which Peter quotes Joel's very words to explain that the apostles aren't drunk, but filled with the Holy Spirit. When Peter says, "this is what was spoken by the prophet Joel...," he is making the secondary application which God intended all along, but which Joel himself likely would not have understood. (See 1 Peter 1:10-12.)

Nor, for that matter, would Joel have had the benefit of history or hindsight to know that his concluding prophecy turned out not to be literally true after all. With a tone of guaranteed finality, Joel had written: "Jerusalem will be holy, never again will foreigners invade her" (Joel 3:17). In point of fact, Jerusalem was not only invaded, but totally sacked by the Roman army in A.D. 70–one of the very events to which Jesus is alluding in Matthew 24. The unique nature of apocalyptic literature being to exaggerate for effect, we are cautioned by this passage and others not to read more than is warranted into, say, "the moon being turned to blood"–when the point is that God will do equally extraordinary things as that in the furtherance of his kingdom.

Are we living in the "last days"?

Before we leave this passage, we should also take note of Peter's insertion of the words, "in the last days," as he begins the quotation from Joel. That not only Peter, but Paul, James, and the Hebrew writer all refer to their own generation as being in "the last days" should give us pause when we are tempted to assume that our own generation today is uniquely in "the last days." We *are*, of course, but no more so than any other generation living after the advent of Christ. Ushered in by his appearance, the "last days" have continued until now, and will continue until the Lord appears. (See Hebrews 1:2; 2 Timothy 3:1; 2 Peter 3:3.)

Similarly, both "the Day of the Lord" and "that day" are used in a number of Old Testament prophecies to refer to God's judgment which, even then, he was bringing against the nations. Yet, when we come to the Gospels and Epistles, those phrases begin to focus almost exclusively on the final Day of Judgment–the same "that day" on which the Lord will appear, and the same "that day" on which the dead will be raised. What remains constant, however, is the connotation which has always attached to the "Day of the Lord"–which is to say: that predictable and verifiable moment in history when everything will be *put right!*

Variations on theme, but the same day

This *day of the Lord*, which will "come like a thief in the night" (1 Thessalonians 5:2) is the same *day of Christ* on which Paul hoped to boast that he "did not run or labor for nothing" (Philippians 2:16). It is the *day of God* which prompts us to "live holy and godly lives" as we "look forward to it and speed its coming" (2 Peter 3:11-12). It is the *great day* for which the rebellious angels are "bound with everlasting chains for judgment" (Jude 6); and *the day of God's wrath* "when his righteous judgment will be revealed" and "God 'will give to each person according to what he has done'" (Romans 2:5-6). It is the same *day of judgment* on which "the present heavens and earth are reserved for fire" along with "the destruction of ungodly men" (2 Peter 3:7); and the same *day of redemption* for which the Ephesians "were sealed" with the Holy Spirit of God" (Ephesians 4:30). It is simply *the day* "when God will judge men's secrets through Jesus Christ" (Romans 2:16); and the day about which Paul could say with full confidence, "I know whom I have believed, and am convinced that he is able to guard what I have entrusted to him for *that day*" (2 Timothy 1:12); and the day of which Martha said of her brother Lazarus: "I know he will rise again in the resurrection at *the last day*" (John 11:24).

Jesus himself is abundantly clear about there being a day to end all days–the day to which he refers five times as "that day." There is, of course, "that day" on which "many will say to me...'Lord, Lord, did we not prophesy in your name, and in your name drive out demons and perform many miracles?' Then I will tell them plainly, 'I never knew you. Away from me, you evildoers!'" (Matthew 7:22-23). And "that day" on which it will be "more bearable...for Sodom than for [any town which did not welcome the seventy-two whom Jesus commissioned to spread the good news of the kingdom]" (Luke 10:8-12). And also "that day" which "will close on you like a trap" if your hearts are "weighed down with dissipation, drunkenness and the anxieties of life....For it will come upon all those who live on the face of the whole earth. Be always on the watch, and pray that you may be able to escape all that is about to happen, and that you may be able to stand before the Son of Man" (Luke 21:34-36).

A special day before "that day"

Did you catch the significance of what Jesus just said? In one sentence, he gives us the key to unlocking Matthew 24, Mark 13, and Luke 21. Having just pointed us unquestionably to "that day" at the end of time when all who live on the face of the earth will stand before the Son of Man, suddenly Jesus is also speaking of "all that is *about to happen to you.*" If there is a final Judgment for everyone to face, there is also a more immediate, national judgment which is to be centered on Jerusalem.

Listen again (first from Matthew, then from Luke) as Jesus describes the events surrounding that special judgment. Says Jesus: "So when you see standing in the holy place 'the abomination that causes desolation,' spoken of through the prophet Daniel—let the reader understand—then let those who are in Judea flee to the mountains. Let no one on the roof of his house go down to take anything out of the house. Let no one in the field go back to get his cloak" (Matthew 24:15-18).

As Jesus indicates, Daniel had written centuries earlier concerning those who would later desecrate the temple. "His armed forces," said Daniel of one particular adversary, "will rise up to desecrate the temple fortress and will abolish the daily sacrifice. Then they will set up the abomination that causes desolation" (Daniel 11:31). No mystery here! In the person of Antiochus IV, that prophecy had already been fulfilled in 168 B.C. when Antiochus desecrated the temple by sacrificing a pig on the altar. But soon, says Jesus, the temple itself will be completely desecrated—not simply by the sacrifice of a pig, but by its total destruction!

And as Luke picks up the action, how could we possibly miss what Jesus has in mind? "When you see Jerusalem being surrounded by armies," he says, specifically, "you will know that its desolation is near. Then let those who are in Judea flee to the mountains, let those in the city get out, and let those in the country not enter the city. For this is the time of punishment in fulfillment of all that has been written. How dreadful it will be in those days for pregnant women and nursing mothers! There will be great distress in the land and wrath against this people. They will fall by the sword and will be taken as prisoners to all the nations. Jerusalem will be trampled on by the Gentiles until the times of the Gentiles are fulfilled" (Luke 21:20-24).

That the events described here could be anything other than those which would occur forty years later seems most unlikely. When else would the mammoth stones of the temple be thrown down on top of one another?

Two for the price of one

Among the many details found in Luke's parallel account of Matthew's gospel is one of particular significance. Remember what Matthew said earlier about the rooftops? (Don't go down into the house. Get out quickly....) While Luke also records those words from Jesus, he doesn't present them in Chapter 21, which otherwise parallels Matthew's account. Instead, he places that warning in Chapter 17, where the context is completely different. Nothing at all there about the temple's destruction, only about "the day the Son of Man is revealed." The day when "the Son of Man...will be like the lightning, which flashes and lights up the sky from one end to the other."

Although this often-overlooked detail tends to confirm what we have already said about there being two different judgments under consideration in Matthew 24, in the process it also raises an interesting question about those "house-top" verses which appear–in Matthew's gospel, as related to Jerusalem's destruction, and in Luke's gospel, as related to Christ's appearing. So which of the two events was Jesus talking about: the destruction of Jerusalem or the destruction of the wicked at the final Judgment? Is it not clear by now? The answer is *both*! Without getting lost in the technicalities of just how "rooftops" would figure in either case (neither seems to fit neatly), the obvious point is that each of the two events would happen so suddenly that there would be no time to spare!

So it is that, in Matthew 24 and Luke 21, Jesus is following the time-honored tradition of the prophets, simultaneously blending together two separate warnings. One is about Jerusalem's imminent destruction by the Romans; and the other, about the universal Judgment at the end of time. Nor should we find this in the least surprising. After all, it was the disciples' expansive questions (knowing or unknowing) which prompted Jesus' dialogue in the first place. You'll recall their questions were prompted by Jesus' observation about the massive stones of the temple, when he said: "I tell you the truth, not one stone here will be left on another; every one will be thrown down." Whereupon some of the disciples came privately to Jesus and asked: "Tell us....when will *this happen*, and *what will be the sign of your coming and of the end of the age?*" (Matthew 24:2-3).

Whereas the focus in both Mark and Luke is on the timing of the temple's destruction and the signs which would precede that event, Matthew's account suggests that the disciples may also have been curious about signs which would accompany "the end of the age." Whether, in fact, that is the case, it appears that Jesus responded *as if* there were two distinct questions.

End of age, or end of time?

By "end of the age," incidentally, the disciples probably didn't mean (as we might) "the end of time" or "the end of the world," as it's sometimes translated–simply the final fulfillment of all the kingdom prophecies, as they understood them. Indeed, they may have assumed that the temple's destruction would be part and parcel of one, cataclysmic event bringing with it the "end of the age." But, as he often did, it appears that Jesus used their question as a "teachable moment," stretching them still further.

Remarkably enough, the disciples' likely belief that Christ's coming and the "end of the age" would coincide with the temple's destruction mirrors the mass confusion which survives even to this day regarding what Jesus said on that occasion. Not only have we mostly missed the dual nature of Christ's prophecy, but–more importantly–we've missed what surely must be the object lesson Jesus intended by mixing the two events so intimately. Not only was the destruction of Jerusalem and the temple the clearest possible signal that the whole of the Jewish religious system and Israel's national life was forever abrogated by the blood of Christ, but it was also a graphic picture of the complete destruction awaiting the wicked at the end of time.

Incarnate prophecy

Then again, to speak of Jerusalem's destruction merely as a picture of God's *future* judgment, or even to talk about a *dual prophecy* (as if Jesus were referring to two, totally unrelated events), falls far short. The destruction of Jerusalem–as with the earlier destruction of the nations–was to be a partial fulfillment of God' total and final judgment against evil. A down payment. A reminder that, although God's sovereignty permits his delay, his righteousness is not oblivious to the evil which takes advantage of his patience. In response to the cry of the sufferer–"How long, O Lord?"–God replies, "Not yet, but even now." What he *will* do, he *has* done. What he *has* done, he even now *continues* to do.

The fierce "battle of Armageddon" between preterists (most of whom believe that Jesus' Olivet Discourse and Revelation depict the events of A.D. 70 exclusively) and futurists (most of whom believe these texts exclusively–or substantially–predict events yet to come at the end of time) are two prophetic extremes which seem not to have taken fully into account how prophecy works. Like the Lord himself, *prophecy is incarnate*. In much the same way as the infinite, eternal God wrapped himself in finite, temporal flesh, what we see throughout prophecy is the future wrapped in the present–a greater spiritual reality to come couched in more immediate, historically-verifiable reality. Prophecy is the untouchable which you can touch; the indescribable which you can understand.

Was Jesus God or man? To choose is to lose. He was both, simultaneously: the God-man. So it is with prophecy. It is both present and future, simultaneously: now, but not yet. "Incarnational prophecy" is inherently apocalyptic, revealing the distant future through the eyes of the near future. When we try to make sense of the Olivet Discourse, the temptation is to focus on the extremes: either to fixate on the Lord's coming in judgment against Jerusalem and deny rich overtones which speak of a much greater Coming; or to fixate on a supposed future earthly reign and miss the heavenly reign which already has begun and will never end.

Sorting out the mysterious, multi-dimensional incarnation of prophecy can be no less challenging than figuring out how God and man could have occupied the same space and time in the person of Jesus. Not unlike a children's movie with lines appreciated only by adults, prophecy is for the truly discerning. To that extent, "incarnational prophecy" shares the same problem as parables: its apparent simplicity belies the profound. Seeing, we do not see; hearing, we do not hear. (Or, more often with prophecy, we see and hear what we *want* to see and hear!)

Seen through the eyes of incarnational prophecy, one "day of the Lord" bespeaks another. An immediate, earthly judgment is likely to be a present embodiment of God's greater judgment yet to come. Just as this present "fleshly" earth is a parable to explain the spiritual world to come, and just as the incarnate "Word made flesh" was a parable to explain the pre-existent and ascended Christ, so too was Jerusalem's destruction an incarnation of another, far greater Day of Judgment. It was a visible "now" in order that we might more clearly see the "not yet."

Too bad we couldn't have witnessed the literal "before" and "after" of A.D. 70. For those Jews who did, Jerusalem lying in ruins must have been a sobering parable of God's wrath. And, with that in mind, who dares think further about the resemblance between that decimated temple and the "temple" of our own body which, one day soon, will disintegrate in the grave? Are we prepared for the sudden coming of *that* day?

Everybody wants to know!

Naturally, it's not just the disciples who wanted to know about the timing. We do, too. So can you tell us, Jesus: When, exactly, *will* "that day" come? Well, if we're talking about Jerusalem's destruction, *"I tell you the truth, this generation will certainly not pass away until all these things have happened"* (Matthew 24:36). But if we're talking about the final Judgment, *"No one knows about that day or hour, not even the angels in heaven, nor the Son, but only the Father"* (Matthew 24:36). And since that's the case, then it stands to reason that you should *"watch out that you are not deceived. For many will come in my name, claiming...'The time is near.' Do not follow them. When you hear of wars and revolutions, do not be frightened. These things must happen first, but the end will not come right away"* (Luke 21:8-9).

All it takes today, of course, is for there to be some catastrophic event and, suddenly, well-meaning prophets of the end time tell us with indubitable certainty: "The end is near! The end is near!" What does it say of us that this phenomenon of end-times prophecies occurs year in and year out with predictable regularity, yet nobody seems to remember that the world didn't come to an end during either of the world wars–as predicted–nor with the rise of communism, nor at the institution of the United Nations, nor following the latest earthquake? Have we so quickly forgotten what Jesus said? "No one knows!" Paul underscores Jesus' caveat, saying, "Now brothers, about times and dates we do not need to write to you, for you know very well that the day of the Lord will come like a thief in the night" (1 Thessalonians 5:1-2). Could it be any plainer? If anyone claims to know when the Lord is coming again, he is proved wrong by making that very claim!

Without question, the further along in time we are from Jesus' appearance on the earth, the nearer we are to his reappearance. (Lord, come quickly!) But Jesus' mention of wars and rumors of wars, earthquakes, famines, and pestilence was not meant to signal his imminent appearing (and not likely even signaling the destruction of Jerusalem). Quite the opposite, Jesus is telling us that these are *false signs*! (Remember, the day of the Lord will come "like a thief"...when we *least* expect it!)

As the ongoing march of history has proved, these cataclysmic events are common occurrences which will remain as part of the fabric of time on earth until Christ's appearing–which is the one event that will be accompanied by *never-before-experienced* wonders of such magnitude that no one will mistake it! In the meantime, wars and natural disasters are but the "beginning of birth pains" for the indescribable glory yet to be delivered.

Same day service

Whenever that spectacular day comes, what we know for certain is that everything will happen in rapid succession, as if one fully-integrated consummation. Listen to Jesus' own words (which–importantly–follow in the wake of Matthew 24): "When the Son of Man comes in his glory, and all the angels with him, he will sit on his throne in heavenly glory. All the nations will be gathered before him, and he will separate the people one from another as a shepherd separates the sheep from the goats. He will put the sheep on his right and the goats on the left" (Matthew 25:31-46).

Note that Jesus speaks, here, in one breath about 1) his coming, 2) the "gathering of all nations," and 3) the dividing of the sheep and the goats–obviously a description of his Appearing, the Resurrection, and Judgment. It is crucial to understand that, in terms of timing, when one happens, they all happen. Since all three major events occur within the scope of "that day," there is neither space nor time for intervening circumstances of any kind. Nor is there the slightest mention of such from Paul or Peter, or from Jesus himself.

What about the man of lawlessness?

Addressing a rumor among some of the Christians in Thessalonia that "the day of the Lord has already come (2 Thessalonians 2:1-12)," Paul reassures them: "...that day will not come, until the rebellion occurs and the man of lawlessness is revealed, the man doomed to destruction." Just as in the Olivet Discourse, this rebellion speaks of a judgment which would take place prior to "the coming of the Lord Jesus Christ and our being gathered to him."

Despite all the debate over the identity of "the man of lawlessness," two things are noteworthy. First, there seems to be a direct correlation between Jesus' reference in Matthew 24:15 to "the abomination that causes desolation...standing in the holy place" and Paul's depiction of the man of lawlessness, who "will oppose and will exalt himself over everything that is called God or is worshiped, so that he sets himself up in God's temple, proclaiming himself to be God." There could hardly be a more apt description of the desecration of the temple by the Romans in A.D. 70, or of the abominable Caesar-worship which would threaten Christians as far away as Thessalonica.

Second, is that the Thessalonians themselves knew who he was. "Don't you remember that when I was with you I used to tell you these things?" Paul says. "And now you know what is holding him back, so that he may be revealed at the proper time. For the secret power of lawlessness *is already at work*; but the one who now holds it back will continue to do so till he is taken out of the way. And then the lawless one will be revealed, whom the Lord Jesus will overthrow with the breath of his mouth and destroy by the splendor of his coming."[1]

The striking parallel here with Jesus' Olivet Discourse continues when Paul, like Jesus, links this more-immediate, special judgment with the final, universal judgment of the world. Speaking of their ultimate vindication at the end of time, Paul tells the Thessalonians:

1 For those who would see the "man of lawlessness" as referring to a particular end-times figure, why tell these Thessalonians about some far distant fulfillment of this prophecy when they are clearly wondering about events that will affect their world? Why, at the conclusion to this discussion, admonish them in light of what has been said to "stand firm and hold to the teachings we passed on to you"? Whoever the "man of lawlessness" was, he was an imminent, first-century threat. In fact, Acts 17:7 specifically pinpoints the persecution which came as a result of their violating Caesar's decrees. (A wider discussion of related end-times scenarios follows in Chapter 12.)

"God is just: He will pay back trouble to those who trouble you and give relief to you who are troubled, and to us as well. This will happen when the Lord Jesus is revealed from heaven in blazing fire with his powerful angels. He will punish those who do not know God and do not obey the gospel of our Lord Jesus. They will be punished with everlasting destruction and shut out from the presence of the Lord and from the majesty of his power *on the day he comes to be glorified* in his holy people and to be marveled at among all those who have believed" (2 Thessalonians 1:6-10).

It's as if we're listening to a broken record, playing over and over again. When Christ comes, the Resurrection of both the righteous and the wicked will occur. When Christ comes, the Judgment will take place for everyone who's ever lived. The day for one is the day for the other. End-time theories which propose a millennial reign on earth between Christ's coming and the day of Judgment simply run out of room. God has no *time* for such theories. (Where Revelation 20:1-10 fits into all of this will be the subject of discussion in Chapter 12. Suffice it to say, it will have to fit in conjunction with the anchor-points of time which have been established beyond any reasonable doubt in the many passages we've already reviewed.)

Sound the trumpet!

If we need yet further corroboration, listen again to the trumpet call of the angels which Jesus mentioned in Matthew 24. In a passage unquestionably addressing the resurrection, Paul also says, "For the trumpet will sound, the dead will be raised imperishable, and we will be changed" (1 Corinthians 15:52). Whenever the trumpet sounds, Christ's appearing and the one and only Day of Resurrection are joined inextricably together.

There is, incidentally, a serendipitous symbolism between this trumpet call and the one which God commanded of Israel each time the wandering nation would set out for a new destination. "The blast will be a signal for setting out," God said to Moses (Numbers 10:6, 17). Then the tabernacle of the Lord would be taken down and carried to its appointed place, where once again it would be re-erected. Is it only coincidence that Paul (in 2 Corinthians 5:1-5) speaks of our "tent" being taken down in death, as it were, in anticipation of our resurrection? When the great trumpet sounds at the Lord's appearing, rest assured we'll be on the move!

That Christ's coming is to be associated with the Day of Resurrection, as opposed to other suggested scenarios, is also implied by the Hebrew writer, when he tells us, first, that Christ "has appeared once for all time at the end of the ages to do away with sin by the sacrifice of himself" (Hebrews 9:26). This happened, of course, during Jesus' incarnation on earth. But the Hebrew writer continues, saying, "Just as man is destined to die once, and after that to face judgment, so Christ...will appear a second time, not to bear sin, but to bring salvation to those who are waiting for him" (9:27-28). When he appears at the time of man's eternal judgment, Christ will redeem all those who have been saved as a result of what he did on the cross when he first appeared. In but two descents to the earth, Christ has now already made *possible* what, on that day, he will make *permanent*.

Last stop: the end of the world

If we have difficulty grasping the coming reality of our own death, at least we can see it happening to others. Even if we don't take time to read the obituaries, page after page in the morning newspaper is a constant reminder of our mortality. And night after night, the six o'clock news brings grim reports of the day's shocking murders and tragic accidents, filling our living rooms even further with gruesome scenes of the latest victims of violence, famine, and disease. But, still, we pretty much expect that the world will go on forever, even without us. The earth doesn't stop spinning when someone dies, and the sun will always rise somewhere on the globe.

So for us to look out on a vast ocean at sunset, or snow-capped peaks in the Alps, or a blanket of stars in the southern African skies, and to think that one day all of that could just disappear, *now* we've approached the truly unthinkable! Yet, that is precisely what the Scriptures tells us will happen...*on the very same day as Christ's coming, and our own resurrection and judgment.* It's going to be a busy day, indeed. And a catastrophic day!

As we have seen repeatedly in one Old Testament prophecy after another, there is an abundance of language which seems to point to a time when the earth will be totally destroyed. For instance, Isaiah says, "Lift your eyes to the heavens, look at the earth beneath; the heavens will vanish like smoke, the earth will wear out like a garment" (Isaiah 51:6). However, by now we've also seen enough hyperbole in prophecy to be wary of automatically taking all of those metaphors literally. Even so, Peter leaves us in no doubt about what will happen to this present universe at the coming of our Lord. His lengthy treatise on the subject (in 2 Peter 3:3-13) may be apocalyptic, but it's not just figurative.

An urgent message from Peter

Our first indication of the literal nature of Peter's commentary is that he is specifically responding to some who were scoffing about the world's not yet having come to an end. (If that was a problem in the first century, no wonder there are so many skeptics some twenty centuries down the line! In a slight twist on the adage that "justice delayed is justice denied," it seems woefully true as well that the Day of Judgment delayed is the Day of Judgment denied.)

As for the delay, itself, Peter begins by saying that God doesn't operate in terms of human time. "With the Lord," he says, "a day is like a thousand years, and a thousand years are like a day" (2 Peter 3:8). Then Peter repeats exactly what Paul had told the Thessalonians about the Day of the Lord coming "like a thief," and reminds his cynics of those *other* scoffers who had wrongly assumed that God was only crying "Wolf!" Had they forgotten Noah's contemporaries, for whom–despite all the warnings–the Flood had come as a huge surprise? In Noah's day, of course, it was water which God used to destroy mankind. Next time, says Peter, it will be fire–a Sodom-like fire which will consume the heavens and the earth, and water itself, for that matter. Strangely, too...even fire!

Complete and utter destruction

In one simple sentence, Peter describes the indescribable. "The heavens will disappear with a roar; the elements will be destroyed by fire, and the earth and everything in it will be laid bare" (2 Peter 3:10). What, no fanfare? No drum roll? For all the times we've quipped, "It's not the end of the world," this time it is!

If you'll recall, we've seen the earth being "laid bare" before in apocalyptic literature, the idea being (at least metaphorically) that

God would wipe the earth clean of all living things. What we haven't seen before is mention of the *elements* being destroyed. That is, presumably, the protons and neutrons and the sub-atomic particles that are fundamental to life. The chemical elements, from actinium to zirconium, of the Periodic Tables. The carbon, hydrogen, and oxygen without which there would be no universe. These very elements, says Peter, "will melt in the heat."

So how complete will the destruction be on the Day of the Lord? There is nothing so distant as can be seen through the most powerful telescope that won't be destroyed; and there is nothing so small as can be seen through the most illuminating microscope that will survive. No earth, no seas, no clouds, no stars. No air, no light, no heat. If you can imagine it, think *total nothingness.* A complete void. The end of all Creation.

Once again, this raises insurmountable problems for any end-time theory that assumes the continuing existence of the earth for any purpose following the Lord's appearing. For the day of his appearing is not only the Day of Resurrection and the Day of Judgment, but it is also the very day upon which the whole universe will be utterly and completely destroyed. There will be nothing left of the earth for apocalyptic battles, or an earthly kingdom reign, or "heaven on earth." If there is no longer any *earth,* how can any of these things happen?

In the same way that man's history is "dust to dust," when all that elemental "dust" is fully and finally destroyed, the Creation itself will have come full cycle, from *nothing* back to *nothing.* Is this not the obvious assumption underlying the psalmist's comparison between a temporal earth and its eternal Creator (in Psalm 102:25-27)?

In the beginning you laid the foundations of the earth,
and the heavens are the work of your hands.
They will perish, but you remain;
they will all wear out like a garment.
Like clothing you will change them and they will be discarded.
But you remain the same, and your years will never end.[2]

2 Compare Isaiah 34:4, which, though clearly apocalyptic language, corroborates both Peter and the psalmist.

Also, when the writer of Ecclesiastes says: "Generations come and generations go, but the earth remains forever" (Ecclesiastes 1:4), the comparison is between the brevity of human existence and the ongoing continuity of the earth. We are not to understand from such a comparison that the writer is addressing the question of whether a time will come when the earth itself will no longer exist.

When the heavens and the earth finally "perish" and are "discarded," all that will remain is the eternal realm of God which was, and is, and is to come–the eternal realm for which man was always destined in the hopeful heart of God. And the same eternal realm from which the faithless, the unrighteous, and the wicked will be forever barred.

Destruction of the universe; destruction of souls

The final, apocalyptic end to God's Creation, suggests Peter, is itself a sobering parable. For it is a dire warning about the fate of those who will not be permitted entrance into the world beyond. Restrained only by his longsuffering patience towards mankind, says Peter, God is not rushing to Judgment, "...not wanting anyone to perish, but everyone to come to repentance" (2 Peter 3:9). But when that day finally arrives, it will set in motion not only the obliteration of the cosmos, but at some point–sooner or later–the destruction of the lost as well.

Note carefully how Peter pairs the two, saying, "The present heavens and earth are reserved for fire, being kept for the day of judgment and destruction of ungodly men" (2 Peter 3:7). If the heavens and the earth (which haven't in the least rebelled against their Maker) are to be destroyed in this way, how could we possibly think that God's wrath against the objects of his love who have ignored him, or even spit in his face, could be anything less?

John's vision of judgment

If the prospect of God's great judgment strikes fear in any heart, it is understandable. Just being in God's presence will be more "totally awesome" than that overworked phrase could ever mean today. Merely consider John's own reaction when he received the visions contained in what we now know as the Book of Revelation. When John relays what it was like to see "the Alpha and the Omega, the First and the Last, the Living One," he says, "I fell at his feet as though dead. Then he placed his right hand on me and said: 'Do not be afraid.'" (Revelation 1:17-18). Thereafter, John describes what he sees...but, interestingly, he doesn't tell us whether his knees ever stopped shaking!

It is, of course, the spectacular cinematic Judgment scene from John's surreal revelation that sticks in our minds. Its similarity to Daniel's vision (in 7:9-10) means that there are all the usual questions to be asked: Is it apocalyptic in style? Undoubtedly. Is it figurative? Without question. But is it nevertheless spine-tingling in its graphic reality? Absolutely!

So tell us again, John, what did you see? "I saw a great white throne and him who was seated on it. Earth and sky fled from his presence, and there was no place for them. And I saw the dead, great and small, standing before the throne, and books were opened. Another book was opened, which is the book of life. The dead were judged according to what they had done as recorded in the books. The sea gave up the dead that were in it, and death and Hades gave up the dead that were in them, and each person was judged according to what he had done. Then death and Hades were thrown into the lake of fire. The lake of fire is the second death. If anyone's name was not found written in the book of life, he was thrown into the lake of fire" (Revelation 20:11-15).

Metaphorical though it may be, John's Judgment scene before the "great white throne" gives us a visual confirmation of what all the other scriptures have indicated. After the heavens and the earth have been dispatched into nothingness, all that remains are the resurrected souls of the dead being judged according to their deeds. What John's vision adds to the other passages is the imagery of death and Hades being destroyed, and also the intriguing opening of the books.

That there will be no more death, nor any further need of a waiting room for the dead is obvious. As Jesus had promised (Matthew 16:18), the gates of Hades would be no match for the power of the resurrection! And so it is that both death and Hades, having served their appointed purpose like the heavens and the earth, will be consumed in the apocalyptic fire.

What about those "books"?

As for the symbolic significance of the "books," we can't be entirely sure. Perhaps they were meant to be innumerable volumes in which the deeds, both good and bad, of all mankind were meticulously recorded. Something like courthouse records. John did say that the dead would be judged by their deeds "as recorded in the books."

But it is also possible, as intimated in Deuteronomy 29:20-21, that they represent the inspired books of Scripture by which man is to be judged: the statutes and commands; the principles and precepts. Referring to any Israelite who might turn away from God, Moses said: "All the curses written in this book will fall upon him, and the LORD will blot out his name from under heaven. The LORD will single him out from all the tribes of Israel for disaster, according to all the curses of the covenant written in this Book of the Law."

In any normal court proceedings, the statutes alleged to have been violated are read out before the court so that the judge or jury can decide how the defendant's conduct matches up to what is expected under the law. As a reminder that God's righteous judgment will not be whimsical, but judicial, this particular interpretation of "the books" would not go amiss.

Yet, it's interesting that, even here, Moses speaks of names being "blotted out," as if from a book. Had God and Moses ever talked about such a book? We know of at least one conversation they had on the subject. While interceding on behalf of the Israelites after they had danced before the golden calf, Moses begs God magnanimously, "Please forgive their sin—but if not, then blot me out of the book you have written." To which the LORD replies: "Whoever has sinned against me I will blot out of my book. Now go, lead the people to the place I spoke of, and my angel will go before you. However, when the time comes for me to punish, I will punish them for their sin" (Exodus 32:32-34).

So God carries a book, does he? David seemed to think so. Indeed, he *hoped so*! Of his enemies, David said, wishfully, "May they be blotted out of the book of life and not be listed with the righteous" (Psalm 69:28). And then, as if it had already happened, David rejoiced to say, "You have sat on your throne, judging righteously; you have rebuked the nations and destroyed the wicked; you have blotted out their name for ever and ever" (Psalm 9:4-5). Evidently, David put considerable weight in this "book of life," as he called it—especially as it pertained to who was "in" and who was "out."

Whether this is the same volume David had in mind when he said, "All the days ordained for me were written in your book before one of them came to be" (Psalm 139:16) is unclear. Since he was speaking about God's having seen his unformed body in the womb, it probably suggests nothing more than that God, being God, would have had prescient foreknowledge of David's entire life. Yet, some would eagerly point us to that fascinating passage in Revelation 17:8, where the angel (explaining to John about the mystery woman and the beast) says: "The inhabitants of the earth whose names have not been written in the book of life *from the creation of the world* will be astonished when they see the beast...."

Questions, questions...

Has a list of all the saved been in the book of life from the very beginning? If so, was it a matter of *predestination* (God's choosing) or *prescience* (God's knowing)? And if the answer to that question is *predestination*, then what does John mean when he tells us—not once, but twice—that in his vision he saw each person being judged according to what he had done? Are we to believe that God is responsible for the very deeds of hatred, violence, and evil by which those whom he intentionally predestined for punishment will be judged?

All of this raises any number of tangential questions about the nature of the final judgment: Has each soul's verdict already been sealed? Might there be any last-minute acts of clemency? Should we expect anything like a trial, or will we simply be in the sentencing phase at that point?

Naturally, we could hardly imagine that the Judge of all mankind would have to deliberate his verdicts as human judges must do. Even now, he knows us backwards and forwards, inside and out. But what John's reference to "the books" does suggest is that, unless the whole Judgment scene is a complete sham, we ourselves are responsible for whatever records there may be of our lives and for whatever adverse judgment befalls us as a result.

What, if anything, this says about predestination and "the elect," one will have to decide. Only a fool would suggest that a single passage (especially one that is patently metaphorical) will put an end to the heated debate. Yet, the obvious must be said. The idea that God chose the "sheep" and the "goats" even before they were born, and then—at the end of time—will arbitrarily consign the "goats" to eternal destruction (all the while telling them it's their fault) makes a mockery of the very idea of judgment. Nor, for that matter, does it speak nobly of God's unquestioned sovereignty.

What John's Judgment scene does speak well of is God's mercy and grace. For there is yet another way to think about those *many* "books" and that *other* book, the book of life. If, in fact, what those first "books" contain is the record of my life and yours, we're condemned before we ever reach the great white throne. "For all have sinned and fall short of the glory of God!" As sinners, we deserve nothing better than the lake of fire. But just about the time we're expecting to be thrown into the lake, the other book is opened–the book of life. And, lo and behold, suddenly we hear the Judge calling out our name. Can you even begin to imagine it? One moment we have every reason to believe we should be lost; the next moment we're wearing a crown!

Praise God for keeping two sets of books, especially the one with all the erasures. For the saved in Christ, it's not our *names* he has blotted out, but our *sins*. What words can possibly tell that story? We're in the book! We're in the book! By the grace of God, we're in the book!

Anchor Verse - Revelation 21:4-5

"For the old order of things has passed away....I am making everything new!"

Chapter Preview

How possibly does God communicate a reality of which we are completely unaware? Life in heaven will be a qualitatively different kind of life from the one we have known in earth's space and time. Even thinking of heaven as "an unending eternity for ever and ever" is to think in human terms, not God's. To be eternal is to have the kind of qualities which endure outside of time.

Whatever new bodies we are given will be tailor-made for heaven. Just right for what we're meant to do there, whatever that is. No need to worry about it before we get there. Function will automatically follow form, just as our heavenly form will reflect the function which God intended from the moment he first conceived to create us.

7

GIVE ME HEAVEN; YOU CAN HAVE THE STREETS OF GOLD

Heaven would hardly be heaven if we could define it.

–William E. Biederwolf

Do you not find it dismaying that we may know more *jokes* about heaven than we know about heaven itself? St. Peter keeps us all laughing, there at the Pearly Gates; but what, in all seriousness, do we know about the eternal state of the saved? Perhaps the single greatest disappointment in our reading of the Scriptures is just how little we are told of heaven. There it is, the final destination of the righteous, the place everybody wants to go when they die, the home of God and the angels–and what we know about it, really, could be put in a thimble.

Sure, there are images, and visions, and analogies, but it's mostly "pie in the sky by and by," not hard news or factual detail. Nothing, say, one could write a long chapter about! Right off the bat, it makes you wonder if the Scriptures' reticence to talk about heaven isn't itself a clue–as if the eternal state of the saved is really and truly indescribable. As if, to think of it as a *place* which you could take a picture of and send to your friends, would be like thinking of a refreshing autumn breeze, or a cozy feeling, or a precious memory, as a "place." How do you take a picture of any of those? Indeed, how do you *go* to any of those? Surely, then, heaven must be the ultimate metaphor, simile, and allegory, all wrapped up into one. A desperate grasping for straws when words fail.

And yet, there are words. And pictures. And talk about "going there." And descriptions, as if it's a real place. So what *do* we know of heaven? What *can* we know?

What the ancients thought

Surely, there must have been early rumors and conjecture...something at least about the glory of being in God's presence. For example, what are we to make of Moses' report that he and Aaron, Nadab and Abihu, and the seventy elders of Israel "went up and *saw the God of Israel*" (Exodus 24:9-11)? His description at the beginning of Scripture has the familiar ring of that which we are given centuries later at the end of Scripture: "Under his feet was something like a pavement made of sapphire, clear as the sky itself." Yet, we know these men of Israel weren't *in* heaven at the time (to think of it again as a place), so this can only be an opening entrée.

Then there is Isaiah's prophecy of Israel's eventual restoration, with its usual overlay of events to come far past the time of his own generation (Isaiah 33:17-24):

> *Your eyes will see the king in his beauty*
> *and view a land that stretches afar....*
>
> *Look upon Zion, the city of our festivals;*
> *your eyes will see Jerusalem,*
> *a peaceful abode, a tent that will not be moved;*
> *its stakes will never be pulled up,*
> *nor any of its ropes broken.*
> *There the LORD will be our Mighty One.*
> *It will be a place of broad rivers and streams....*
>
> *No one living in Zion will say, "I am ill";*
> *and the sins of those who dwell there will be forgiven.*

"Zion," with no more illness or sin? Whatever more-immediate "heaven" Isaiah may have had in mind, the picture he paints is right out of Revelation. (Or...a more intriguing possibility...the picture in Revelation is right out of Isaiah!) And from Moses to Isaiah to John's

Revelation, there's always those jewels and precious gems glittering in the Holy City. Isaiah seems bedazzled by them (Isaiah 54:11-12):

"O afflicted city, lashed by storms and not comforted,
I will build you with stones of turquoise,
your foundations with sapphires.
I will make your battlements of rubies,
your gates of sparking jewels,
and all your walls of precious stones."

Would anyone reading these words within even a few centuries of Isaiah's day have imagined them to be a description of *heaven*? Would they not simply have thought Isaiah was embellishing the picture of a restored Jerusalem after the exile? And yet, from our perspective in time, we can hardly read that description without thinking of anything other than heaven itself. For confirmation, all we have to do is add Isaiah's words in Isaiah 35:8-10:

...only the redeemed will walk there,
and the ransomed of the LORD will return.
They will enter Zion with singing;
everlasting joy will crown their heads.
Gladness and joy will overtake them,
and sorrow and sighing will flee away.

Never mind that Isaiah is obviously talking about what it will be like when the prisoners in foreign captivity finally return to Jerusalem. We now claim this passage for ourselves as a promise of our own no-more-tears, heavenly Jerusalem. It is *we ourselves* who will enter heaven singing and wearing crowns of joy. And perhaps that's exactly what God *wants* us to anticipate. Not all of his parables are drawn from nature. Some are from history.

Reading between the lines

The problem is, it's just difficult to tell how much we are reading back into the consciousness of the ancients. Is there any way of knowing how clearly the idea of heaven may have been articulated in their own minds? Apparently, it was enough for David simply to know that, following all the days of his life, he would "dwell in the house of the LORD forever" (Psalm 23:6). Did he ask for more details? Did he need pearly gates and streets of gold, or was he content to know that "You will fill me with joy in your presence, with eternal pleasures at your right hand" (Psalm 16:11)? For David, *joy* and *pleasure* would not likely have been a geographically-identifiable destination with picture post cards, but the intangible, inexpressible blessings of an intimacy with God not possible in our present reality.

There was, of course, the "land of milk and honey"–that promised land which foreshadows the bliss of heaven. But David was a *king* in that very land, and yet he was looking ahead to still a *better* Promised Land, as were all the other ancient men and women of faith. If they lacked the benefit of John's Revelation, they nevertheless had their own vision of the "heaven" to come. Take that nomadic tent-dweller Abraham, for example. He "was looking forward to the city with foundations, whose architect and builder is God" (Hebrews 11:10). Are we to believe that Abraham was expecting a literal city; a walled, fortified Jerusalem on earth? Surely, what he anticipated was a sense of eternal belonging–the security which comes from knowing there's nowhere else you'd rather be.

We are told that, along with Abraham, all of the patriarchs "admitted they were aliens and strangers on earth." They knew that life on this terrestrial ball was never intended to be their eternal state of existence. "People who say such things show that they are looking for a country of their own. If they had been thinking of the country they had left, they would have had opportunity to return. Instead, they were longing for a better country–a heavenly one. Therefore God is not ashamed to be called their God, for he has prepared a city for them" (Hebrews 11:13-16).

To say they were looking for a *better* country is to say they were looking for a *different kind* of country. Not a country with geographical, political, and economic realities, but a spiritual reality distinctly *without* those things! A spiritual city *without* walls and fortifications and houses and streets. Not even golden streets!

What Jesus *didn't* say about heaven

When we come to the gospels, once again we couldn't be more disappointed. Jesus is frustratingly silent about what heaven is like.

Oh, there is plenty of talk about what the *kingdom* of heaven is like. Indeed, there are all sorts of parables about the kingdom, which Jesus said was both "near" and "within you." And, of course, there is the "heaven" in which we ought to store up our treasures (Matthew 6:20); and in which the names of the righteous are written (Luke 10:20).

He tells us, too, what we really already knew: that heaven is where his Father is...and ours–"Our father who art in heaven"–to whom we pray, "thy will be done, on earth as it is in heaven" (Matthew 6:9-10). And, certainly, heaven is the "throne" of God (Matthew 5:34); but because the earth is also "his footstool" (Matthew 5:35), we find ourselves once again mired in frustrating metaphorical bogs. Nor do we learn much from when heaven was "opened" at the point of Jesus' baptism in the Jordan, when he saw the Spirit of God descending like a dove and heard the "voice from heaven" confirming his sonship (Matthew 3:16-17). Indeed, was "heaven" (or, "the heavens" KJV) here anything more than a reference to the "skies above"?

It comes as no surprise, either, that Jesus tells us heaven is the eternal abode of the angels–the same angels who, says Jesus, "always see the face of my Father in heaven" (Matthew 18:10). And the same angels *in heaven* among whom there is rejoicing when even one sinner repents (Luke 15:10). But what news is that? The youngest among us can tell us where the angels live! (And, of course, they know all about their golden harps and majestic wings, as well....)

We do perk up a bit when we briefly overhear Jesus telling his disciples that he is going to prepare a place for them (which we like to think applies to us as well). "In my Father's house are many rooms; if it were not so, I would have told you. I am going there to prepare a place for you. And if I go and prepare a place for you, I will come back and take you to be with me that you also may be where I am" (John 14:2-4).

Sure *sounds like* a place, doesn't it? And a place to which we can *go*! Unfortunately, Jesus didn't pass out any four-color brochures giving us glossy photos of the heavenly mansion and its celestial amenities. We just have to take the travel agent's word that it's going to be great when we get there.

Beyond what we learn in those few passages (with one additional observation to be discussed momentarily), Jesus was virtually silent about the nature of heaven. If anything, he may well have spoken with more clarity about the nature of hell.

Some revelations about Revelation

So it seems we are left almost entirely with the apocalyptic imagery of John's Revelation to satisfy any curiosity we may have about heaven. Yet, here as before, all the normal warnings about apocalyptic language apply. It is metaphor and imagery, not cold fact. It is suggestive, not definitive. To take each detail as literal is to miss the message. In fact, we cannot even be completely certain when John is sharing a vision of heaven and when he is not.

A case in point is John's repeated reference to seeing a temple in heaven. "Then *God's temple in heaven* was opened," John first says (in 11:19), "and within his temple was seen the ark of his covenant. And there came flashes of lightning, rumblings, peals of thunder, an earthquake and a great hailstorm." Then (in 14:17) he tells us that "Another angel came out of *the temple in heaven*, and he too had a sharp sickle." And finally (in 15:5), "After this I looked and *in heaven the temple*, that is, the tabernacle of the Testimony, was opened. Out of the temple came the seven angels with the seven plagues." And so on.

Listening excitedly to those scenes being described, we could be forgiven for thinking there is actually a "temple" in heaven. But when John begins to describe his vision of "the Holy City, Jerusalem" (which appears to be John's clearest vision of heaven), John stumps us entirely, saying, "I did not see a temple in the city, because the Lord God Almighty and the Lamb are its temple" (Revelation 21:22). One minute we have a temple in heaven; the next minute we don't!

Another caution comes in the very language John employs when he introduces his vision of "a new heaven and a new earth" (21:1-5). Listen carefully to what John says: "Then I saw a new heaven and a new earth, for the first heaven and the first earth had passed away and there was no longer any sea." So far so good. As we've already seen from Peter's writing, this present earth and the heavens above it will vanish into nothingness on the day of the Lord's appearing.

But now we hear John saying: "I saw the Holy City, the new Jerusalem, coming down out of heaven from God....," and he proceeds to describe that city in great detail. Are we to take all these details literally? Have we not seen repeatedly that apocalyptic imagery was never meant to be taken as anything other than a figurative picture of an underlying reality? The only fact we can take literally is that Revelation has become a minefield of biblical interpretation for the very fact that people take it as literal fact! Or—more pernicious yet—*selectively* as literal fact.

For example, those who take John's mention of a "thousand year reign" as literal fact are not likely to agree with others who take it as literal fact that only 144,000 will be taken up into heaven. Nor are they likely to accept that John's picture of pearly gates and golden streets is to be taken literally; but they might well be happy to believe that those who are thrown into the (literal) lake of fire (literally) will be tormented day and night for ever.

We're a funny bunch of folks when it comes to deciding what we will pick and choose from the smorgasbord of possible literal interpretations among all the apocalyptic language spread before us. This is not to say there isn't a factual reality underlying all of the vivid imagery. There is! But as Jesus, himself, cautioned in Matthew 24, "let the reader understand." As with all apocalyptic literature, *discernment* must ever be the watchword. Or perhaps *humility*.

What Revelation reveals about heaven

Because of its sequencing (immediately after the Judgment scene and the total destruction of the earth and sky), John's description of the "new heaven and new earth" (in Chapter 21) is likely our most reliable beginning point in Revelation to attribute his vision directly to what heaven might be like. Before that point, we have imagery overload in so many different directions we can't be completely sure what is meant to be past, present, or future. Any number of fantastic scenes "come down out of heaven" into John's view, but whether any of them is meant to describe *heaven itself* is difficult to say.

Of course, even the phrase —"a new heaven and a new earth"—suggests that a whole new reality will replace virtually everything we've ever known in this present world. Certainly everything of a physical nature. That being the case, how possibly does God communicate a reality of which we are completely unaware? It's like a parent talking to a two-year-old about the danger of electricity. Using word-pictures is about the best one can do.

Certainly, God could make some headway through a process of elimination, revealing what heaven is *not*. And this he does, telling John that "there will be no more death or mourning or crying or pain" (Revelation 21:4). Every tear will be wiped from the eye. Nor will there be any night there (Revelation 21:25). What's more, "nothing impure will ever enter it" (Revelation 21:27); and "no longer will there be any curse" (Revelation 22:3).

But the number one question—What we will actually *do* in heaven?—gets short shrift. In a single, terse statement, John is told: "The throne of God and of the Lamb will be in the city, and his servants [presumably *the saved*] will serve him" (Revelation 22:3). At the very least, this brief mention might give some illumination as to what the Hebrew writer meant when he said: "We...have such a high priest, who sat down at the right hand of the throne of the Majesty in heaven, and who serves in the sanctuary, the true tabernacle set up by the Lord, not man" (Hebrews 8:1-2). And then, referring to earthly priests, the writer continues, saying, "They serve at a sanctuary that is a copy and shadow of what is in heaven" (Hebrews 8:5).

Yet, just how we might serve as priests in the heavenly tabernacle remains as much a mystery as ever. Certainly there would be no animals to sacrifice, and, more importantly, *no need* of further sacrifice for sin. In heaven, we will be in the very presence of the Lamb slain for the sins of the world! If that is meant to be a snapshot of heaven's activities, it falls far short of what we might wish.

Is it about a place, or about a relationship?

There are other snapshots which seem equally mysterious. However, importantly, they take us less in the direction of what we will *do*, and more towards what we might *be*. For example, John's opening impression of the Holy City coming as a "bride beautifully dressed for her husband" (Revelation 21:2), speaks about new beginnings...about an intimacy with God which we've never before known.

We often speak of a "marriage made in heaven." What John envisions is a heaven made for marriage, in which the Holy City itself is the bride. As John goes on to say, "One of the seven angels who had the seven bowls full of the seven last plagues came and said to me, 'Come, I will show you the bride, the wife of the Lamb.' And he carried me away in the Spirit to a mountain great and high, and showed me the Holy City, Jerusalem, coming down out of heaven from God. It shown with the glory of God, and its brilliance was like that of a very precious jewel, like a jasper, clear as crystal" (Revelation 21:9-11).

The Holy City as a *bride*? What words come quickly to mind? Beauty. Purity. Joy. Anticipation. Consummation. Bliss. It would be hard to think of a better analogy.

Somewhat more straightforwardly at this point, John tells us that the time finally has arrived for the wedding couple to begin their life together. It's then that he shifts the focus back to us, reminding us that we ourselves are the bride! "Now the dwelling of God is with men, and he will live with them. They will be his people, and God himself will be with them and be their God" (Revelation 21:3). So to think of the Holy City merely as a *place* (complete with measurable walls and beautiful gates) is to miss the beauty of the *relationship* which John's vision was meant to describe. (Who really cares where you live, as long as you're together!)

Being versus *doing*

If, therefore, heaven is to be a new relationship with God–like a radiant bride, ineffably beautiful–are we not being told that heaven is a reality where *being* is at least as important as *doing*? And yet, that must surely be our very problem with heaven. To most folks, heaven just seems downright boring. How can you possibly compare it to "the good life" right here, right now? We'd rather be jet-setting it in United's "friendly skies" than twiddling our thumbs in God's humdrum heaven...through "endless years the same."

Ever wonder why the early-American slaves sang so many "spirituals" about heaven? For that matter, why most white folks also sang more about heaven in days gone by? Naturally, the prospect of no more pain or tears would have looked mighty good to slaves spending backbreaking days in the cotton fields under the whips of their masters. But, that aside, no one in earlier times, whether black or white, seemed to be as frenetically obsessed with "doing" as we are today. Beyond the long hours of hard work demanded of life back then, folks appear to have been far more content simply to *be*. In view of what we know about heaven, might we do well even now to give greater focus to *being*, not *doing*?

Of course, there will always be things in this life we still must *do*, even for the advancement of the kingdom. And more things yet which we must endure, whether major illnesses, the death of loved ones, rebellious children, painful divorces, financial downturns, or emotional upheavals. Life can be overwhelming at times, even exhausting. Seen from that perspective, heaven's calm may well be a more welcomed alternative. There are any number of tumultuous moments in our lives when that ominous "silence in heaven for about half an hour" begins to look pretty good.

For those who long for relief from their daily struggles, the Hebrew writer brings the wonderful promise: "There remains, then, a Sabbath-rest for the people of God; for anyone who enters God's rest also rests from his own work, just as God did from his" (Hebrews 4:9-10). If there are those who might think heaven a bit boring, there are multitudes of others for whom heaven's promised "rest" is the only hope that gets them through the day.

What about the pearly gates and golden streets?

The next snapshot John shares with us is of the Holy City, the "heavenly Jerusalem." That it is *not* the ancient City of David which John sees, nor the present center of political controversy in the State of Israel, nor the future site of some perceived kingdom reign on earth, is suggested by John's incredible imagery, surpassing even that of Moses and Isaiah. For starters, we're talking about a "city" in the shape of a cube (1,400 miles wide, long and high), with walls 200 feet thick. We're also talking about a city of pure gold (but transparent); walls of jasper; foundations decorated with every imaginable gemstone; gates made out of pearls; that great street (not actually "streets") of gold; a river flowing from the throne down the middle of the great street; and so on (Revelation 21:15-22:5).

To say from all of this that heaven will be utterly magnificent is an understatement. In fact, *perfect* is the perfect word for heaven, as seen in the numerical symbolism of the twelve gates and twelve angels, and the names of the twelve tribes of Israel over the gates; not to mention the twelve foundations on which were written the names of the twelve apostles (Revelation 21:9-14). If twelve is the number of perfection, *perfection* just became even more perfect!

But in the midst of this magnificent perfection, don't miss the point of it all. The operative words ought to be highlighted, underlined, and starred: "For the old order of things has passed away....I am making everything new!"

Can't wait to see all that gold?

Take that great street of gold, for example. Do you really think there will be streets in heaven, much less a street of pure gold? Isn't God using that street to tell us that, in heaven, all of our present values will be turned on their head? Gary Cooper's character "Hooker" just about had it right in his line from the 1954 classic, "The Garden of Evil": "If earth were made of gold, men would kill each other for a handful of dirt."

It doesn't take a genius to know that, among other reasons, we pave our streets with asphalt or concrete rather than gold because of gold's relative scarcity. Gold is precious because it's rare! But in heaven, that which is rare will be in abundance; and that which is in abundance will be rare. Ever covet a pot of gold here on earth? In heaven, we'll be walking on the stuff!

That is, *if* we were walking on streets at all. Which we won't be. For streets are as much a part of this "old order" as anything else. As is gold itself. And pearls. And jasper and crystals; emeralds and sapphires.

Do you not find it fascinating that God created a physical universe of wondrous beauty, which one day he is going to completely destroy in order that we might experience a far superior reality; but that he uses the beauty of this lesser creation to tell us something of a sublime existence yet to come? More intriguing yet, why would God appeal to our love of the material (which so often ends up becoming the root of all evil) to describe a non-material sphere of total righteousness? Or, to put it another way, if we were attracted to heaven because of all those glittering gemstones and the dazzling "streets of gold," would we be the right people to be there?

Surely, God has not used such materialistic imagery to appeal to our baser earth-bound instincts for wealth and power and glory, but rather to underscore that heaven will be as different as asphalt and gold. As revolutionary as "cubed" cities. As extraordinary as bright daylight without the sun. Behold, all things are new!

Heaven on earth?

So why do some insist that heaven will be right here on the earth? That, somehow, there will be a rejuvenated (or perhaps entirely re-created), "heavenly earth" where ferocious lions will lie down next to gentle lambs without the slightest thought of lamb chops for supper? Where we will live in a familiar universe, except that we won't die, and all will be peace and love? Where there will be government, and business, and family life, but all in a perfect utopia? Apart from the fact that the Scriptures are crystal clear about the total extinction of this planet and its very elements, isn't there something fundamentally unworthy about wanting to live in a perfected but perpetuated earth?

Hear again the words from Peter: "That day will bring about the destruction of the heavens by fire, and the elements will melt in the heat. But in keeping with his promise we are looking forward to a new heaven and a new earth, the home of the righteous" (2 Peter 3:12-13). As with our own resurrection bodies, the idea is *new*, not *renewed*–so new and different, indeed, that the eternal sphere of heaven defies imagination.

That the earth-like language purporting to describe heaven is not to be taken literally is confirmed by similar language in passages which are clearly talking about the *kingdom of heaven* in the "here and now," not the eternity of heaven in the "there and then." For example, the "new heaven and new earth," described so vividly by John, corresponds perfectly with the Hebrew writer's portrait of what we already experience as kingdom people.

Contrasting the *spiritual* kingdom of Christ with their former Jewish heritage and "a mountain that can be touched," he says to these Hebrew Christians: "You *have come* to Mount Zion, to the heavenly Jerusalem, the city of the living God. You *have come* to thousands upon thousands of angels in joyful assembly, to the church of the firstborn, whose names are written in heaven. You *have come* to God, the judge of all men, to the spirits of righteous men made perfect, to Jesus the mediator of a new covenant, and to the sprinkled blood that speaks a better word than the blood of Abel" (Hebrews 12:22-24).

The present spiritual kingdom of God is already "the heavenly Jerusalem" for those here on earth whose names are written in heaven–a heaven which, like the present kingdom itself, cannot be

156

touched, or seen, or experienced as we think of touching, seeing, and experiencing in our present physical environment. Our confusion about an ethereal, spiritual heaven versus a tangible, physical "heaven on earth" is but an extension of our convoluted usage of the word *church*. Heaven in the afterlife will no more be a *place* of any kind than the church of the living God is the stain-glassed and steepled building in which the church congregates.

If one just insists on having heaven on earth, it's already here in the kingdom of heaven. Now. In the present. Here today; never gone tomorrow. Already a present reality in this world; yet not to be fully consummated until the marriage of the Lamb and his bride...which is *heaven*!

A final word from Jesus

Thinking about heaven this way is all very interesting. Colorful snapshots, intriguing analogies, comforting promises. But we still aren't given any direct answers to most of our questions. Will stillborn children recognize their mothers in heaven; or talk with adults on the same level of maturity? How can we possibly be joyful in the presence of God, knowing that loved ones have been eternally damned? What common language, if any, will we all speak? Will we be singing and praising God day in and day out? Will we wear white robes, or possibly have wings? Will we know Moses, and Abraham, and Elijah? Will they know *us*? And what will our relationship be with our earthly husbands and wives and parents and children?

We can speculate, of course, attempting to read between the lines. For example, it's difficult to imagine that we won't retain some memory of our life on earth, else why would we want to praise God as our Savior? Yet, if we were to have complete recall of the past, how could we possibly move beyond the unpleasant memories of difficult relationships or perhaps traumatic experiences of war, hunger, rape and murder? Then again, without our earthly memory, how could we possibly recognize each other? Many, in particular, who have lost a spouse or a child seem haunted by the question: Will we know each other there?

Want a heavenly body?

Of course, that question opens Pandora's box regarding the form and nature of our celestial bodies. Despite our earlier analogy of seeds and watermelons, it remains next to impossible to avoid the wishful thought that, in heaven, we will still look pretty much like what we see in the mirror. But, surely, that can't be the case, given the range of earthly bodies all the way from aborted fetuses and still-born infants to wrinkly octogenarians and amputees; from husky body builders to the blind and the lame.[1] And have we stopped to consider that, given centuries of infant mortality, a huge percentage of those in heaven will never have lived beyond the age of ten? Equally intriguing, will there be racial features to our heavenly bodies, or even the usual masculine and feminine body traits?

The further you go down this road, the more likely it seems that our heavenly bodies might well be both uniform and strangely unfamiliar. When Paul said of our natural body, "it is raised a spiritual body" (1 Corinthians 15:44), did he mean a spiritual body which is solid and opaque like our present bodies, or perhaps something more akin to the shadowy figures in C. S. Lewis' *The Great Divorce*? Does the spiritual body have need of food and drink, or have sexual desires (or even the capacity for sex)? Does it need regular sleep? Surely, we'll not need sleep in heaven!

It seems like a simple thing, but will we be called by our names? Or perhaps be given *new* names, like Abram and Sarai were given the names Abraham and Sarah? The angels have names (at least there's Michael and Gabriel), and since we are to be like them, will we not also have names?

There's simply no end to all the questions, but hardly any beginning to the answers. Paul wasn't speaking about heaven when he paraphrased Isaiah 64:4, but his words could hardly be more fitting: "No eye has seen, no ear has heard, no mind has conceived what God has prepared for those who love him" (1 Corinthians 2:9).

Perhaps our many unanswered questions partially explain the skepticism of the Sadducees (and others to this day) about whether there is even an afterlife, much less a heaven. In fairness to the skeptics, it does seem a bit unreal, doesn't it? Unless, of course, we open ourselves to the possibility of a major paradigm shift in values and realities. As from children to adults. As from the world's being flat to the world being round. As from the Stone Age to the computer age.

---

1 Contrary to unofficial but widespread Catholic belief, the souls of unbaptized fetuses and infants do not end up in limbo, a hypothesized state of existence somewhere between heaven and hell. See Chapter 11.

In an earlier chapter we listened in on that conversation Jesus had with the Sadducees when he answered their hypothetical about the woman with the seven husbands. Rebuking both their ignorance of Scripture and their lack of appreciation for God's power to totally transform, Jesus told the Sadducees that, "At the resurrection people will neither marry nor be given in marriage; they will be like the angels in heaven" (Matthew 22:30). Surely, Jesus' startling response puts us on notice that who we will be in heaven, and what our relationships will be, and even what we will *do*, will be a paradigm shift of the highest order. Not only will it require a complete metamorphosis of our present, earthly bodies, but also a revolutionary transformation of how we think.

Check out this body!

As for the metamorphosis, Paul assures us that we will have just the right bodies for our eternal existence. For "our citizenship is in heaven. And we eagerly await a Savior from there, the Lord Jesus Christ, who, by the power that enables him to bring everything under his control, will transform our lowly bodies so that they will be like his glorious body" (Philippians 3:20-21). If all we take away from that passage is the idea that having a glorified body like the ascended Christ is an exciting prospect, we are missing the greater significance of its wider implications. That our *bodies* will be profoundly different will itself make all the difference in how we think, how we act, and even in what we are capable of doing.

You have to wonder if God didn't purposely create the caterpillar-cum-butterfly as the perfect example of the relationship between the form of a body and how that body functions. When caterpillars are around, no one is surprised to discover holes in any nearby leaves. Munching its way through the day, the caterpillar has little or no regard for the consequences, and ends up being one destructive little creature. But then the most amazing thing happens. One day, that same unlovable larva wraps itself in a cocoon, takes a long nap, and mysteriously re-emerges as the most beautiful, delightful creature you've ever seen. And what does it *do*? It spreads beauty all around the garden. Couldn't destroy a leaf if it had to! Its glorious reconstituted body wouldn't let it. Behold, the old has passed away, and all things are new!

If that's not a perfect picture of our own metamorphosis, what is? Sinful, selfish, and destructive in this life, eventually one day we die, take a long nap in the cocoon of *hades*, and re-emerge at the Day of Resurrection to receive a heavenly body so glorious that we couldn't be sinful, selfish, or destructive if we had to! Whatever new bodies we are given will be tailor-made for heaven. Just right for what we're meant to do there, whatever that is. No need to worry about it before we get there. Function will automatically follow form, just as our heavenly form will reflect the function which God intended from the moment he first conceived to create us.

Who knows whether we'll have wings? If butterflies have them, maybe angels do too. And didn't Jesus say we'd be like the angels in heaven? But don't take flying lessons quite yet. It would just give you one more thing to *do*. If you really want to get a head start on heaven, don't think about wings, and harps, and streets of gold. Or what you will do, or who you will know. "Dear friends, now we are the children of God, and *what we will be* has not yet been made known" (1 John 3:2). Is it not enough to know that "when he appears, we shall be like him"? And also like the angels?

Getting a handle on "eternity"

Interestingly, the answer for most of us is either a hesitant "Not so sure" or perhaps a resounding "No!" Even if somehow we could be convinced that heaven was filled with exciting, interesting, and robust activity—not just contemplative piety in the presence of God—we still have major difficulty getting our heads around the idea of being in heaven for an eternity. Doing *anything* for an eternity would have to get old, wouldn't it? Just how much "Wow!" can we stand?

Sure, faced with the option of death followed by non-existence, we'll take eternal life every time, thank you very much. But it's not as if we are greatly enthralled by the idea. Or so motivated by the expectation of experiencing it that we will sell everything we have to buy the field in which the treasure of eternal life is buried. Just think about all the bad times when we've said, "It seemed like an eternity." By contrast, "time flies when you're having fun." Let's face it, eternity just doesn't sound fun. Try as we might, we can't think of having enough "fun" in heaven for eternity to fly by! Remember all those pulpit illustrations about how interminably long eternity is?

One does wonder what folks are thinking when they talk about eternity in such temporal terms. Have we been so easily seduced by "a day being a thousand years" in the eyes of God? Or is it the companion word *forever* that throws us off? For all the misunderstanding about "eternity," interestingly, the word itself is used only once in the entire King James Version (Isaiah 57:15), and only three times in the NIV. With the exception of Ecclesiastes' observation that God has "set eternity in the hearts of man," each of the other references is to God (or to the personified "Wisdom" of the Book of Proverbs). You, O LORD, are "from all eternity," says the psalmist (Psalm 93:2). "I [Wisdom] was appointed from eternity, from the beginning, before the world began," we learn from Proverbs 8:23.

Is there some *continuity of time* that we're supposed to see here, but don't? Surely the idea is not eons of time, but, quite the opposite, God's very *timelessness!* Eternity stands outside of time. In the incarnation of Christ, God's eternal nature has intersected with time, but he is not bound by it. Or defined by it. Or driven by it, as we are.

So to think of heaven as "an unending eternity for ever and ever" is to think in human terms, not God's. That's best seen when we examine the Scripture's use of the word *eternal*. Of course, if we're already thinking in terms of eons, then the Ecclesiastes' reference to man's "eternal home" (Ecclesiastes 12:5) sounds like heaven will last...well... for eons! The same is true when we hear the master's advice to the dishonest manager: "I tell you, use worldly wealth to gain friends for yourselves, so that when it is gone, you will be welcomed into eternal dwellings" (Luke 16:9).

The other, timeless face of "eternity"

However, we begin to sense the true meaning of the word *eternal* in connection with "dwellings" when Paul uses it with reference to our resurrected bodies. "Now we know that if the earthly tent we live in is destroyed, we have a building from God, an eternal house in heaven, not built by human hands" (2 Corinthians 5:1). Time, here, is not even remotely a consideration. Paul is talking about the *nature* of the bodies we will have in heaven. Unlike man-made structures which deteriorate over time, in heaven we will have bodies not subject to time—nor, consequently, to deterioration. There are *mortal* bodies; and there are *eternal* bodies. Just as *mortal* bodies are fit for time on earth, *eternal* bodies will be fit for heaven, where man's time will be swallowed up in God's eternity.

W. R. Matthews drew an insightful distinction in saying, "There really are two ideas: life which goes on, and life which has some quality or value in it which lifts it above time. We might use 'everlasting' for the first idea and 'eternal' for the second." Even if the root words are essentially the same, their distinctive connotations are as distanced from each other as is heaven from earth.

If you have a computer Bible program (or an antiquated concordance!), pull up the word *eternal* and be prepared for a shock. In all of its many associations, there is not a single hint of time. To save you time, here's a quick list: eternal God, eternal love, eternal pleasures, eternal praise, eternal laws, eternal kingdom, eternal dominion, eternal ways, eternal fire, eternal sin, eternal punishment, eternal glory, eternal purpose, eternal encouragement, eternal judgment, eternal redemption, eternal covenant, and eternal gospel. Surprised? Most people would be. To be *eternal* is to have a *lasting nature*. To have the kind of qualities which endure *despite the passing of time* (if, in fact, there is any time at all).

So what do we learn when we add "eternal life" to that long list if not that the word *eternal* has to do with the *nature and quality* of life in heaven, not heaven's duration in time? As a bonus, what we understand about the word *eternal* tells us yet more about heaven itself. By sheer word association, we learn that heaven is all about God, love, pleasure, praise, dominion, purpose, and redemption. But nothing about "endless years the same," because all things heavenly are as timeless as God's love for us.

Indeed, it is God's love for us which gives ultimate meaning to eternal life. Without the slightest mention of time, Jesus himself defined the very essence of eternal life in his prayer to the Father. "Now this is eternal life: that they may know you, the only true God, and Jesus Christ, whom you have sent" (John 17:3). What's there to know about God? Simply that he "so loved the world that he gave his one and only Son, that whoever believes in him shall not perish but have eternal life" (John 3:16).

Life before life in the here and now

Even that juxtaposition tells us something significant. As the opposite of "perish" (in which there is no continuity), eternal life is *characterized* by its very continuity. Therefore, to live eternally is to live immortally, in stark contrast to the wicked, upon whom immortal life will not be bestowed. Far from indicating the *length* of immortality, "eternal life" for the righteous affirms the promised *fact* of immortality, as compared with its unthinkable alternative.

Word connotations cannot always be reliable arguments, especially in any given language. But it may be helpful to think of two similar words in English which have significantly different connotations. Whereas the word *continual* suggests that which occurs repeatedly over a long period of time (as in the continual temple sacrifices, year after year, century after century), the word *continuous* suggests that which extends forward, uninterrupted by time. It has *lasting effect*. If it happens once, it is for all time, as in "the blood of the eternal covenant" (Hebrews 13:20). Unlike the continuous temple sacrifices, Jesus died *once...for all eternity*. He doesn't die *continually*.

It is for that very reason, praise God, that we *already have* "eternal life." (Already, but not yet!) The paradox of already having eternal life before we enter the eternal realm is explained in Jesus' ghoulish-sounding words: "Whoever eats my flesh and drinks my blood *has* eternal life, and I *will* raise him up at the last day" (John 6:54).

It is not unlike the unborn baby in the womb, who already has life, but hasn't yet been born. And who could possibly explain to that developing little person about life outside the womb? Or about the nature of time? The irony is that, in the womb, we've already experienced a timelessness in which we were perfectly content. An "eternity," as far as we knew, in which our every need was met without our ever asking!

To say, then, that we will have eternal life in heaven says nothing about *how long* we will live in heaven. It's already begun before we get there! The point is that life in heaven will be a qualitatively *different kind of life* from the one we have known in earth's space and time. So different, in fact, there'll be no such thing as "boring."

As much *being* as *doing*, perhaps, but never boring!

Anchor Verse - Matthew 10:28

"Do not be afraid of those who kill the body but cannot kill the soul.
Rather, be afraid of the one who can destroy both soul
and body in hell."

Chapter Preview

What is the nature of the "fire" associated with hell? Whereas you can count on one hand the number of times the word *torment* is used, you can hardly count the endless number of times you read of *destruction, perishing, blotting out, cutting off,* and *consuming* in connection both with God's judgment and hell itself.

"Eternal fire" bespeaks the *nature* of hell's fire, not its *duration.* "Eternal punishment" will no more be punishment throughout an endless eternity than was the immediate, devastating punishment suffered by the people of Sodom and Gomorrah. At some point—sooner or later—hell will mean the everlasting destruction of the soul and its resurrection body.

8

THE TORMENTING CONUNDRUM OF HELL

*Hell was not made for men. It is in no sense parallel to heaven:
It is "the darkness outside," the outer rim where being fades away
into nonentity.*

–C.S. Lewis
The Problem of Pain

Ask a random sampling of people about hell, and what you'll invariably hear is that it's the place you *don't* want to go when you die. Ask them to *describe* hell, and odds are that you'll quickly hear talk of fire and brimstone, and the weeping and gnashing of teeth for an eternity in the midst of hell's leaping flames. Yet, ask them if they take the prospect of such a hell seriously, and you are as likely as not to hear evasiveness, uncertainty, or even derision. If pressed, of course, most folks could live with the thought that there is some future fiery furnace for child-molesters, serial killers, and all the maniacal "Hitlers" of the world. But to think that "broad is the way and wide is the gate" that leads to the torture chamber of hell is cause for increasing embarrassment even among many believers.

Indeed, in church after church today, there would be shock and dismay if Sunday's sermon were to be a good-old-fashioned "hell fire and damnation" thrashing. Heaven forbid there should be any mention of Jonathan Edwards' "blowing brick-kiln" in which "after millions of ages, your torment would be no nearer to an end than it ever was." Or Charles Spurgeon's horrifying vision of your being "put in a vessel of hot oil...all thy veins becoming a road for the hot feet of pain to travel on." Our current aversion to such vivid depictions of hell may have more to do with today's never-frowning God of contemporary Christian culture (or even politically-correct notions of non-judgmentalism and tolerance) than with any scholarly rejection of the traditional view of hell's unending agony. But, for whatever reasons, hell's literal flames have gradually given way in the view of many to an everlasting *mental* or *emotional* suffering. Or to the eternal absence of God's love, or some vaguely-defined "separation from God" which lasts forever.

If for many folks the "literal" music of hell's licking flames has ended, the melody of ongoing, never-ending suffering of some kind manages tenaciously to linger on. After all, even if there is absolutely no basis in fact for identifying the story with hell, how does one possibly erase from his mind that fiery furnace of the rich man and Lazarus? And, as many would argue from other, more relevant references, there's just too much fire associated with hell to ignore the flames. So whether the imagery is taken literally or metaphorically, the idea of non-stop torment continues to dominate both the believing and non-believing world's conversation about hell.

Thinking outside the box

Of course, there are two things about hell of which we can be altogether certain: first, that hell will be whatever hell turns out to be, whether or not our understanding of its reality is anywhere close to being correct; and second, that whatever it turns out to be will be appropriate punishment inflicted by a righteous and holy God. Given those two verities, debating the nature of hell could be seen by some as nothing more than an interesting academic exercise which, in the end, is entirely moot and therefore a needless waste of time. But can anything of which God has spoken ever be a waste of time? In light of the many scriptures which address the subject of hell, surely God intends that we have *some* understanding about the fate of the wicked. Indeed, the Hebrew writer assumes basic knowledge of the resurrection and eternal judgment to be elementary (Hebrews 6:1-2).

It's always possible, of course, that the consensus view of hell's ongoing conscience torment is entirely accurate. Given the descriptive imagery in the text, all one has to do is point to the words! The biblical language is so familiar that we can close our eyes and almost see the fire and smell the smoke. But have we possibly missed something about all those flames? Is there, perhaps, another way that we are meant to understand the purpose and effect of hell's fire? And, if so, might it make an important difference in how we respond to the reality of hell?

One of the most intriguing questions in all this discussion is what the earliest disciples themselves might have understood about the nature of hell. On the one hand, despite a dearth of overt Old Testament references to hell, it doesn't appear that Jesus had to explain to his listeners what it was all about. They must have had *some* idea of hell, if nothing more than the word associations which Jesus made with the prophets' ancient apocalyptic images of unquenchable fire, never-dying worms, and gnashing of teeth. All of that easily would have been connected with "the day of the Lord," which for the Jews was past and future all at once! And, of course, there would have been no mystery about the parallel Jesus made between hell and the smoldering garbage dump just outside Jerusalem. Everyone would have understood that picture instantly.

On the other hand, it would be decades before John received his Revelation with its unique vision of the "fiery lake of burning sulphur." In the meantime (as will be discussed momentarily), the popular image of hell so familiar today seems to have had little or no impact on the teaching or functioning of the church in those vibrant early years. So just how much weight can be put on the traditional view of hell?

What follows is a case for understanding hell's punishment as ultimately culminating in the complete and total destruction of the wicked, body and soul. The primary scriptural cornerstone for the case is Matthew 10:28, in which Jesus warned: "Do not be afraid of those who kill the body but cannot kill the soul. Rather, be afraid of the one who can destroy both soul and body in hell."[1]

To immediately put a label on this position would be less than helpful, since no well-recognized school of thought is monolithic. Among those who advance this general position are many who hold

---

1 The destruction of "body and soul" here may refer either to the totality of the *person*, or more specifically to destruction of the resurrection body along with the soul. Jesus' similar warning in the Sermon on the Mount, set within the context of his discussion of adultery (Matthew 5:29-30), appears to be a variation on theme, focusing as it does on our present physical bodies. Within that context, the idea is not that the earthly body will be thrown into hell (for it will long since have deteriorated), nor that one ought literally to gouge out his eye or cut off his hand. It appears, rather, that Jesus is underscoring the seriousness of the eternal consequences for what we do while we are in our earthly bodies. Comparatively speaking, it would be better to go through life maimed than to have one's body intact, yet end up losing everything in hell's destruction.

significantly different views on various aspects of it. Nor would they necessarily endorse the entire afterlife perspective offered in this book. It remains, then, for you to evaluate the case presented here on its own merits and to decide for yourself whether it best reflects what the Scriptures teach on the subject. As with a number of other afterlife issues, hell is sufficiently shrouded in mystery that one would be foolish indeed to go to the wall even for a time-honored hypothesis, much less one that is out of step with so broad a consensus. So in the spirit of open and honest pursuit of God's truth, come, let us reason together.

What kind of fire is it?

Instantly, of course, there are problems with taking the fire of hell literally. Like heaven, hell is a spiritual state in which souls are no longer in flesh-and-blood, earthly bodies. Those physical bodies will long since have deteriorated, replaced at the resurrection with *spiritual* bodies fit for an ethereal realm. So, whatever "fire" there might be in hell would certainly have to be such as would punish spiritually-embodied souls, not physically-embodied souls. (When you think about it, the combination of literal earthly bodies and literal flames of fire would hardly bode well for the idea of a continual burning. Just how long could a body of flesh last when licked by literal flames? At the very least, God would have to transform our present physical bodies to accommodate a reality never before experienced...which would mean that we would no longer be talking about literal earthly bodies, much less literal fire.)

However, to move the discussion along, let's assume for the moment that the fire is absolutely, finger-scorching literal—or, at the very least, perfectly descriptive of whatever "spiritual fire" God intends. The question remains: What is the *nature* of all the biblical fire associated with hell? Is it a fire which *torments*, or a fire which *consumes*?

Although not a single Old Testament passage overtly purports to describe hell for us, the imagery of fire in association with God's judgment against both nations and individuals is inescapable. Beyond all doubt, for example, it was literal fire which consumed, not only the burnt offering, but also Aaron's sons who offered "strange fire" before the Lord. "Fire came out from the presence of the LORD and consumed the burnt offering and the fat portions on the altar." And then, "Aaron's sons Nadab and Abihu took their censers, put fire in them and added incense; and they offered unauthorized fire before the LORD, contrary to his command. So fire came out from the presence of the LORD and consumed them, and they died before the LORD" (Leviticus 9:24-10:2).

Was fire used as God's agency of punishment? No doubt about it. Did it have lasting effect? Unquestionably. But did the pain of the flames last forever? Clearly not. In one brief moment, God's judgment had been executed on the wicked, through fire. What could be clearer? Nadab and Abihu were not *tormented* in the fire, but *consumed* by it.

The same is true of the 250 men who had joined with Korah in his rebellion. After the earth opened up and swallowed Korah and his family, "fire came out from the LORD and consumed the 250 men who were offering the incense" (Numbers 16:35). Again, the word is *consumed*, not *tormented*.

And then there is Achan who, after being stoned for bringing sin into the camp at Ai, was burned along with his entire family. For God had said: "He who is caught with the devoted things shall be *destroyed* by fire, along with all that belongs to him" (Joshua 7:15).

There are also those two different captains, along with their men, who were sent by the king of Samaria to the prophet Elijah. "'If I am a man of God,' said an indignant Elijah to first one captain then the next, 'may fire come down from heaven and *consume* you and your fifty men!' Then fire fell from heaven and *consumed* the captain and his men" (2 Kings 1:9-14).

Fiery destruction was also the fate of Israel's enemies, and even Israel herself. As for Israel and Judah, God said: "I will send fire upon their cities that will *consume* their fortresses" (Hosea 8:14). Virtually the same language is used regarding Israel's many enemies, including the Philistines (Amos 1:7); the Ammonites (Amos 1:14); Damascus (Jeremiah 49:27); the Moabites (Amos 2:2) and the citizens of Ar of Moab (Numbers 21:28). Obviously, none of these fortresses were *tormented* by fire, but totally *destroyed*.

Of stubble, straw, and dung

Throughout the Scriptures, we see numerous variations on a single theme—the burning of waste—which changes only with the particular substance being consumed. Most often, that substance is stubble, which quickly catches fire and just as quickly is gone. For example, Obadiah predicts that "the house of Jacob will be a fire and...the house of Esau will be stubble, and they will set it on fire and *consume* it." What follows is even more significant. "There will be no survivors from the house of Esau" (Obadiah 18). When stubble is placed into the fire, nothing is left. Applying the metaphor to human victims, there are no survivors. If perhaps there is suffering in the fire, more importantly there is no one left to tell about it!

The picture is the same when Joel warns of the coming day of the LORD, saying, "Before them fire devours, behind them a flame blazes....like a crackling fire *consuming* stubble" (Joel 2:3-5). And again comes the metaphor when Isaiah speaks of Babylon's destruction, specifically including its astrologers and stargazers: "Surely they are like stubble; the fire will *burn them up*" (Isaiah 47:14). Same again when Nahum assures Judah of the fall of the Ninevites, saying: "they will be *consumed* like dry stubble" (Nahum 1:10).

If ever there were any doubt about what happens to the "stubble" which is burned, that doubt vanishes as Malachi describes the day of the LORD when the wicked will get their due. Crucially, among all the Old Testament references which have apparent allusions to the Day of Judgment, heaven, and hell, perhaps none is more direct than this passage. Says God, "'You will again see the distinction between the righteous and the wicked, between those who serve God and those who do not. Surely the day is coming; it will burn like a furnace. All the arrogant and every evildoer will be stubble, and that day that is coming will set them on fire,' says the LORD Almighty."

And what is the result of the fire in the furnace of God's judgment? "'Not a root or a branch will be left to them....Then you will trample down the wicked; they will be ashes under the soles of your feet on the day when I do these things,' says the LORD Almighty" (Malachi 4:1-3). If this is meant as a picture of hell, the furnace can roar for as long as one might wish, but it will take no time at all before someone's got a job carrying out the ashes!

So when at last we come to what Jesus said to his disciples about the danger of forsaking him, we know exactly what he is talking about. "If anyone does not remain in me," warned Jesus, "he is like a branch that is thrown away and withers; such branches are picked up, thrown in the fire and burned" (John 15:6). Burned in *unending agony*, or *completely destroyed*? The destruction Jesus implies could not be clearer. Nor that of the Hebrew writer who, warning against our own falling away, speaks of land that produces thorns and thistles being worthless and in danger of being cursed. "In the end it will be burned"–which again is to say, totally destroyed (Hebrews 6:8). These images are but distant echoes of what God had said centuries earlier regarding the lineage of Jeroboam: "I will burn up the house of Jeroboam as one burns dung, *until it is all gone*" (1 Kings 14:10).[2]

Burn, baby, burn!

But, still, some will ask, "Doesn't the fire of hell last forever?" They may even point us to any number of passages which speak of "unquenchable" fire. For instance, there is that reference in Isaiah to the mighty man who will become tinder, and his work a spark. "Both will burn together, with no one to quench the fire" (Isaiah 1:31). Or perhaps to Isaiah's description of Edom's pending punishment (Isaiah 34:9-10):

> *Edom's streams will be turned into pitch,*
> *her dust into burning sulphur;*
> *her land will become blazing pitch!*
> *It will not be quenched night and day;*
> *its smoke will rise forever.*

Day and night forever sounds like a lot of burning, doesn't it? Yet, don't forget the ending:

> *From generation to generation it will lie desolate;*
> *no one will ever pass through it again.*

The fire itself may never be quenched, but its work has been completed, with lasting effect. Nothing survives in the blazing pitch! Far from "unquenchable fire" suggesting the endless suffering of whatever is put into it, the idea is that nothing can hold back the fire of God's judgment. It will do its work!

---

2 To suggest, as some have, that the burning bush which Moses saw on Mount Horeb (Exodus 3:1-4) proves there can be a fire which does *not* consume, is merely to highlight the rule by pointing to an exception. When we see "fire" combined in context with words like "destroy" or "consumed," we are no longer dealing with some exception, but rather with the natural meaning which ought to apply to those words, even if they happen to be used symbolically.

...circumcise your hearts,
you men of Judah and people of Jerusalem,
or my wrath will break out and burn like fire
because of the evil you have done–
burn with no one to quench it (Jeremiah 4:4).

And again Jeremiah gives the proper emphasis as the focus shifts away from the fire itself to the inflamed judgment of God which lies behind it: "My anger and my wrath will be poured out on this place...and it will burn and *not be quenched*" (Jeremiah 7:20). The unmistakable point of all this "unquenched fire" is that God's righteous wrath will have its day. Nothing and no one can stop it!

Indeed, Jeremiah provides us with a direct link between "unquenchable fire" and "fire which consumes." Pens the prophet, "The LORD said to me...I will kindle an *unquenchable* fire in the gates of Jerusalem that will *consume* her fortresses" (Jeremiah 17:27). Ezekiel, too, corroborates the connection, saying: "'This is what the Sovereign LORD says: I am about to set fire to you, and it will *consume* all your trees, both green and dry. The blazing flame will *not be quenched*, and every face from south to north will be scorched by it. Everyone will see that I the LORD have kindled it; it will not be quenched'" (Ezekiel 20:47-48).

We see this same word association yet again in the dramatic announcement of the Messiah's long-awaited appearance. John the Baptizer says of Christ: "He will baptize you with the Holy Spirit and with fire. His winnowing fork is in his hand to clear his threshing floor and to gather the wheat into his barn, but he will *burn up* the chaff with *unquenchable* fire" (Luke 3:16-17).

What, then, does "unquenchable fire" do? It makes desolate, it consumes, and it burns up whatever is put into it. If perhaps you still believe that the "fire" literally burns forever, even so, don't get hung up on how long the fire burns. Concentrate on what it *does*.

A fire of total destruction

Of course, it's not just Old Testament prophecy that speaks of consuming fire. The Hebrew writer tell us that, even under the new covenant, "If we deliberately keep on sinning after we have received the knowledge of the truth, no sacrifice for sins is left, but only a fearful expectation of judgment and of raging fire that will *consume* the enemies of God" (Hebrews 10:26-27). Lest we miss the significance of this passage, it is important to note that the language here cannot possibly be confused with ancient prophecies against Israel's political and military enemies in which fire might be symbolic of their overthrow. Clearly, the Hebrew writer is talking about God's judgment against individuals...and where else but in hell? But if hell's "fire" is the subject of the warning, what that fire does is *consume*, not *torment*.

In the same way that the present heavens and earth are reserved for destruction by fire, Peter tells us that ungodly men are also being kept for the day of judgment and *destruction* (2 Peter 3:7). Like the cataclysmic fire which will completely obliterate the universe on that day, hell is also a fire that consumes. A fire that destroys. A fire that causes the wicked to perish.

And to what would you liken it, Peter? To the fire that destroyed Sodom and Gomorrah, comes Peter's quick reply. "If he condemned the cities of Sodom and Gomorrah by burning them to ashes, and made them an example of what is going to happen to the ungodly...." then he knows how to hold the unrighteous for the day of judgment (2 Peter 2:6-9). And, of course, Jude concurs, saying that Sodom and Gomorrah "serve as an example of those who suffer the punishment of eternal fire" (Jude 7).

Eternal fire? You mean fire that keeps on burning its victims forever? Not if Sodom and Gomorrah are anything to go by. The fate of those two abominable cities stands as the quintessential illustration of a *consuming* fire. In the wake of that catastrophic fire–however long it burned–nothing was left of the two cities, not even a trace! For anyone still insisting that hell is all about ongoing torment in fire and brimstone, serious thought needs to be given to a specific day in history when fire and brimstone literally rained down on the wicked.

To be sure, there would have been suffering in the process– undoubtedly even some "weeping and gnashing of teeth." But their suffering would not have lasted for long. Only long enough for the rain of hot sulfur to do what needed to be done: to assuage God's righteous wrath and rid the land of its evil. As Jesus himself put it: "...in the days of Lot, people were eating and drinking, buying and selling, planting and building. But the day Lot left Sodom, fire and sulphur rained down from heaven and *destroyed* them all" (Luke 17:28-29).

"Eternal fire" bespeaks the *nature* of hell's fire, not its *duration*. Need we reiterate our discussion in the previous chapter about the meaning of "eternal"? (Eternal love, eternal praise, eternal laws, eternal kingdom, eternal dominion, eternal ways, eternal sin, eternal glory, eternal purpose, eternal encouragement, eternal redemption, eternal covenant, and eternal gospel....) So, when we hear Jesus speaking about "eternal fire," there's no reason to think in terms of clocks or calendars. Time is not the issue. *Effect* is the issue.

Is "eternal" really "forever"?

Maybe we're thrown off track by words which are the equivalent of "eternal" but different. Words like *forever* or *everlasting*. Yet even those don't necessarily mean *without end*. Merely consider the many uses of the Hebrew word *olam* and the Greek word *aionios*, both of which mean the same as "eternal." Through the use of those two words, any number of things are described as "eternal" which did not last forever. For example, speaking of the sprinkling of blood at Passover, God said to Moses: "Obey these instructions as a lasting [eternal] ordinance for you and your descendants" (Exodus 12:24). Is that old covenant requirement still in force today? Then there is "eternal" Aaronic priesthood. "The priesthood is theirs by a lasting [eternal] ordinance" (Exodus 29:9). And, "...their anointing shall surely be an everlasting [eternal] priesthood throughout their generations" (Exodus 40:15, KJV). Does an eternal Aaronic priesthood square with our even now being priests under the great High Priest, Christ?

Consider also the servant whose ear has been drilled to a door symbolically indicating that "he shall be thy servant for ever [eternally]" (Deuteronomy 15:17, KJV). And there's Caleb's inheritance that was to last "forever" (Joshua 14:9); and Samuel's apprenticeship which was to last "always" (1 Samuel 1:22); and Solomon's temple which was a place for God to dwell "forever" (1 Kings 8:13); and Gehazi's leprosy which was to "cling to you and your descendants forever" (2 Kings 5:27). Are any of these situations and occurrences ongoing, continuous, and unending? Is Samuel still an apprentice, or Solomon's temple still standing? Are Gehazi's descendants (if any remain) still afflicted with leprosy? In all these instances, equivalent words to "eternal" were not intended to mean there would never be an end to the effect described, only that their certainty was guaranteed for so long as God intended it within his purposes.

So it is that when Jesus talks about the great dividing of the sheep from the goats, and says of those on his left, "Depart from me, you who are cursed, into the eternal fire prepared for the devil and his angels," the point is *destination*, not *duration*. Likewise, when Jesus says, "Then they will go away to eternal punishment, but the righteous to eternal life" (Matthew 25:41,46), he's speaking of the kind of punishment—namely *destruction*—which has everlasting consequences.

Obligingly, Jesus even provides us with a graphic illustration of his use of the Greek root word *ainon*, when he cursed the unfruitful fig tree on his way into Jerusalem. "Let no fruit grow on thee henceforward for ever," Jesus commanded. "And presently the fig tree withered away" (Matthew 21:19 KJV). The desired effect was not something that happened over and over again throughout eons of time, but once for all time. Apply the imagery of *immediate withering* to "eternal fire" and you get the picture.

"Eternal punishment" will no more be punishment throughout an endless eternity than was the immediate, devastating punishment suffered by the people of Sodom and Gomorrah. Nor, for that matter, will it be any *less* lasting in its effect. For the punishment of "eternal fire" has eternal, lasting, never-ending repercussions. That which is consumed is forever consumed. That which is totally destroyed, is everlastingly—*eternally*—destroyed.

Dramatic confirmation of this point comes when Isaiah asks: "Who of us can dwell with everlasting burning?" (Isaiah 33:14). If our first thought conjures the prospect of ceaseless torment in such burning, we've overlooked the obvious. For in the same verse, Isaiah asks the question another way: "Who of us can dwell with the *consuming* fire?" And only two verses earlier, we see that the people are to be burned "as if to lime." Everlasting fire, then, is self-defined by the very answer implied in Isaiah's rhetorical question. It's obviously the kind of fire in which *no one can dwell!* It's the kind of fire Nebuchadnezzar put into his blazing furnace hoping to utterly wipe out Shadrach, Meshach, and Abednego; and the kind of apocalyptic fire in which nothing can possibly withstand God's fierce and final judgment.

More objections; more to think about

But someone undoubtedly will point us to Jesus' description of hell where he doesn't use the word *eternal*, but rather speaks of a hell "where the fire never goes out" (Mark 9:43). Moreover, he adds to that: "It is better for you to enter the kingdom of God with one eye than to have two eyes and be thrown into hell, where

> *"'their worm does not die,*
> *and the fire is not quenched.'*
> *Everyone will be salted with fire"* (Mark 9:47-49).

Taken alone and at face value, these words might well imply the kind of continual torment contemplated in the popular image of hell. However, we have already seen that what takes place in "unquenchable fire" is destruction, not unending anguish. We also know that in the earthly model for hell–Jerusalem's burning garbage dump in the valley of Gehenna–although the fire never went out, whatever was thrown into it was ultimately consumed. And, finally, it should come as no surprise that those in hell would be "salted" with fire. Given the molten sulfur which undoubtedly was associated with Lot's wife becoming a "pillar of salt," hell will also see the wicked permanently "salted." No wonder Jesus cautioned: "Remember Lot's wife!"

What about those worms?

Apart from these three particular aspects of hell's "fire," the only additional element in this passage is Jesus' mention of the "worm" that never dies. It should be enough to know that we're clearly in the realm of figurative language at this point. What worm is going to live forever, especially in the midst of literal fire? Beyond that, however, is a far more significant explanation for Jesus' mention of the worm. As it happens, Jesus' reference is a direct quotation from Isaiah 66:22-24, where Isaiah's prophecy about the coming destruction of Israel's enemies has obvious overtones regarding the final destruction of the wicked.

As we have seen elsewhere, this particular passage in Isaiah foreshadows John's vision of "the new heaven and new earth." Says Isaiah: "'As the new heavens and the new earth that I make will endure before me,' declares the LORD, 'so will your name and descendants endure. From one New Moon to another and from one Sabbath to another, all mankind will come and bow down before me,' says the LORD." Then comes the passage from which the words in question are drawn: "'And they will go out and look upon the *dead bodies* of those who rebelled against me; their worm will not die, nor will their fire be quenched, and they will be loathsome to all mankind.'"

Even considering the apocalyptic nature of the language, it is clear that the "worm" and the "fire" are simply putting the finishing touches to the destruction which has already taken place in the death of the wicked. There is no suggestion whatsoever of agony, pain, torture, or torment. As always, it's context, context, context.

And how did these wicked die? The prophet gives us this vivid description (in Isaiah 66:15-17):

See, the LORD is coming with fire,
and his chariots are like a whirlwind;
he will bring down his anger with fury,
and his rebuke with flames of fire.
For with fire and with his sword
the LORD will execute judgment upon all men,
and many will be those slain by the LORD.

In Isaiah's running commentary—replayed by Jesus—the wicked were killed by sword and by fire. The idea may be capital punishment by fire; or, more likely, the same fate as the beast in Daniel 7:11, which first was destroyed and then was thrown into the fire. In this instance, it would mean execution by the sword, followed by the bodies being dumped into a Gehenna-like waste site where worms and licking flames would consume the bodies of the slain. But torment? Not here! Agonizing suffering for ever and ever? Only Dante could wring such a tortured conclusion out of this passage!

And all that weeping and gnashing?

There are, of course, those passages where Jesus talks about the "weeping and gnashing of teeth." In two parables—"the weeds" (Matthew 13:42) and "the net" (Matthew 13:50)—Jesus specifically links "weeping and gnashing" with a fiery furnace, making us think he must be talking about hell. In the parable of the net, for example, Jesus says: "This is how it will be at the end of the age. The angels will come and separate the wicked from the righteous and throw them into the fiery furnace, where there will be weeping and gnashing of teeth." Arguably, hell is also the intended venue in the parable of the wicked servant (Matthew 24:51), when Jesus says that the master "will cut him to pieces and assign him a place with the hypocrites, where there will be weeping and gnashing of teeth."

However, when Jesus uses the phrase elsewhere, the imagery radically changes from a *fiery furnace* to complete *darkness*. In two parables–"the wedding banquet" (Matthew 22:13); and "the talents" (Matthew 25:30)–Jesus talks about the wicked and unfaithful being "thrown outside, into the darkness, where there will be weeping and gnashing of teeth." The same words are used when Jesus upbraids Israel's lack of faith compared with that of the centurion whose servant Jesus healed (Matthew 8:12).

If hell is the "darkness" under consideration, to say the least, any literal rendering would be incompatible with a literal fiery furnace which would be ablaze with light as well as with heat. But without quibbling about the details, the question remains: What is the "weeping and gnashing of teeth" all about? If one accepts the traditional assumption–that it is caused by physical agony from leaping flames day and night forever in hell's fiery furnace–what explains the same "weeping and gnashing of teeth" merely from being cast into outer darkness?

It is Luke who records the likely answer. Remember the question Jesus was asked about how many people were going to be saved (Luke 13:22-30)? Jesus first responded by talking about the door that would be slammed shut on those evildoers, despite their pleas for entry. Then he concluded, saying, "There will be weeping there, and gnashing of teeth, when you see Abraham, Isaac and Jacob and all the prophets in the kingdom of God, but you yourselves thrown out." (And don't forget that this passage introduces the long build-up to the story of the rich man and Lazarus, in which the teaching point is about the rich man's regret over his wasted opportunities to repent.)

Whether the imagery is of the wicked being thrown into a fiery furnace, or into outer darkness, Jesus obviously is talking about how people will react when they come face to face with the reality that their eternal destiny is not a life with God, but rejection from his presence and eternal destruction. Isaiah paints a perfect picture of that horrifying moment (Isaiah 13:6-8):

> *Wail, for the day of the LORD is near;*
> *it will come like destruction from the Almighty.*
> *Because of this, all hands will go limp,*
> *every man's heart will melt.*
> *Terror will seize them,*
> *pain and anguish will grip them;*
> *they will writhe like a woman in labor.*
> *They will look aghast at each other,*
> *their faces aflame.*

Shades of Jesus' own prediction, really: "Many will say to me on that day, 'Lord, Lord, did we not prophesy in your name, and in your name drive out demons and perform many miracles?' Then I will say to them plainly, 'I never knew you. Away from me, you evil doers!'" (Matthew 7:22-23). Can't you just imagine them turning and looking aghast at one another when, instead of a crown, a death sentence is handed down by the Judge! It is *that* painful realization–and the awful, "death row" anticipation of hell's fury–which will cause the rueful (perhaps even *angry*) "weeping and gnashing of teeth." Not endless torment.[3]

Of torture and torment

Of course, someone is sure to point out that Scripture itself uses the word *torment*, and even *torture*. For instance, there is that Gadarene demon who asked Jesus: "Have you come here to torture us before the appointed time?" (Matthew 8:29). Sure sounds like the demon was expecting to be tortured *sometime* in the future! And what about the possible implication of Jesus' parable of the servants in debt (Matthew 18:23-35), in which the master turns his wicked servant over to the jailor "to be tortured" until he pays back what he owes. Says Jesus, "This is how my heavenly Father will treat each of you unless you for-

---

3 The aspect of anger being associated with "weeping and gnashing of teeth" can be seen in Acts 7:54 on the part of Stephen's antagonists who were "gnashing their teeth at him"; in Job 16:9, where Job characterizes God's anger toward him as gnashing with his teeth; in Psalm 35:16, where David speaks of those who gnash at him with their teeth; and in Lamentations 2:16, where Jeremiah describes how Jerusalem's enemies "hiss and gnash their teeth."

give your brother from your heart." Are we forced to assume from this comparison that God will employ actual, agonizing torture; or might we more reasonably understand the intent of the passage to be that God will *punish harshly* in the same way that torture is harsh?

And then there is also the word *torment*, as used, for example, by the "third angel" in Revelation 14:9-12, referring to anyone who worships the beast. "He will be tormented with burning sulfur in the presence of the holy angels and of the Lamb. And the smoke of their torment rises for ever and ever. There is no rest day or night for those who worship the beast and his image...."

As always with the apocalyptic language of Revelation, we must choose whether to take the language literally or figuratively. And further, we must decide whether it is even a description of hell, or perhaps some other judgment which would take place in the lifetime of John's immediate readers. (We tend to forget that first-century readers had to make some sense of all this strange language for their own immediate application.)

If we take John's vision literally, and further associate that torment with hell itself, then we are left with the improbable situation where the "torment of the wicked for ever and ever" will be in the literal presence of the angels and of the Lamb (and, presumably, also in the presence of all the righteous souls with them). Can that even remotely be the case? Didn't we just hear Christ saying, "*Away from me*, all you evildoers"? And how could heaven be heaven if just off the back porch of heaven is a fiery pit of screaming souls!

What about Babylon?

Both *torture* and *torment* crop up again in Chapter 18, where John records the revelation of God's special judgment against "Babylon." In John's vision, a voice from heaven says: "Give her as much torture and grief as the glory and luxury she gave herself." And only a few verses later: "When the kings of the earth who committed adultery with her and shared her luxury see the smoke of her burning, they will weep and mourn over her. Terrified at her torment, they will stand far off and cry:

> "'Woe! Woe, O great city,
> O Babylon, city of power!
> In one hour your doom has come!'"

Even if this language were meant to describe hell, which does not appear to be the case, the "torture" and "torment" turn out to be anything but ongoing agony in fire. As we have seen time and time again in the apocalyptic language of God's fierce judgment, John says of this "Babylon" (in 18:8), "She will be *consumed* by fire, for mighty is the Lord God who judges her." What's more, it is clear that the "torment" initially came in the loss of all her worldly splendor and wealth (18:15-17), but was finally culminated when "a mighty angel picked up a boulder the size of a small millstone and threw it into the sea and said:

"With such violence
the great city of Babylon will be thrown down,
never to be found again."

Whatever torture or torment is involved with this special judgment of "Babylon," the end result is total destruction. Three times we are told: "She has been brought to ruin"...never to be seen again!

The strongest case for torment in hell

This brings us to the only passage using the word *torment* which seems to have a direct association with the fire of hell. After the nations have been deceived and fire comes down from heaven and devours them, John sees in his vision, that "the devil who deceived them, was thrown into the lake of burning sulfur, where the beast and the false prophet had been thrown" (Revelation 20:10). Whereupon John tells us: "They will be tormented day and night for ever and ever."

The case for unending conscious torment in hell doesn't get any better than in this passage. If we were to take this language literally, then all the other many scriptures speaking of hell's destruction, death, and consuming fire would have to be tossed out, *for ever and ever*! Certainly, one might attempt to distinguish the fate of the devil, the beast, and the false prophet from all the other wicked–as if unending torment were a special punishment just for the three of them. But there's really no need even for that. All we have to do in order to reconcile this seemingly disparate passage with the many others we've examined, is to consider parallel apocalyptic language elsewhere, wholly unassociated with the punishment of hell.

Turning once again to Isaiah 34:10, we see virtually the same language being applied to the imminent destruction of Edom (even the words *night and day*):

> *Edom's streams will be turned into pitch,*
> *her dust into burning sulfur;*
> *her land will become blazing pitch!*
> *It will not be quenched night and day;*
> *its smoke will rise forever.*

The only thing missing is the word *torment* itself, which in other passages has stood comfortably alongside consuming fire and total destruction. What, in Revelation 20, initially looks so much like unending, night-and-day torment turns out by comparison with Isaiah 34 to be nothing more than typical apocalyptic language describing the complete and utter ruination of the object of God's judgment.

Indeed, unending torment seems ever so far from what may be yet another apocalyptic description of the devil's ultimate fate. Ezekiel's judgment against the king of Tyre (Ezekiel 28:1-19) is widely thought to be an allusion to Satan and his prideful fall from heaven. If that is the case, then we are back to familiar territory in terms of the nature of hell's punishment:

> *"'You were the model of perfection,*
> *full of wisdom and perfect in beauty.*
> *You were in Eden,*
> *the garden of God....*
> *You were anointed as a guardian cherub,*
> *for so I ordained you.*
> *You were on the holy mount of God....*
> *You were blameless in your ways*
> *from the day you were created*
> *till wickedness was found in you....*
> *So I drove you in disgrace from the mount of God....*
> *So I threw you to the earth....*
> *So I made a fire come out of you,*
> *and it consumed you,*
> *and I reduced you to ashes on the ground*

in the sight of all who were watching.
All the nations who knew you
are appalled at you;
you have come to a horrible end
and will be no more.'"

If, in fact, this is a picture of Satan's ultimate doom, it portends nothing of endless torment, but total, final, and horrendous destruction—the same fate that awaits those who are forever cursed—whom Jesus said will be cast into "the eternal fire prepared for the devil and his angels" (Matthew 25:41).[4]

Hell's fire reflects God's wrath

It doesn't play all that well in Poughkeepsie or Peoria these days, but what we learn from all of this is that "the LORD your God is a *consuming* fire, a jealous God" (Deuteronomy 4:24). "Fire goes before him and consumes his foes on every side" (Psalm 97:3). Call it hyperbole if you wish, but "in the fire of his jealousy the whole world will be consumed, for he will make a sudden end of all who live in the earth" (Zephaniah 1:18). For "I will pour out my wrath upon you and breathe out my fiery anger against you; I will hand you over to brutal men, men skilled in destruction. You will be fuel for the fire...." (Ezekiel 21:31). Over and over, we hear God saying, "I will pour out my wrath on them and consume them with my fiery anger" (Ezekiel 22:31). Is it such a stretch to think that the nature of hell's fire reflects the nature of God's wrath itself? His *consuming* wrath?

Or do we somehow think that the God of the Old Testament takes on a kinder, gentler nature in the Gospels and Epistles? If so, hear again the words of the Hebrew writer as he concludes: "Therefore, since we are receiving a kingdom that cannot be shaken, let us be thankful, and so worship God acceptably with reverence and awe, for our God is a consuming fire" (Hebrews 12:29). No, not a twisted, cruel God who tortures the wicked, dangling them over licking flames,

---

4 An argument is made that since the lake of fire was prepared for the devil and his angels (Matthew 25:41), then, by virtue of their inherent immortality, the lake's torment must necessarily last without end. But the argument founders on the shoals of its misunderstanding of Luke 20:36, where Jesus says of the resurrected righteous: "they can no longer die, for they are like the angels in heaven." That angels do not die physically as man dies on this earth is light years away from saying that God is powerless to destroy them! The devil and his angels may not be mortal as we are mortal, but no scripture comes anywhere close to suggesting that they are "immortal" in the platonic sense of inherent, indestructible immortality.

but a God who, "choosing to show his wrath and make his power known, bore with great patience the objects of his wrath–prepared for destruction" (Romans 9:22).

The language of destruction

Whereas you can count on one hand the number of times the word *torment* is used (and not always referring to hell), you can hardly count the endless number of times you read of *destruction, perishing, blotting out, cutting off,* and *death* in connection both with God's judgment and hell itself.

Think about it. How possibly could God have signaled his seriousness about sin any better than through the Flood, in which he literally destroyed all but eight people out of the entire population of the earth? Do we dare take lightly God's promise *back then*, which presages his promise even *now*? "I am going to put an end to all people," God said in Noah's generation, "for the earth is filled with violence because of them. I am surely going to destroy both them and the earth" (Genesis 6:13). Far from being mythical, or ancient history which is of no concern to us, the Flood remains, even today, a dire warning of the wrath yet to come.

When Jesus presented his case regarding the coming Day of Judgment (Luke 17:26-27), the devastating destruction brought through the Flood stood alongside the desolation of Sodom and Gomorrah as Exhibit A. In hell, just as in the Flood, those who have rejected God and have refused to believe in his Son will be totally wiped out! Completely eradicated. Their existence will come to an abrupt end.

Crucial clues from David

There is certainly no pretension that David is consciously describing hell's destruction in Psalm 37, but just look at the words he uses regarding the wicked:

For evil men will be cut off,
but those who hope in the LORD will inherit the land....

But the wicked will perish:
The LORD's enemies will be like the beauty of the fields,

they will vanish–vanish like smoke....
But all sinners will be destroyed;
the future of the wicked will be cut off.

When you consider that *everyone* dies–and to that extent is "cut off"–there must surely be another "cutting off" for the wicked if David's warning is to have any punch at all. And where else is that "cutting off" to happen, but in hell?

Using language which certainly seems to point to the final judgment, David again writes (in Psalm 9:4-5):

...you have sat on your throne, judging righteously,
You have rebuked the nations and destroyed the wicked;
you have blotted out their name for ever and ever.

David, the warrior, had seen with his own eyes how God literally had destroyed the enemies of Israel; but "blotting out their name" for all time suggests a punishment far beyond merely slain soldiers and sacked cities. That would take a more profound and permanent destruction, like this description in Isaiah 13:9-11:

See, the day of the LORD is coming
–a cruel day, with wrath and fierce anger–
to make the land desolate
and destroy the sinners within it....
I will punish the world for its evil,
the wicked for their sins.

When destruction is punishment

Take careful note, here, of the significant connection between *destruction* and *punishment*. Perhaps to the surprise of some, destruction *is itself punishment!* Hence, there is no cause to insist that Jesus' reference to "eternal punishment" (Matthew 25:46) must mean ongoing torment for an eternity. Just as capital punishment has a lasting, irreversible effect (which those on death row will do almost anything to avoid), so too the destruction of the wicked. Hell is God's spiritual version of capital punishment.

Or, as Isaiah tells us elsewhere (Isaiah 26:14):

They are now dead, they live no more;
those departed spirits do not rise.
You punished them and brought them to ruin;
you wiped out all memory of them.

Here again, the punishment of the wicked is the very destruction that wipes them from all memory. Unlike the righteous, whose spirits rise to life eternal, the spirits of the unrighteous are punished by being cut off forever.

As we all know, there was Another who was also "cut off"—at least from the land of the living (Isaiah 53:8). That, of course, was Jesus Christ, of whom Isaiah said (in 53:5):

But he was pierced for our transgressions,
he was crushed for our iniquities;
the punishment that brought us peace was upon him,
and by his wounds we are healed.

No one doubts the tortuous, agonizing suffering of Jesus on the cross. Yet, it was not his *suffering*, but his *death*, that was the punishment which has brought us peace. Although "it was the Lord's will to crush him and cause him to suffer," it is because "he poured out his life unto death" that we ourselves have hope of eternal life rather than being destroyed forever.

Before Jesus went to the cross and "suffered death" for us, he himself told us where the "broad road" leads (Matthew 7:13-14): "It leads to *destruction*." He also told us whom should we fear and why: "Be afraid of the One who can *destroy* both soul and body in hell" (Matthew 10:28).[5]

---

5 When you compare Matthew 10:28 with Matthew 7:13-14 any argument that the word *destruction* means only "lost" (as in the lost coin), or "wasted" (as in the "wasted" perfume Mary poured over Jesus), or perhaps simply "useless," is shown for the fraud that it is. Unlike the highly-figurative apocalyptic passages in which we find words like "torment" and "torture," use of the word *destruction* in straightforward passages like these argues for the natural, most-obvious meaning of the word. Indeed, in Matthew 7:13-14, the logical contrast with "the road that leads to *life*," must surely be the road that leads to *non-life*, which is to say *destruction*.

How can one possibly miss the plain meaning of Matthew 10:28 which derives from the contrast between the power of man and the power of God? Jesus is saying that *man* cannot kill the soul, but *God* can! Therefore, what God can do to the soul that man can't is the logical equivalent of what man can do to the body, which is to *kill* it, not just "lose" it, or "waste" it, or make it "useless." Rendering "destroy" as anything less than its plain meaning in this passage is to play linguistic games while ignoring the obvious context.

Paul weighs in on the issue

And what say you, Paul? Is there such a thing as "eternal punishment"? Yes, indeed. "When the Lord Jesus is revealed from heaven in blazing fire with his powerful angels...He will punish those who do not know God and do not obey the gospel of our Lord Jesus." And how will they be punished, Paul? Will it be with ongoing, continual, everlasting torment? No, "they will be punished with *everlasting destruction* and shut out from the presence of the Lord and from the majesty of his power on the day he comes to be glorified...." (2 Thessalonians 1:7-10).

As with all other questions, Jesus and Paul are on the same page about the nature of hell. Hell's everlasting destruction won't be at all like the cartoon cliche, with a red-suited devil, pitch fork in hand, grinning sadistically as creatures around him roast forever amid leaping flames and curling smoke.

And amazingly enough, considering all the weight given to Revelation's description of the "lake of fire," if we listen carefully (in Revelation 11:18), we can hear the same language we've heard throughout Scripture from beginning to end:

> *"The time has come for judging the dead,*
> *and for rewarding your servants the prophets*
> *and your saints and those who reverence your name,*
> *both small and great–*
> *and for destroying those who destroy the earth."*

Not tormenting them. Not torturing them. But destroying them.

The second death

All of this best explains that other pivotal passage, in Revelation 20:12-15, where John describes his "great white throne" vision. After each person was "judged according to what he had done...Then death and Hades were thrown into the lake of fire. The lake of fire is the *second death*. If anyone's name was not found written in the book of life, he was thrown into the lake of fire." Then, as if to underscore the fate of the wicked, John repeats himself even more specifically (in Revelation 21:8), telling us that "the cowardly, the unbelieving, the vile, the murderers, the sexually immoral, those who practice magic arts, the idolaters and all liars–their place will be in the fiery lake of burning sulfur. This is the *second death*."

If we are disposed to take the "lake of fire" literally, then we must also take John's candid explanation of that lake just as literally. Certainly, John could well have chosen to use the same apocalyptic language as before. ("They will be tormented day and night for ever and ever.") But he chooses, instead, to give us a straightforward interpretation of that for which the lake is symbolic, which is *death*. Not just death of the body, which is the *first* death. But the *second* death–death of the resurrected and spiritually re-embodied soul.[6]

Look how John uses the same expression so matter-of-factly in the opening pages of Revelation before his more apocalyptic vision begins. Writing to the persecuted Christians in Smyrna (Revelation 2:10-11), John says, "Do not be afraid of what you are about to suffer....Be faithful, even to the point of death, and I will give you the crown of life....He who overcomes will not be hurt at all by the second death."

The beseiged disciples in Smyrna were facing the very real possibility of being martyred, suffering death for the name of Christ. Therefore, John exhorts them to remain faithful, no matter what happens, and then underscores what Jesus had said about those who could kill the body, but not the soul. Says John, there is a *second death* from which those who are faithful will be spared; but not those who renounce their faith when met with this world's pressures, nor those unrighteous sinners in John's earlier list. For both the unrighteous and the unfaithful, hell will mean the eternal death of their souls.

Now it all makes sense!

Can we not now begin to see the whole of Scripture more clearly? "There is a way that seems right to a man, but in the end it leads to death" (Proverbs 14:12). Ah...to the *second* death. And "the truly righteous man attains life, but he who pursues evil goes to his death" (Proverbs 11:19). Again, the *second* death. And, of course, there's the oft-repeated punch line of Ezekiel's powerful Chapter 18: "The soul that sins, it will die"...in the consuming fire of hell, forever!

---

6 Unlike the "first death," where there is continued existence of the soul beyond the demise of the fleshly body, in the "second death" of hell there can be no continued existence beyond what Jesus said would be the destruction of both body and soul (Matthew 10:28).

And on and on the Scriptures go. "The evil man has no future hope, and the lamp of the wicked will be *snuffed out*" (Proverbs 24:20). "Whoever believes in the Son has eternal life, but whoever rejects the Son *will not see life*, for God's wrath remains on him" (John 3:36). "If you do not believe that I am the one I claim to be, you will indeed die in your sins" (John 8:24). Not just die *in* your sins (in the first death), but *because of* your sins (in the second death).

So, finally, we have come full circle back to the opening chapter and to God's warning to Adam and Eve: "You must not eat from the tree of the knowledge of good and evil, for when you eat of it, you will surely die." God wasn't referring to the *first* death, which was inevitable because of man's created mortality, but rather to the *second* death. He was warning them (and us) that sin has, not just earthly consequences, but eternal consequences. What is at stake for every one of us is nothing less than *eternal life* or *eternal death*.

What, after all, is the opposite of *life*, if not *death*; and the opposite of *eternal life*, if not *eternal death*? "For God so loved the world that he gave his one and only son, that whoever believes in him shall not *perish* but have *eternal life*" (John 3:16). To insist that the contrast is between eternal life and eternal torment misses the point altogether. Eternal life finds its greatest significance in the very fact that there *is life* where otherwise *there would be no life*! Our eternal destiny is not a matter of better or worse. It's nothing less than a matter of life and death!

Is that not what the "book of life" is all about? Those whose names are found written in the book will inherit life with God forever. For those whose names are missing, there is no lasting life whatsoever, tormented or otherwise. Only death. The second and final death.

This is also precisely what being "saved" or "lost" is all about. The very existence of our souls is at risk. Will we be saved for eternal life, or forever lost? What else is the good news of the gospel, if not that we who otherwise would be eternally lost because of our sins can be saved through the atoning blood of Jesus? So "go into all the world and preach the good news to all creation. Whoever believes and is baptized will be *saved*, but whoever does not believe will be *condemned*" (Mark 16:15-16).

Why, again, should we be evangelistic? Because through us, God "spreads the fragrance of the knowledge of him. For we are the aroma of Christ among those who are being *saved* and those who are *perishing*. To the one we are the smell of *death*; to the other, the fragrance of *life*" (2 Corinthians 2:14-16).

To be saved is to have life eternal in heaven. To be lost is to perish forever in the fiery destruction of hell. Or as Paul prints it in unmistakable, 25-point bold type: "The wages of sin is death, but the gift of God is eternal life in Christ Jesus our Lord" (Romans 6:23).

Does it really matter what hell is like?

Whether hell is permeated with the acrid smell of burning flesh, or is some kind of mental and emotional torment, or is an empty void of everlasting death, may seem to some folks as much ado about nothing. Whatever the case, it's not a destiny anyone in his right mind would choose (though millions in their right minds have chosen to ignore any or all such possibilities).

Yet, there are many others who would consider eternal destruction an "easy way out" when compared with unending conscious torment. Which would *you* choose, for instance, if given the option? On the other hand, we may have greatly underestimated the primal urge for survival at virtually all cost, as suggested in P. J. Bailey's observation that "hell is more bearable than nothingness."

Devoted "Trekkies" may recall the "Deja Q" episode from "Star Trek: the Next Generation" (the third season), in which Q, an alien from a multi-dimensional race called the Q-Continuum is stripped of his immortality and made mortal before being put on the USS Enterprise. After he is nearly killed in an attack from other aliens, Q gives an insightful soliloquy on non-existence, in which the chilling punch line of unacceptable extinction is: "No more me." For every atheist or agnostic who seems happy to launch himself into hopeless oblivion, many more people would be willing to endure almost anything one could imagine rather than contemplate the thought of "no more me." The very fact that the writers of this episode even raise the issue tells us that *someone* out there is thinking long and hard about the dread of total, permanent loss of personhood.

The problem, however, is that oblivion versus torment is simply not the option we are given. As the greater weight of scriptural evidence indicates, the only option is eternal life versus eternal death. Blessed existence versus non-existence. (So *now* which would you choose?)

Yet why, someone asks, would God hold the wicked in sheol's dark prison, then raise their souls and re-embody them in some spiritual form, only at some point to put them to death again for all eternity? Who knows? (For that matter, why have an intermediate state of the *righteous* dead before resurrecting them to glory? And why should there be a "judgment" before the throne when God already knows our eternal destiny?) In this study of the afterlife, we've just been reporting the news, not speculating about God's motives or reasons, or second-guessing his eternal purposes. Once we go down that path, the questions are endless.

If, for example, you take a literal view of hell's agony, why would a loving God subject any of his creatures to endless torment, fully aware that we are as weak as "dust"? And why create us as mortal humans in a transient world in the first place instead of creating us like the angels in heaven? Indeed, why endow us with the freedom of will that permits our spiritual rebellion and triggers his wrath? (Or—more difficult yet for those who believe in predestination—why would God go to all this trouble if he has already predestined some to glory and others to eternal damnation, however you choose to define it? How can that be anything other than a divinely manipulated puppet show in which judgment is merely a charade and punishment of any kind is monstrously undeserved?)

There is always the possibility, of course, that God has in mind some form of conscious punishment in addition to the ultimate destruction of the soul. Maybe that's what all the imagery of suffering in hell is about. But if that is the case, we aren't told anything further about it. The only thing which seems certain is that, for his own reasons, God has prepared hell as an obliterating punishment in which, at some point—sooner or later—the wicked will be forever purged from his sight.

Punishment by degrees?

As you probably know, some have surmised from Jesus' words in Luke 12:47-48 that there might possibly be degrees of punishment in hell. To get a sense of context, we have to begin reading in verse 42, where Jesus tells a parable about a slothful and evil manager who, when his master didn't return on the day expected, got drunk and beat all the lesser servants in the house. When the master finally appeared, not surprisingly, the manager was in big trouble.

Turning then to make his point, Jesus says: "That servant who knows his master's will and does not get ready or does not do what his master wants will be beaten with many blows. But the one who does not know and does things deserving punishment will be beaten with few blows. From everyone who has been given much, much will be demanded; and from the one who has been entrusted with much, much more will be asked."

Since the context has nothing at all to do with the afterlife, it's highly unlikely that Jesus is hinting at degrees of punishment in hell. Instead, the last line seems to be a perfect answer to the question posed by Peter (in verse 41) which began the whole discourse: "Lord, are you telling this parable to us, or to everyone?"

Who, if not the twelve, has been entrusted with much? Well, actually the answer is *us*! And so Jesus says to all of us who know the Lord that we bear a far greater responsibility to live in expectation of his appearing than those who do not yet know the Lord. Our own judgment will not be based on the same standards which might be applied to the ignorant and unknowing, but on the higher standard of moral and spiritual excellence patterned for us by Christ. At issue here is not so much the Judge's *sentence* but his *verdict*.

And on what will his verdict be based? Among other things, undoubtedly, it will include the earnestness with which we have shared the Lord with the ignorant and unknowing. But degrees of punishment in hell? If so, the evidence for it could certainly be far stronger than it is.

Does "more bearable" suggest degrees?

Some have suggested Luke 10:13-15 as that stronger evidence: "Woe to you, Korazin! Woe to you Bethsaida!....it will be more bearable for Tyre and Sidon at the judgment than for you." Yet, clearly this language is hyperbole. To begin with, Jesus was talking about whole cities, not individual persons. But far more instructive is the immediately preceding verse (vs. 12) in which there is parallel structure. Speaking of any town that would not receive one of the seventy-two special envoys Jesus was sending out to spread the news of the kingdom, Jesus said: "I tell you, it will be more bearable on that day for Sodom than for that town."

Using a city that was totally and utterly destroyed as his point of comparison, Jesus is simply underscoring the severity of the punishment that awaits those who reject his kingship. Whereas the people of Sodom did not have Christ himself in their midst, these towns had seen Jesus perform miracles in their presence but still not believed. How, by any means, would they escape God's punishment? But to use this as a proof-text for degrees of punishment in hell is a real stretch.

Doesn't justice demand degrees?

To repeat what we said earlier, if God chooses to punish the unrighteous and the unbelieving in some way before their final destruction—even by degrees—that is certainly his prerogative. It's just that there is little textual evidence to suggest it. That we like to think there would be degrees of punishment in hell undoubtedly reflects more of a hopeful sense of justice than anything strictly biblical.

Merely consider the two words we just lumped together: the *unrighteous* and the *unbelieving*. Should those who are morally upright people, but who didn't put their faith in Jesus Christ, be punished with the same severity as those who do wickedly bad things to others in this life? And should God take into account the fact that millions of people grew up in families or cultures which did not honor God, or honored God through the wrong prophet or teacher?

Given almost limitless degrees of spiritual ignorance and rebellion, proportionate degrees of punishment is an appealing thought. Yet one does have to wonder whether the worst-case scenario of hell—eons upon eons of physical and mental torment—could have *any* degrees which would be justly proportionate for those who should be "beaten with fewer stripes." Would it really make much difference if you were in the upper oven at 250 degrees rather than in the lower oven at 475 degrees? At least with total destruction there is an arguable rationality that accompanies the uniform extinction of all souls who, for whatever reason, are unfit for eternal life with God. But all of that is nothing more than humans talking to humans about matters more properly pertaining to God.

Is hell's horror at risk?

Finally, many folks undoubtedly will protest that everlasting destruction in hell is not as effective a deterrent to sin as is the fiery image of ongoing torment. Unfortunately, after all this laborious effort to understand and honor what God has revealed to us on the subject, such an argument serves merely to inject an element of pragmatism into the discussion. But if one insists on having that discussion, he must be prepared to explain why the current, popular notion of hell's tormenting fire has become the object of jokes, derision, and outright rejection by millions upon millions of non-believers. If the traditional imagery of agonizing souls frying in hell's fiery furnace doesn't capture their imagination, pray tell, what will?

Indeed, one has to ask whether an oversold caricature of hell's torment isn't so inconsistent with what folks intuitively sense would be the character of a righteous God that they reject such an image out of hand. If perhaps they might reconcile some form of harsh punishment with a righteous God–even a kind of "capital punishment"–endless torture seems beyond the pale.

Naturally, the fact that God himself gives us the imagery of hell's fire may tell us that we *need* some alarming wake-up call beyond the cold, hard fact of potential non-existence. But that God went beyond merely getting our attention with all that talk of fire and flames and went on to clarify what he *really* meant about the "second death" must surely tell us that he wants a rational, informed, and serious decision from us, not one that is strictly visceral.

Resounding silence in the epistles

Perhaps this explains one of the greatest of all curiosities regarding what the Scriptures have to say about the punishment of those who will be eternally condemned. Even after all that Jesus himself had to say about hell, the writers of the Epistles are ominously silent about it. Quite incredibly, Paul never once mentions hell! Not once! Did Paul not understand, as we seem to, that ongoing conscious torment in the raging cauldron of hell is an indispensable deterrent to man's spiritual rebellion? Apparently not. Instead of even a single mention of eternal fire, or torment, or worms, or gnashing of teeth, what we hear from Paul is a litany of words describing the fate of wicked with crisp, clear finality. There is "perishing" (2 Corinthians

2:15; 2 Thessalonians 2:10); "death" (Romans 1:32; 6:23; 8:13; 2 Corinthians 2:16); "destruction" (Galatians 6:8; Romans 9:22); and "everlasting destruction" (2 Thessalonians 1:9); but no torment.

Of those who "live as enemies of the cross of Christ," Paul says not a word about some endless agonizing existence in a lake of fire, but simply that "their destiny is destruction." How did Paul ever expect to evangelize the world and never once preach a sermon about the flames, and worms, and gnashing of teeth? What possibly was he (or the Holy Spirit!) thinking, not giving folks a more chilling reason to be good!

The same goes for the writer of Hebrews, despite warning after warning about the judgment to come. We see mention of thorns and thistles being burned up (6:8); "acts that lead to death" (9:14); "raging fire that will consume the enemies of God" (10:27); those who shrink back being "destroyed" (10:39); and a God who is "a consuming fire" (12:29); but, again, not the first word about pain, agony, or torment.

Not even James, the Lord's brother, dwells on hell. Characterizing a dissembling or slanderous tongue as a destructive "fire," James makes a play on words, saying that such a tongue itself will be "set on fire by hell" (James 3:6). But when he refers to the tongue's slander being brought to account, his reminder is that "There is one Lawgiver and Judge, the one who is able to save and *destroy*" (James 4:12). And Peter and Jude join in the chorus, linking their brief references to the "eternal fire" with the *destruction* of unbelieving Israel and the people of Sodom and Gomorrah. But, just as with Paul, there's not the slightest hint, subtle allusion, or faintest whisper of "torment day and night for ever and ever." Simply destruction.

Still think that warnings about death and destruction in hell don't have the same "punch" as vivid images of torment in hell? How, then, explain this glaring omission in the Holy Spirit's handling of the subject?

Maybe we've missed the whole point of hell

Perhaps this is a new idea for most of us, but is it possible that deterrence might not be the primary purpose for hell's existence as we have supposed? When Moses spoke to the people of Israel and said, "See, I set before you today life and prosperity, death and destruction" (Deuteronomy 30:15), there were no images of pearly gates in heaven nor a "lake of fire" in hell to act as "carrot" and "stick." Even so, we know that the Israelites had repeatedly seen (and would see over and over again in the centuries to come) instance after shocking instance where God struck down, destroyed, and cut off the wicked—not in some future nether world, but before their very eyes!

Yet, did God's harsh punishment in their immediate presence put an end to their sinning and rebellion? Quite unbelievably, *no*! So for us to debate the relative merits of eternal torment versus everlasting destruction as a deterrent to sin is spitting into the wind. The only question can be: What, in fact, has God revealed about the fate of the wicked? If we get that right, then we automatically know what God himself deems to be the most effective deterrent—if, indeed, deterrence is hell's primary purpose, or purpose at all.

There is something to be said for the idea that hell is as much a promise as a threat. Considering that God is a holy God, and that in the heavenly city which he has prepared for his holy ones "nothing impure will ever enter it," hell's destruction of the wicked may be God's way of insuring his own holiness and the purity of heaven. With the universe destroyed, and death and Hades along with it, the souls of the wicked would have no place to exist except in the presence of God. Unless, that is, they are extinguished forever.[7]

Seen in this light, God's consuming wrath is not vindictiveness, but moral outrage against all that is unholy. The fire of his jealously is fanned by his knowledge that evil and holiness cannot coexist. And so he promises that one day he will judge the world in righteousness and holiness, ridding even the remotest corner of the cosmos of all evil, wickedness, and spiritual impurity of every kind.

What seems like a threat, therefore, is but a warning of that which cannot help but happen in the final cleansing of God's temple. Faced with the cold fact of that inevitability, we can choose to be holy as he is holy and enjoy eternal life in God's presence, or we can reject God's holiness and know even now that we will be cast into oblivion. God gives us a lifetime to make up our minds, and does everything he can—short of making the choice for us—to make heaven look inviting and hell seem unthinkable. If either "eternal torment"

---

7 For those who insist that hell is principally an eternal separation from the presence of God, where could that isolated corner of the heavenly realm possibly be? Since God is omnipresent, how could anything having existence of any kind ever be totally separated from him?

or "everlasting destruction" helps anyone to make the right choice, so much the better.

Yet, make no mistake. Simply running away from hell's fire won't make anyone the slightest bit holier, only exhausted and fearful. But by understanding the importance of being holy, and inviting God to bestow his own divine holiness on us, we can insure that when God begins driving the wicked and impure from his holy presence, we will have nothing to fear.

And the best news yet...because of Jesus Christ, we won't have to personally test whatever theory of hell's fire we or others might have been wrong about here on earth!

Anchor Verse - 2 Peter 3:11-12

"Since everything will be destroyed in this way, what kind of people ought you to be? You ought to live holy and godly lives as you look forward to the day of God and speed its coming."

Chapter Preview

It is not just God's avowed enemies who will stand before the throne. Each of us will have to give an account of our lives. That most of the warnings about hell are directed to Jesus' own disciples ought to get our attention. If that seems fearsome, our boldness to approach the judgment seat with confidence comes in knowing the love of God for his children, if indeed we *are* his children. To know God's grace is not to diminish our fear of him; and to fear God does not diminish his grace.

If we truly wish to identify with Christ's resurrection, we can no longer live in the sinful way we once lived before we died with him. Our greatest challenge as Christians is to actually live each day as dead sinners who have been spiritually resurrected for finer things than the sin which has brought us condemnation.

9

LIVING IN THE ETERNAL PRESENT

Until a man finds meaning in his death, he should never expect to find meaning in his life.

–Victor Frankl

So what are we to take away from this study of the afterlife? What fresh insights, if any, have we gleaned? And what practical difference might this glimpse of eternity make in how we live the rest of our fleeting days here on earth?

After all we have considered about the afterlife, *how then should we live in view of eternity?* Or, as Peter put it (having just described the cataclysmic destruction of the earth at the time of Christ's appearing): "Since everything will be destroyed in this way, *what kind of people ought you to be?*" Peter's own answer to that question might surprise some, implying, as it does that those who are in Christ might have more to consider than normally is thought. Says Peter: "You ought to live holy and godly lives as you look forward to the day of God and speed its coming" (2 Peter 3:11-12).

Seen in its most positive light, of course, Peter's admonition may be telling us nothing more than that living holy and godly lives ought to be our natural response to God's mercy. Yet, the obvious association between the destruction of the unrighteous and how we ourselves should live, suggests that even those of us who are saved have some serious thinking to do about our eternal destiny.

Rumors persist that this simply cannot be the case–that once we are saved, there is no possibility of our being lost. Did not Jesus himself say, "My sheep listen to my voice; I know them, and they follow me. I give them eternal life, and they shall never perish; no one can snatch them out of my hand" (John 10:27-28)?

Some will eagerly assure us that, if any are lost, they never were his sheep in the first place. Others will suggest a distinction between being "snatched away" and "falling away." Whatever your particular theology, room will have to be made for several passages—unquestionably addressed to those who are in Christ—which are unambiguous in their warning to the saved about the possibility of eternal punishment.

Not the least of these warnings comes from the same Jesus who just told us that no one can snatch away his sheep. Addressing his innermost circle of disciples on their way to the Mount of Olives, Jesus warned: "If anyone does not remain in me, he is like a branch that is thrown away and withers; such branches are picked up, thrown into the fire and burned" (John 15:6). To separate ourselves from the Vine into which we've been grafted is to be cut off and burned in the fire of eternal destruction.

Lest we think, as we often do, that God's judgment is reserved only for robbers, rapists, and serial killers, the writer of Hebrews reminds us that, "if we deliberately keep on sinning after we have received the knowledge of the truth, no sacrifice for sins is left, but only a fearful expectation of judgment and of raging fire that will consume the enemies of God" (Hebrews 10:26-27).

It is not just God's avowed enemies who will stand before the throne, for as Paul reminded the saints in Rome, "we will all stand before God's judgment seat" and "each of us will give an account of himself to God" (Romans 14:10-12).

When the warnings hit close to home

If that is a challenging (even troubling) thought—and it is—what explains how we can live our entire lives making such little specific preparation for the most ominous moment of truth we will ever face? Maybe we just take it for granted that only "the bad guys" will be put on trial and punished. If so, we need to reconsider. These particular warnings from Scripture are not addressed to mass murderers, child abusers, or political terrorists—or even to atheists, agnostics, or religious pagans—but to God-fearing, Scripture-believing, blood-bought and baptized disciples of Christ. Have we forgotten that it was not the unsaved but his own twelve apostles whom Jesus warned: "Be afraid of the one who can destroy both soul and body in hell" (Matthew 10:28)?

As he always has, "the Lord will judge *his people.*" And it is regarding God's own people that the Hebrew writer says, "It is a dreadful thing to fall into the hands of the living God" (Hebrews 10:30-31). If we don't believe that, there are some rebellious angels who might suggest we think again. (Who more than angels could be said to have "known the Lord," and yet they fell. Literally fell.)

Certainly, we will not be judged on that day simply on the basis of what we profess by way of faith. For Paul says (once again, to justified, sanctified Christians) the day is coming when "God will judge men's secrets" (Romans 2:16). Hands up all of you who would like our reservoir of secret sins to be Exhibit A upon which we would wish our eternal destiny to be judged. What, no takers?

As it was for the ancients, Ecclesiastes' concluding wisdom is equally worthy of consideration by the saved today: "Fear God and keep his commandments, for this is the *whole* of man. For God will bring every deed into judgment, including every hidden thing, whether it is good or evil" (Ecclesiastes 12:13-14).

Do those in Christ have reason to fear?

Do you think the writer of Ecclesiastes might have used a different word than *fear* if he had been better informed about God's grace through Christ? Don't count on it. Remember, it was the Hebrew writer who used that word "dreadful" when referring to the believer who has "insulted the Spirit of grace." *Dreadful* sounds a lot like *fear*, doesn't it? So, should Christians really fear the judgment to come, or is that just a warning to Christians who "deliberately keep on sinning?" (And, if so, which of us is immune from that!)

To know God's grace is not to diminish our fear of him; and to fear God does not diminish his grace. In a way, it's one of those parent-child mysteries: fearing and trusting at the same time. What child wants to face up to a parent's judgment, knowing that the forbidden cookie jar lies shattered in pieces on the floor? But whose judgment will be more measured and appropriate than that of a loving parent–a truth which, in time, a child grows to appreciate?

Perhaps something in that analogy helps make sense of what otherwise might appear to be godly gibberish from the apostle John. "And so we know and rely on the love God has for us," John writes reassuringly. "God is love. Whoever lives in love lives in God, and God in him. In this way, love is made complete among us *so that we will have confidence on the day of judgment*, because in this world we are like him. There is no fear in love. But perfect love drives out fear, because fear has to do with punishment. The one who fears is not made perfect in love" (1 John 4:16-19).

It is only because of God's love for us that we have any hope of not being fearful on that great day. By any measure (whether by sins that are secret or by sins that are well-known to others), each and every one of us will approach our moment of judgment fully deserving of punishment. If that isn't cause for fear, what is? Yet, our boldness to approach the judgment seat with confidence comes in knowing the love of God for his children, if indeed we *are* his children. (Is that possibly a matter you have yet to take up with God?)

Renouncing our inheritance

That God is loving and faithful to his children goes without saying. The question is: Are we, in turn, faithful to God? Have we remained true to our covenant vows, or have we turned our back on them, despising God's love? "Since the promise of entering his rest still stands," warns the Hebrew writer, "let us be careful that none of you be found to have fallen short of it....Let us, therefore, make every effort to enter that rest, so that no one will fall by following their example of disobedience" (Hebrews 4:1,11).

To whom is the writer referring as our "example of disobedience"? To God's chosen people of Israel, who–though God's children all–did not all inherit the promised land.

In view of such a striking example of unfaithfulness, surely "we must pay more careful attention, therefore, to what we have heard, so that we do not drift away. For if the message spoken by angels was binding, and every violation and disobedience received its just punishment, how shall we escape if we ignore such a great salvation?" (Hebrews 2:1-3). It is to *us*–the saved–that the reminder comes: "Nothing in all creation is hidden from God's sight.

Everything is uncovered and laid bare before the eyes of him to whom we must give account" (Hebrews 4:13).

How can we be both saved and lost?

But didn't we earlier rejoice that God keeps two sets of books–one filled with the deeds by which all of us deserve eternal death, and the other, the book of life, in which our names are found only by the grace and mercy of God? There's no question about it: without God's grace and mercy, not a single soul could ever have the hope of eternal life with God. Even so, it is equally certain that we ourselves can cause our names to be blotted out of the book of life by rejecting the grace we once knew. In fact, *we* even more than those who have never named the name of Christ are at risk. If perhaps unbelievers might plead ignorance, we who have put our faith in Christ clearly have no excuse!

Hear again, as if never before, these words of warning addressed to first-century Christians: "It is impossible for those who have once been enlightened, who have tasted the heavenly gift, who have shared in the Holy Spirit, who have tasted the goodness of the word of God and the powers of the coming age, *if they fall away*, to be brought back to repentance, because to their loss they are crucifying the Son of God all over again and subjecting him to public disgrace" (Hebrews 6:4-8).

Dare anyone suggest this warning is not to the saved? Or that the saved cannot fall away? Surely, one would have to be wearing theological blinders to miss the obvious. And what are we told about the eternal fate of unfaithful Christians whose names were once written in the book of life? It's the same theme we've seen over and over again in association with hell: "Land that produces thorns and thistles is worthless and is in danger of being cursed. In the end it will be burned" (Hebrews 6:8).

Indeed, who is more deserving of hell's destructive fire than the child of God who has seen the light of Christ, has tasted of God's grace, and been filled with the Holy Spirit–only to throw it all away because, like Demas, he has loved this world too much to follow through with his commitment to Christ (2 Timothy 4:10)?

Peter was so concerned about the possibility that we could lose our promised inheritance that he wrote an entire letter about it. His second epistle reminds us, first of all, of the "very great and precious promises" we have in Christ, "so that through them you may participate in the divine nature and escape the corruption in the world caused by evil desires" (2 Peter 1:4). Then he urges his readers to add to their faith all those Christ-like qualities with which we are so familiar (1:5-7). "But if anyone does not have them," Peter observes, "he is nearsighted and blind, and has forgotten that *he has been cleansed from his past sins*" (1:9).

To those whose sins have been forgiven in Christ—which is to say *the saved*—Peter then says straightforwardly: "Therefore, my brothers, be all the more eager to *make your calling and election sure*. For *if you do these things* you will never fall, and you will receive a rich welcome into the eternal kingdom of our Lord and Savior Jesus Christ" (1:10-11). How can we possibly miss what Peter is saying? Eternal life with God is not a slam-dunk, even for those who may have been "dunked"!

It's interesting that Peter seems to be more than ever conscious of the possibility of our falling away as he himself approaches the threshold of eternity. "I think it is right to refresh your memory as long as I live in the tent of this body, because I know that I will soon put it aside, as our Lord Jesus Christ has made clear to me" (1:13-14). Knowing that a person's last words tend to be their most solemn and important, it wouldn't be a bad time to perk up our ears.

Snapshots of those who fell away

Peter's subsequent warning about false teachers within the primitive church resounds to all of God's people, both then and now. Turning our backs on God after being saved and receiving the promise of eternal life is not a pretty picture. In fact, here's the picture which Peter paints of brothers and sisters in Christ who fall away:

> If they have escaped the corruption of the world by knowing our Lord and Savior Jesus Christ and are again entangled in it and overcome, they are worse off at the end than they were at the beginning. It would have been better for them not to have known the way of righteousness than to have known it and then to turn their backs on the sacred command that was passed on to them. Of them the proverbs are true: "A dog returns to its vomit," and

"A sow that is washed goes back to her wallowing in the mud" (2 Peter 2:20-22).

Vomit? Mud? Any doctrine of eternal security worthy of Scripture must first be filtered through the disgusting images Peter presents in this passage, as well as this stirring conclusion to his letter: "Be on your guard so that you may not be carried away by the error of lawless men and *fall from your secure position*" (3:17).[1]

Is our position in heaven secure? You can count on it! Is it possible to fall so far as to lose that position? You can count on it! But which of these is right? Peter's clear, unmistakable, and provocative answer is *both*!

Is that so strange? If we show up at the theater with tickets to the royal box, we can be assured of being ushered to the best seats in the house. They're reserved for us! But if, tickets in hand, we turn and drive away from the theater before we get there, who would think it strange that we missed the performance?

God's promises are certain. His love never wavers. His hope for us never wanes. It is we who are fickle and unfaithful.

Our brother's keeper

Not only are we admonished to give renewed attention to our own eternal salvation, but we are shouldered with an equally-great burden of responsibility to watch for the souls of our brothers and sisters in Christ. Consider, for example, Paul's admonition to the Corinthians regarding the brother living openly in sin with his father's wife (1 Corinthians 5:1-5). "Hand this man over to Satan," says Paul sharply, "so that the sinful nature may be destroyed and his spirit saved on the day of the Lord."

Here was a brother in Christ whose soul was in jeopardy. He was one of the Lord's sheep gone badly astray–a child of God who was sniffing at his promised inheritance. And yet, his fellow Christians in Corinth seemed wholly unfazed by his spiritual peril.

---

1 Calvinism is a vulnerable five-story structure which collapses in on itself when the top floor fails to hold. If on Floor 5 there is no automatic perseverance of the saints, but rather the possibility that we can fall from grace, then it means that Floor 4 also collapses, since grace obviously *can* be resisted. Which also means, then, that Floor 3 no longer holds because Christ's atonement would not be limited to those who are unable to resist it; that Floor 2 is the next to go, since election could no longer be unconditional, but contingent upon one's faith; and that, finally, Floor 1 gives way, since no one is so totally depraved that they lack the free will to choose faith and salvation. No one can escape the inevitable. Once the top floor of irreversible eternal security buckles under the weight of biblical teaching, all the supporting assumptions collapse as well, leaving nothing but rubble at ground zero.

Had they been enticed by the seductive notion of "once saved, always saved"? Were they, perhaps, afflicted with something of the obsessive non-judgmentalism prevalent in our own day? If the latter, Paul's response is: "God will judge those outside...Are you not to judge those inside?" (1 Corinthians 5:12-13). There is too much at stake eternally for us to stand back and let a brother or sister throw it all away. Judgment not only *will* begin with the family of God (1 Peter 4:17-18), but it *must* begin with the family of God. Within the family!2

To be raised is to be forever dead

If there is any passage from which Paul has earned his reputation as a deep thinker and writer, it may well be Romans, Chapter 6. Sandwiched between Chapters 5 and 7, where Paul writes passionately about death of the soul *because of* sin, Chapter 6 introduces a mixed metaphor of sorts, wherein Paul speaks, instead, of our being dead *to* sin.

The metaphor becomes even more complex when Paul draws a parallel between Christ's physical death, burial, and resurrection, and our own spiritual death, burial, and resurrection, witnessed graphically in the act of immersion. Our "watery grave" reflects his borrowed tomb. As we go down into the water, we die to our sins (as he died *for* our sins), are buried in the water of baptism (as he was buried in Joseph's tomb), and are raised to walk a new life (just as he was resurrected when the stone was rolled away).

Because we have died to sin in that act of symbolic identity with Christ's own death, Paul asks how we can possibly continue to take a casual attitude toward the sin in our lives. "Or don't you know," he observes, "that all of us who were baptized into Christ Jesus were bap-

---

2 Having just told the Corinthians that they were not to judge those outside the church, but those within, Paul suddenly suggests (in 6:1-8) that "the saints will judge the world" and even angels! It's possible he has reference to Daniel 7:22, where "the Ancient of Days came and pronounced judgment in favor of the saints of the Most High, and the time came when they possessed the kingdom."

It's also possible that Paul is anticipating the final Judgment, when the saints themselves will appear before the throne of judgment. If so, he may be suggesting that the righteousness of the saints will set the standard by which an unrighteous world will be judged. (See, e.g., Hebrews 11:7, in which it is said that Noah's faith condemned the world.) It seems unlikely that human discretion will have any place in God's own judging of either the wicked or angels.

References in both Jude 14-15 and 1 Thessalonians 3:13 to the Lord coming with his "holy ones" in judgment on the world likely refers to his faithful angels, mentioned in other resurrection passages.

Jesus' promise to the Twelve (in Matthew 19:28) that they would sit on twelve thrones judging the twelve tribes of Israel may speak of their heavenly exaltation, but more likely to their leadership role in the fledgling church. Yet the reference is not wholly clear.

tized into his death? We were therefore buried with him through baptism into death in order that, just as Christ was raised from the dead through the glory of the Father, we too may live a new life" (6:1-4).

In the symbolism of immersion, the *old man of sin* dies and is buried, and a *new man* is given life—which is to say, born again. That's the very mystery Jesus was trying to explain to Nicodemus when he talked to him about being born again of the water and the Spirit (John 3:5). Or, as Paul puts it here in terms of our baptism: "If we have been united with him like this in his death, we will certainly also be united with him in his resurrection. For we know that our old self was crucified with him so that the body of sin might be done away with, that we should no longer be slaves to sin—because anyone who has died has been freed from sin" (6:5-7).

Here, then, is the progression: 1) Our sin has brought upon us the consequence of spiritual death. 2) As an act of atonement, Christ shed his blood for us on the cross, whereupon he was buried and then powerfully resurrected. 3) In response to his mercy and grace, we reenact Christ's own death, burial and resurrection by going down into water, being buried in it, and being raised up from it. 4) Having thus identified with Christ in baptism, we become obligated to live *as if we were already dead and resurrected*—which is to say, dead to sin, but alive to the Spirit of Christ.

So it is that Christ's resurrection is not simply proof of life after death for all mankind—the righteous and wicked alike. For those of us who have emerged from the waters of baptism with excited expectations of our new life in Christ, his resurrection serves as a powerful, ever-present admonition. We must never forget, says Paul, that "since Christ was raised from the dead, he cannot die again; death no longer has mastery over him. The death he died, he died to sin *once for all*; but the life he lives, he lives to God" (6:9-10).

In like manner, if we truly wish to identify with Christ's resurrection, we can no longer live in the sinful way we once lived before we died with him. Having been raised with Christ, returning to the sin which led to our death in the first place is simply out of the question. Sin must no longer has mastery over us, for we are people who have died and been given a new life! To be spiritually resurrected, Paul argues, is to turn onto a one-way street—a street leading home for the righteous, and away from lives that are unworthy of our eternal destiny.

The real challenge

It's one thing, of course, to understand in some academic sense the significance of our physical death and future resurrection, as we've tried to do in this book. Relatively speaking, that part is child's play. What's eminently more difficult is to actually live each day as dead sinners who have been spiritually resurrected for finer things than the sin which has brought us condemnation. We may have been justified by faith and saved by grace; but, if we're honest about it, old habits die hard. Even if the spirit is willing, we know all too painfully that the flesh is still frustratingly weak.

Worse yet, it is ever so clever, rationalizing our sins (excuse me, *weaknesses*) with the comforting thought that, after all, "we're only human;" whispering in our ear, perhaps at the very moment of moral rebellion, that God's grace has no boundaries beyond which we can go; and even preaching from our pulpits that, once we know the Lord and are saved, we couldn't possibly end up in hell.

In view of eternity, all such thinking is madness. Not just theological confusion on the part of some, but sheer, high-risk madness on the part of all of us who play down the seriousness of our sin in the wishful or arrogant belief that God will turn and wink at us when we stand before him at the throne as if he didn't know. As if he never sees. As if, even now, he isn't eyeing the book of life and reaching reluctantly for his pen. "What shall we say, then? Shall we go on sinning that grace may increase? By no means! We died to sin; how can we live in it any longer?"

Hope for the suffering Christian

As difficult as it is to really and truly "die with Christ" in this way, there is at least one challenge of potentially greater difficulty–which is dying *for* Christ. Hope of the afterlife will never have the meaning for most of us modern-day Christians as it did for those thousands, perhaps millions, of believers who lived in earlier centuries marked by widespread brutal persecution. Nor should we forget the persecution experienced by many believers still today in hostile, non-Christian cultures. So what is their secret for faithfulness under fire? In the face of torture, deprivation, and death, surely nothing sustains a person quite like his conviction that justice ultimately will prevail and that life after death will be worth any suffering he might experience for the name of Christ.

Listen solemnly as we remember again those who, because of their faith, "were tortured and refused to be released, *so that they might gain a better resurrection.* Some faced jeers and flogging, while still others were chained and put in prison. They were stoned; they were sawed in two; they were put to death by the sword. They went about in sheepskins and goatskins, destitute, persecuted and mistreated....They wandered in deserts and mountains, and in caves and holes in the ground" (Hebrews 11:35-38).

Take off your shoes and humble yourself in the presence of these courageous men and women of faith, for this is holy ground on which we're standing. Poignant beyond measure is their simple epitaph: "The world was not worthy of them."

Paul's own inspiring example

If there were an icon for them other than Jesus Christ himself, it would be Paul. Who among us can even begin to appreciate the trials and tribulations of this venerable apostle? Sometimes it's easy to forget what this scholarly giant in the faith endured for the sake of the cross even before his apparent martyrdom. With embarrassed reluctance, Paul defended his apostleship by recounting his frequent imprisonment; the five times he had received the 39 lashes; the three times he was beaten with rods; that time he was stoned; and the three times he was shipwrecked; not to mention the constant danger he was in, and the lack of sleep, and the many times he was hungry and cold—all for the sake of Christ.

So what does a Christian think about in the midst of such suffering? What possibly sustains him? According to Paul, it's *the Resurrection!*

To his young protégé Timothy, Paul writes (in 2 Timothy 2:8-13): "Remember Christ Jesus, *raised from the dead*....This is my gospel, for which I am suffering even to the point of being chained like a criminal. Therefore I endure everything for the sake of the elect, that they too may obtain the salvation that is in Christ Jesus, with eternal glory. Here is a trustworthy saying:

If we died with him,
we will also live with him;

if we endure, we will also reign with him.
If we disown him,
he will also disown us;
if we are faithless,
he will remain faithful,
for he cannot disown himself.

Ironically, what sustained Paul in the midst of persecution was the very heart of the gospel for which he was being persecuted–which was the hope of resurrection! Counting all things as loss for the sake of Christ, Paul pens those majestic words which have sustained countless believers facing suffering of every kind: "I want to know Christ and the power of his resurrection and the fellowship of sharing in his sufferings, becoming like him in his death, and so, somehow, to attain to the resurrection from the dead" (Philippians 3:10-11).

Surrounded by martyrs

As courageous as it is to step down into the waters of baptism, committing one's life to Christ and symbolically identifying in a personal way with Christ's own death, burial, and resurrection, it is nothing to compare with the courage of those who literally have gone to their death for the sake of their Savior. For them, knowing Christ and the power of his resurrection was not just a popular mantra for daily inspiration, but a real sharing in Christ's suffering and death. Who more than these martyrs would have thought long and hard about the afterlife issues we've confronted in the pages of this book perhaps while sitting comfortably in an "easy chair"?

For persecuted Christians throughout the centuries, the hope of resurrection was not simply grist for theological debate, but a last-ditch safety line to which they held on with every ounce of ebbing strength they could muster. For them, the prospect of resurrection was a hope when all hope was gone. An assurance in the midst of doubt and despair. A compelling reason to do what otherwise would have been impossible.

And don't think for a minute that it wouldn't have been tempting to take the easy way out. To deny Christ in a thousand ways. Just ask Peter, who lied and cursed and betrayed Jesus there in Annas' courtyard. But that was before the cross. Before the tomb. Before the stone was rolled away....

A divine pep talk

In a stirring passage filled with afterlife references, the Hebrew writer gives a rousing locker room speech at halftime when the scoreboard would suggest little hope for a comeback.

> *Remember those earlier days after you had received the light, when you stood your ground in a great contest in the face of suffering. Sometimes you were publicly exposed to insult and persecution; at other times you stood side by side with those who were so treated. You sympathized with those in prison and joyfully accepted the confiscation of your property, because you knew that you yourselves had better and lasting possessions (Hebrews 10:32-34).*

"So do not throw away your confidence" at this point, the coach continues, "it will be richly rewarded. You need to persevere so that when you have done the will of God, *you will receive what he has promised.* For in just a very little while,

> *"He who is coming will come and will not delay.*
> *But my righteous one will live by faith.*
> *And if he shrinks back,*
> *I will not be pleased with him (Hebrews 10:35-38)*

"But *we are not of those who shrink back and are destroyed,* but of those who believe and are saved" (Hebrews 10:39).

You can almost see the resolution in the players' faces as they leave the locker room and head out onto the field for the second half. You get the feeling that the score is about to change dramatically. Why? Call it motivation. There's everything to win and everything to lose. Persevere, and there's the all the glory that has been promised them. Shrink back, lose heart, give in, and the game will be over.

Except that it's not a game....

From here to eternity

When we step away from the analogy and back into reality, our life on earth is not a game. Between God and Satan, it's a cosmic struggle. For all of us, it's a *spiritual* struggle—between good and evil, morality and immorality, purity and corruption, faith and unbelief, loyalty and betrayal. While persecution and martyrdom obviously puts the struggle in sharper contrast, even so the struggle is there every day, just waiting for us to get out of bed and face it. Moment by moment, we have to decide who we are and who we want to be.

Of course, we can ignore the long-term implications of what we decide, pretending that our youthful bodies will never crash and burn. But pretending gets more and more difficult as the years go by and the aches and pains increase. In our heart of hearts, we know that eternity looms and that there's no escaping death and what follows in its wake. So again comes the question: *How, then, shall we live?* In distraction and denial? In desperation and fear? In confident hope?

One could do worse than taking a cue from Paul. "Since, then, you have been raised with Christ," he told the Colossians, "set your hearts on things above, where Christ is seated at the right hand of God. Set your minds on things above, not on earthly things. For you died, and your life is now hidden with Christ in God. When Christ, who is your life, appears, then you also will appear with him in glory" (Colossians 3:1-4).

Just dying to live

In almost any other generation since the beginning of time, this chapter could have ended comfortably on that note of high expectation. Who possibly could wish for more than appearing with Christ in glory when he comes! (And since we've already "died" in Christ, we've virtually had a dress rehearsal for dying in the flesh.) But if being with Christ in heaven is our confident hope, why do we go to such extraordinary lengths to prolong our life on earth?

Rather amazingly, this is a question which no other generation in the history of the world has had to answer in quite the same way. No previous generation has had anything like our ability to prolong life. Until recent times, most diseases were incurable, and death was relatively swift from such fairly unremarkable causes as pneumonia or even a ruptured appendix. With the advent of modern medicine, the plain fact of the matter is that it's getting harder and harder to die. Intensive care units, artificial life support, and extraordinary means of resuscitation have combined to sustain life interminably, even for those who remain irreversibly terminal.

One unexpected consequence of all this is that "meeting one's Maker" is no longer as fashionable as it once was—nor *preparing* to meet one's Maker. Somewhere along the line, we seem to have gotten the idea that we can beat the odds, cheat the Grim Reaper, and live forever—even if we're comatose and jaundiced, with nothing more than a slow-drip plastic tube acting as our umbilical cord to a womb now eager to be rid of us.

All of which begs a serious question for a people of faith who claim to look forward eagerly to the glory awaiting us in Christ. The question is no longer: How shall we *live* in view of eternity, but how shall we *die* in view of eternity? Whereas other generations didn't have much of a choice in the matter, we do.

There is no suggestion here that it's unbiblical, unChristlike, or immoral to accept even extraordinary medical assistance when there is reason to believe that significant recovery of life is still possible. Jesus himself was the Great Physician healing the sick, the blind and the lame. It doesn't get more extraordinary than a miracle! But when, at last, the time comes to depart this earth, the true believer need not grasp desperately at whatever medical straws might be available (or, worse yet, demand of God undying life on earth!) as if there were no tomorrow. No hope. No resurrection. No promise of glory in the life to come.

None of us knows just how we will respond on our deathbed. Nor should we presume to second-guess anyone's personal or family decisions at so sensitive a point in life. But blessed with the assurance of resurrection and eternal life with God, surely we have every reason to die differently from those who have no hope. Whereas "death with dignity" has become a modern medical mantra (as well as a subtle campaign slogan for immoral euthanasia), "death in perfect peace" better suits the dying Christian. Who, more than Christians, should face death with composure and confident trust? Who, but Christians, can eagerly anticipate the joy of eternal life with God on the other side of death's door?

Whether, then, in sickness or in health, in persecution or in peace, in temptation or in strength–may this brief glimpse of life on the other side of life make us a changed people, even now *eternal*...till death do us part. As James Steward has so elegantly framed the challenge: "Let us live as people who are prepared to die, and die as people who are prepared to live."

PART II
Bedlam On the Brink of Eternity

*For the time will come when men will not put up with sound doctrine.
Instead, to suit their own desires, they will gather around them a great
number of teachers to say what their itching ears want to hear. They will
turn their ears away from the truth and turn aside to myths.*

−2 Timothy 4:3-4

*But there were also false prophets among the people, just as there will be
false teachers among you....In their greed these teachers will exploit you
with stories they have made up.*

−2 Peter 2:1, 3

Anchor Verse - 1 John 1:7

"If we walk in the light, as he is in the light..the blood of Jesus, his Son, purifies us from all sin."

Chapter Preview

Catholic doctrine provides purgatory as a place of spiritual suffering and discipline for those who are not wicked enough to be consigned to hell but aren't quite ready for heaven. The idea of such a place is wholly without biblical support. Christ's blood not only justifies (in the legal sense of paying the debt for our sin), but it also sanctifies (as we respond in kind, allowing his grace to transform our lives).

There's more than one way to slap grace in the face. One way is to trade on God's grace and flaunt our lack of sanctification as if it's all up to him. The other way is to assume that God is so powerless to transform our imperfection into perfection that we must invent a purgatory where somehow we can make ourselves pure enough for heaven.

10

PURGATORY–SLAPPING GRACE IN THE FACE

Too black for heaven, and yet too white for hell.

–John Dryden
The Hind and the Panther, Part I, l. 343

When no less a thinker and writer than C. S. Lewis believed in the Catholic doctrine of purgatory (seen especially in *The Great Divorce*), one can't simply dismiss the concept out of hand. The simple question which underlies the doctrine is an important one: How can those who are justified through the blood of Christ, but who are not fully sanctified in holiness at the time of their deaths, be welcomed into heaven where nothing impure is allowed to enter? To put it more personally...Even assuming our sins have been completely forgiven, do we live morally-pure and spiritually-perfect lives before God? If the answer is "no"–and surely it must be–then how possibly could we enter into heaven's holiness without tainting it?

There's yet another way to think about it. Are we to believe that we have access to eternal life in heaven merely because we have given genuine mental assent to God's saving grace, evidenced perhaps in some ritualistic formality that is thought to put us into a saved state? If there is no real, transforming spiritual growth beyond that point, is heaven still ours to enjoy, or are we just indulging in a delusional form of cheap grace? The alternative is not simply an afterlife version of legalism, "working our way to heaven," as if either in life or in death we could ever put God in our debt. Rather, we're talking about sanctification of the soul. About becoming holy as God is holy. About moral and spiritual *purity*, which is linked directly with the root meaning of *purgatory*, denoting a process of purification.

With very little difficulty, it is easy for us to tell ourselves, in effect: "I try my best; Christ will take care of the rest." But C. S. Lewis, for one, was not so sure about that.

> *Our souls demand purgatory, don't they? Would it not break the heart if God said to us, "It is true, my son, that your breath smells and your rags drip with mud and slime, but we are charitable here and no one will upbraid you with these things, nor draw away from you. Enter into the joy"? Should we not reply, "With submission, sir, and if there is no objection, I'd rather be cleansed first"? "It may hurt, you know." –"Even so, sir."[1]*

Is Lewis onto something important here? Would not our souls themselves *beg* for a final cleansing before entering heaven, as if knowing all too well that we are unworthy *in fact*, even if *deemed* worthy in Christ? At the very least, there is the practical problem of yet-to-be-perfected souls entering into a perfect heaven. At some point, it is obvious that God will have to do *something* to rid us of our ingrained sinful habits. That being the case, are we to be merely passive objects of a wholly divine act of grace, or are we to participate somehow in that process?

Catholic doctrine responds to these crucial questions by providing purgatory as a necessary way station for those who are not wicked enough to be consigned to hell but not quite ready for heaven, either. Having nothing to do with the eternal punishment of the damned, purgatory is the final purification of the elect, the saved, the redeemed.

Threshold of pain

As Lewis suggests in his fictional conversation between the soul and God, central to the idea of purgatory is the necessity of pain acting as something like a "refiner's fire" (Malachi 3:2). For advocates of purgatory, today's popular mantra, "No pain, no gain," translates into "No pain, no sanctification." Thus, purgatory is conceived as a

---

1 C. S. Lewis, *Letters to Malcolm*.

place of spiritual suffering and fatherly discipline for those who are not good enough to enter immediately into heaven. (It begs the question, of course: If all have fallen far short of the glory of God, who *would* be good enough?)

Yet, even the hard edge of purgatory's suffering is often tempered with appeals to New Testament teaching that we are to *rejoice* in adversity because it purifies our faith. St. Catherine of Genoa said, for example, that although purgatory is incomparably painful (confronting us with the horror of our sins), it is also incomparably joyful, because 1) God is in purgatory with the souls who are being purified, and 2) because each soul knows that he is guaranteed eventual entrance into heaven.[2] No doubt few will find much comfort in those reassuring words, but we can hardly deny the underlying principle that suffering can bring spiritual growth, and thus sanctification. (Then again, it can also produce bitterness and rejection–a possible consequence rarely, if ever, acknowledged when purgatory is being defended.)

In support of the idea that purgatory is God's loving parental discipline, we are pointed to Hebrews 12:5-16 which, in summary form, is a restatement of Proverbs 3:11-12.

> *My son, do not make light of the Lord's discipline,*
> *and do not lose heart when he rebukes you,*
> *because the Lord disciplines those he loves,*
> *and he punishes everyone he accepts as a son.*

The Hebrew writer then goes on to elaborate further, using words which seem to echo the earlier sentiments of St. Catherine of Genoa. "God disciplines us for our good," he says, "that we may share in his holiness. No discipline seems pleasant at the time, but painful. Later on, however, it produces a harvest of righteousness and peace for those who have been trained by it." The only problem, of course, is that the Hebrew writer is addressing Christians who are still very much alive and well on earth–not those who are in, or destined for, some afterlife purgatory.

To these living, breathing first-century Christians who are facing the possibility of imminent persecution the writer says: "Let us fix

---

2 Peter Kreeft, *Catholic Christianity–A Complete Catechism of Catholic Beliefs, based on the Catechism of the Catholic Church* (San Francisco: Ignatius Press, 2001), 149.

our eyes on Jesus, the author and perfecter of our faith, who for the joy set before him endured the cross, scorning its shame, and sat down at the right hand of the throne of God. Consider him who endured such opposition from sinful men, so that you will not grow weary and lose heart" (Hebrews 12:2-3).

Contrary to what is often suggested, there is nothing anywhere close to a "hell on earth." But, for many, there very well may be a kind of purgatory right here on earth. To a greater or lesser degree, depending on our particular circumstances, we can be in the midst of it with the next dreaded telephone call, doctor's visit, or gut-wrenching moral dilemma. Whether physical, emotional, or spiritual–our present suffering can indeed be a fire that helps purge our souls of their dross.

That kind of present purging "fire" can be seen in yet another passage cited in support of purgatory: 1 Peter 1:6-7. "In this [the salvation to be revealed in the last time]," says Peter, "you greatly rejoice, though *now* for a little while you may have to suffer grief in all kinds of trials. These have come so that your faith–of greater worth than gold, which perishes even though refined by fire–may be proved genuine and may result in praise, glory, and honor when Jesus is revealed." Lest we miss the present nature and effect of that suffering, Peter wraps up his discussion, saying, "for you *are receiving* the goal of your faith, the salvation of your souls" (1 Peter 1:9).

That our *present* suffering leads to sanctification–or ought to–is seen as Peter gives application to his thesis, saying, "Just as he who called you is holy, so be holy in all you do; for it is written: 'Be holy, because I am holy'" (1 Peter 1:15-16). "Therefore, rid yourselves of all malice and all deceit, hypocrisy, envy, and slander of every kind. Like newborn babies, crave pure spiritual milk, so that by it you may grow up in your salvation, now that you have tasted that the Lord is good" (1 Peter 2:3).

It is *now* that we are to "grow up in our salvation." *Now* that our suffering ought to make us holy people fit for eternity with a holy God. But, if we're honest, that's more theory than reality. And it is precisely this "reality gap" which drives the forces behind purgatory. How much have we *really* suffered as Christians in this life? Just how holy have we *actually* become? When we die, will we be anywhere near as holy as heaven deserves?

A long, controversial history

If perhaps these concerns have accompanied Christian theology from the very beginning, the doctrine of purgatory did not come into its own until the Middle Ages. Although Augustine (354-430) reflected on the doctrine's underlying issues, it was not before the Council of Florence (1439) and the Council of Trent (1563) that purgatory became an official part of Catholic dogma. And, even then, Catholicism has not always had a uniform view of purgatory's nature and purpose. Roman Catholicism, for example, has tended to see purgatory as a place of punishment for sins of which the soul has not sufficiently repented; whereas Eastern Orthodox theologians have placed a greater emphasis on the process of maturing and sanctifying the dead.

Indeed, there have been charges that Catholicism puts on the softer glove of "final sanctification" when explaining purgatory to Protestants, but takes off that glove when preaching the harsher view of "punishment for sins" to its own communicants.[3] To this day, many Catholics tremble at the prospect of dying, only to join the suffering souls in purgatory for having committed even one venial sin. Scant comfort is taken from the teaching that accumulated indulgences can help shorten their torment (which itself militates against the idea of sanctification through suffering).[4]

Worse yet is the ongoing distress of thinking about departed family and friends suffering in purgatory. Nor is it easy to forget their ordeal, since one month each year (November) is a designated time for prayers, novenas, and Masses to be offered for loved ones still writhing in purgatory's agonizing flames.

As is well known, the combination of playing on that very fear and the corrupt sale of indulgences was one of the sparks which lit the fuse of the Reformation movement. Martin Luther was incensed when the Dominican monk John Tetzel began selling papal indulgences, guaranteeing renewal of the spiritual state which the people enjoyed at the point of their baptisms—which is to say, sinless perfection. For yet more money, indulgences could also be bought to free the souls of loved ones from their anguished torture in the fiery inferno of purgatory. "At the very instant the money rattles at the

---

3 For a fuller discussion of these ideas, see Jerry L. Walls, "Purgatory for Everyone," *First Things*, April, 2002, 26-30.
4 Tony Coffey, *Once A Catholic* (Eugene: Harvest House Publishers, 1993), Chapter Nine.

bottom of the chest," Tetzel promised brazenly, "the soul escapes from purgatory, and flies liberated to heaven." And who makes that possible? "The Lord our God no longer reigns," came Tetzel's breathtaking response. "He has given all power to the pope!"

Tetzel's blasphemy led directly to the posting of the ninety-five theses in which Luther challenged the whole system of indulgences, together with the sanctioned avarice which lay behind it.

John Calvin's concern was deeper yet, seeing the doctrine of purgatory as a frontal assault on salvation by faith. Said Calvin in righteous fury: "We must cry out with the shouting not only of our voices but our throats and lungs that purgatory is a deadly fiction of Satan, which nullifies the cross of Christ, inflicts unbearable contempt upon God's mercy, and overturns and destroys our faith."[5]

From Calvin's vitriolic response, we sense that the view of purgatory in his day had far less to do with sanctification toward greater holiness than justification from sin. Even if Calvin had recognized a problem of yet-to-be-perfected sinners entering into a perfect heaven, you get the idea that he would have dismissed it with the assurance that God unilaterally resolves the matter through his sovereign power.

Skirmish over Scripture

Calvin was concerned, not merely about the theology behind purgatory, but about the very existence of a place such as purgatory. Proceeding on the Protestant notion of *sola scriptura* (that Scripture alone is to be our authority in all matters of faith and doctrine), it was clear to Calvin–as indeed it is to any student of the Bible–that Scripture makes no mention of purgatory as a fixture of the afterlife. While this obvious fact is acknowledged by Catholic theologians, a number of passages are presented–seemingly with apology–in an effort to give the doctrine a patina of biblical support. Unlike other afterlife issues which engender a battle of the Scriptures, the debate over purgatory is no more than a minor skirmish, in which its proponents argue almost exclusively from shadowy inference.

In his recent book, *Catholic Christianity–A Complete Catechism of Catholic Beliefs, Based On The Catechism of the Catholic Church*, Peter Kreeft cites six passages as the Church's answer to the question: "Is purgatory found in Scripture?"[6] "The reality of purgatory is found in

---

5 John Calvin, *Institutes*, 3.5.6.
6 Kreeft, 2001, 149-150.

Scripture," says Kreeft, "though not the word–just like the Trinity. For instance, Scripture speaks of a cleansing spiritual fire (I Cor 3:15; I Pet 1:7)."

We have already seen in our earlier analysis that Peter (in 1 Peter 1:7) was speaking about current suffering in this present world–not some future suffering of the soul in the world to come. By contrast, in 1 Corinthians 3:15 Paul is not speaking of suffering at all, but rather about division in the church at Corinth and how God will judge those who cause that division. (The discussion begins in Chapter 1, where Paul says, "I appeal to you, brothers...that there may be no divisions among you....") It is with this ungodly schism in mind that Paul says:

> By the grace God has given me, I laid a foundation as an expert builder, and someone else is building on it. But each one should be careful how he builds. For no one can lay any foundation other than the one already laid, which is Jesus Christ. If any man builds on this foundation using gold, silver, costly stones, wood, hay or straw, his work will be shown for what it is, because the Day will bring it to light. It will be revealed with fire, and the fire will test the quality of each man's work. If what he has built survives, he will receive his reward. If it is burned up, he will suffer loss; he himself will be saved, but only as one escaping through the flames (1 Corinthians 3:10-15).

As the context makes clear, Paul is warning the Corinthians about how they should build upon the doctrinal foundation which he laid when he was among them. If they built upon that foundation with "gold" and "precious stones," then they would be rewarded; but if with "hay" or "straw," it would be to their loss. And how would it be known with which of these they built? Paul says that all will be known at the day of judgment ("the Day"), when their work will be tested as if by fire. If their work for the kingdom has been as gold, it will stand the test. But if it has been as straw, it will be consumed and of no value to them, even if by the grace of God they are saved despite the harm they have caused.

Granting the uncertainty of Paul's words–"he himself will be saved, but only as one escaping through the flames"–it is crystal clear that this could not be a reference to purgatory. To begin with, there is the problem that what the "fire" tests in this passage is tied to a particular antecedent (causing division), not to one's overall purity or holiness. Even more problematic is the fact that the "flames" in question are specifically associated with the day of judgment, which itself follows the resurrection. By Catholic doctrine, purgatory begins at the moment of death for each individual destined to it. (More on this momentarily.)

But the clincher, really, is Paul's conclusion to the discussion: "Therefore judge nothing before the appointed time; wait till the Lord comes. He will bring to light what is hidden in darkness and will expose the motives of men's hearts. At that time each will receive his praise from God" (1 Corinthians 4:5). It is not until the day of judgment (post-purgatory) that the motives of men's hearts will come to light and be judged. If souls had already been fully cleansed in purgatory, there would be no evil motives remaining to be exposed.

An "imperfect" argument

Kreeft's next three passages highlight what we've already discussed about the fact that–as he words it–"at death many of us are still imperfect (I Jn 1:8) and that in heaven we will all be perfect (Mt 5:48; Rev 21:27)." Without question, none of us has lived up to Jesus' challenge: "Be perfect, therefore, as your heavenly Father is perfect" (Matthew 5:48). And it goes without saying that "nothing impure will enter [heaven]" (Revelation 21:27). But is Kreeft correct when he says that, from putting these two principles together, "purgatory necessarily follows"?

There is some irony in Kreeft's reference to 1 John 1:8 for support of the proposition that we are still imperfect at the moment of death. While that is objectively true in terms of our own dismal inattention to sanctification, it is not true subjectively in the eyes of God. As elsewhere, the *Catechism's* pro-purgatory interpretation defies obvious context. Without question, the apostle says here that "if we claim to be without sin, we deceive ourselves and the truth is not in us." But the very next verse reads: "If we confess our sins, he is faithful and just and will forgive us our sins and *purify us from all unrighteousness.*" Not only that, but the immediately preceding verse also tells us that "if we walk in the light, as he is in the light, we have fellowship with one another, and *the blood of Jesus, his Son, purifies us from all sin."*

On the strength of that one passage alone, we can believe in a far greater purgatory than the one presented to us in Catholic doctrine. That all-sufficient purgatory is Christ's blood! Not only does it justify (in the legal sense of paying the debt for our sin), but it also sanctifies by purifying us from *all sin.*

Yes, of course, we must continue to walk in the light, which we do imperfectly. And we must also be willing to confess our sins, which we do all too infrequently. But that's *our* part–our all-too-feeble contribution to the process of sanctification. For *his* part, God bridges the gap between our imperfection and his holiness. It's only when we expect God to do more than his fair share that we reveal hearts unfit for heaven.

There's more than one way to slap grace in the face. One way is to trade on God's grace and flaunt our lack of sanctification as if it's all up to him. The other way is to assume that God is so powerless to transform our imperfection into perfection that we must invent a purgatory where, through extraordinary pain and suffering, we can make ourselves pure enough for heaven.

Dropping the mask of sanctification

Citing Matthew 12:31-32, Kreeft says: "Scripture also distinguishes sins that cannot be forgiven either before or after death from sins that can be forgiven after death."

But even a cursory look at this passage tells us that dodgy logic is being used to prop up a weighty theological proposition for which there is no other support. Listen carefully to Jesus' words. Responding to the charge that his miracles are of Beelzebub–which is to say satanic–Jesus says heatedly: "I tell you, every sin and blasphemy will be forgiven men, but the blasphemy against the Spirit will not be forgiven. Anyone who speaks a word against the Son of Man will be forgiven, but anyone who speaks against the Holy Spirit [by whom his miracles were being performed] will not be forgiven, either in this age or in the age to come."

How at any time, whether now or in the future, could a person ever be forgiven for blaspheming against the only Spirit by whom a person can be forgiven! Could we possibly miss Jesus' point? There is no sin which can't be forgiven except the sin of denying the One who make all forgiveness possible. But to use the fact that this uniquely unforgivable sin won't be forgiven even "in the age to come" as a premise to conclude that other sins can be forgiven after death–namely, in purgatory–is gratuitous illogic of the highest order.[7]

Not only is this passage a futile attempt at artificially breathing life into a dead doctrine, but it also highlights the fact that, at least for the Roman Church, the real, bare-knuckles significance of purgatory is justification–not, as advertised, the soft glove of sanctification. And therein lies the supreme danger of this patently-contrived doctrine: the more purgatory is linked with forgiveness, the greater the risk of denying the saving power of Jesus' blood.

Reaching outside the canon of Scripture

Unfortunately, the focus on justification doesn't change in the final passage offered in defense of purgatory. In Kreeft's words: "Scripture also teaches us to pray for the dead, 'that they might be delivered from their sin'...which is impossible for those in hell and already finished for those in heaven."

If perhaps the words of this passage don't have the ring of familiarity, it is most likely because they are not in your Bible. The citation is to 2 Maccabees 12:46, found only in the Apocrypha, a collection of literature from the inter-testamental period which is not included in the canon of most Protestant Bibles. Apart from the fact that Jesus himself never made approving reference to the books of the Apocrypha, speaking only of the Laws of Moses, the Prophets and the Psalms (Luke 24:44), the book of Maccabees itself makes no claim to being inspired. Far from it, the writer concludes his book, saying apologetically, "At this point I will bring my work to an end. If it is found well written and aptly composed, that is what I myself hoped for; if cheap and mediocre, I could only do my best" (2 Maccabees 15:38-39). Almost as shocking as the book's inclusion in the Catholic canon is the fact that Catholicism would hang its vaunted doctrine of purgatory on so tentative a hook.

Indeed, it is all the more surprising, considering that praying for the particular dead which the writer has in mind would be contrary

---

7 For that matter, we can't even be completely certain that Jesus was talking about what will happen after death. Conceivably, "the age to come" could refer to the kingdom age in which the Holy Spirit now plays a more central role than it played before Jesus ascended.

to Catholic doctrine. In verse 40, we see that those who died were Israel's slain soldiers, who at the time of their death possessed forbidden idols. According to Catholic doctrine, idolatry is a mortal sin for which hell–not purgatory–is the only destiny. Has this problematic detail slipped the Church's attention?

A desperate snatching at straws

Reduced to strained contexts, convoluted logic, and even a questionable canon, Catholicism's defense of purgatory is forced to retreat into its all-too-familiar fallback position. Says Kreeft: "Finally, the Church, which Scripture calls 'the pillar and bulwark of the truth' (I Tim 3:15), has always taught and has solemnly and officially defined purgatory as a divinely revealed dogma (Councils of Florence and Trent)."

While that trump card may work for anyone willing to grant the Roman Church primacy over God's own revealed Scripture, it merely serves to underscore the weakness of the biblical case for purgatory, which for the rest of us is all that matters.

It's not that we don't relate

There is no doubting the natural urge which lies behind prayers for the dead. Who of us isn't concerned with the souls of our friends and loved ones who have died without being in Christ? Who of us hasn't prayed in desperation that God would somehow find a way to grant divine clemency for their souls? As Paul reminds us (1 Corinthians 15:29), there are those (even today) who go so far as to be baptized on behalf of the dead, despite there being no basis whatsoever for thinking that a vicarious immersion could save them.

Yet, to pray for the souls of the dead who supposedly are experiencing a process of purification inexorably leading to heaven doesn't make sense. By Catholic doctrine, there is no danger that such souls can slip downward into hell, nor any reason to fear that they'll miss out on heaven. And if the pain and suffering of purgatory were truly their only hope of entering heaven in a pure state, why should we pray that they might escape such a beneficent ordeal? What, then, is left to pray for, other than begging God to make the required pain somehow less painful?

The very idea of praying for souls in purgatory is as fundamentally flawed as the very notion of such a place itself.

No place for such a place

It may be a problem of "chickens and eggs" (which came first?), but one gets the idea that the doctrine of purgatory has forced some strange accommodations in Catholic afterlife theology. The plain fact is that, once you throw purgatory into the mix of afterlife events, you have to do a lot of pushing and shoving to make room for it. And that is precisely what Catholic dogma has done. Whereas Scripture speaks of but one, universal judgment of the righteous and the wicked on the Last Day–the day of Christ's appearing–Catholicism's tangled web now includes at least two.

As Kreeft explains the *Catechism of the Catholic Church*: "What happens at death is the particular judgment. God infallibly knows and judges each soul as either (a) able to enter heaven immediately, or (b) needing to be purified in purgatory first and then able to enter heaven, or (c) set forever (since our lifetime is over) in unrepented sin and capable only of hell. Then at the general judgment at the end of time, there is the general resurrection of the body, which will share in the soul's eternal destiny."

Does Scripture at any point speak of a "particular judgment" and a "general judgment?" For that matter, does it suggest that some righteous souls go immediately to heaven upon death, whereas other righteous souls must lag behind? As is typically the case–no less than with a child's desperate attempt to bolster the initial deception–one invention (purgatory) demands yet another invention (a "particular judgment"), and on it goes. Get the theology wrong, and practical problems begin to mount up. (One wonders, for instance, whether purgatory is to be dispensed with in the case of those who are still living when the Lord returns....)

This, then, is the Achilles heel of purgatory. It simply doesn't fit within the sequence of afterlife events presented to us in Scripture. Nor is it simply that Paul is silent about purgatory, but that he is silent in the face of specific questioning about afterlife events and their sequence. Nothing even remotely like purgatory has any place in Paul's teaching about afterlife chronology. We hear plenty of talk about Christ's appearing, and the resurrection, and the judgment, but not a word about purgatory, not even by reasonable inference.

The flip sides of sanctification

So, can any good thing come out of purgatory? For all the needless fear and dread the prospect of purgatory has instilled—nigh unto unforgivable itself—nevertheless, a kernel of truth remains: that sanctification is indeed a joint enterprise. We ourselves must participate in our own sanctification, for that is the high calling of a redeemed people. Using almost a throw-away line, Paul presents us with both sides of the coin in the opening words of his first Corinthian letter: "To the church of God in Corinth, to those *sanctified in Christ Jesus* and *called to be holy....*" (1 Corinthians 1:2).

On one side of the coin is the divine transaction whereby the saved have had their sins remitted and their relationship with God radically changed for eternity. Reminding the Corinthians that they once were idolaters, male prostitutes, thieves, and drunkards, Paul then says, "But you were washed, you were sanctified, you were justified in the name of the Lord Jesus Christ and by the Spirit of our God" (1 Corinthians 6:9-11). In God's mercy, they had been both justified and sanctified. Once lost and traveling the road to hell, praise God they were now both saved and cleansed!

But time and again Paul shows us the other side of that marvelous coin, bearing the same imprint of Christ as the first side. Now that you *have been sanctified*, says Paul, "it is God's will that you *should be sanctified*....For God did not call us to be impure, but to live a holy life" (1 Thessalonians 4:3-8).

In the greatest love match ever played, the ball of sanctification was served up by Christ the minute we walked to the base line, prepared to receive it. But now the ball is in our court, and it's up to us to return it. Not in competition, as if we could win the game by any skill or strength of our own; but out of sheer gratitude, and a desire to imitate our Mentor and Coach who wants us to be every bit as good as he is.

If there's not a chance in the world that, apart from his grace, we could ever fully purify ourselves, the divine irony is that we *must* purify ourselves! "Since we have these promises, dear friends, let us purify ourselves from everything that contaminates body and spirit, perfecting holiness out of reverence for God" (2 Corinthians 7:1).

But how possibly could we ever *perfect* holiness, even out of reverence for God? When all is said and done, it's still a matter of grace–still a matter of the Spirit working in and through us–teaching us, rebuking us, loving us. "For the grace of God that brings salvation has appeared to all men. It teaches us to say 'No' to ungodliness and worldly passions, and to live self-controlled, upright and godly lives *in this present age*, while we wait for the blessed hope–the glorious appearing of our great God and Savior, Jesus Christ, who gave himself for us to redeem us from all wickedness and to purify for himself a people that are his very own, eager to do what is good" (Titus 2:11-15).

What a passage! What a picture: One glorious coin...two sides! Whether we see both sides, of course, depends on how we've tossed it. If the hand of purgatory has managed to hide the first side, especially from the unlearned and the vulnerable, the hand of cheap grace has too often hidden the flip side from those of us who are quick to renounce purgatory but slow to seek God's purifying fire here on earth.

In the ordinary coin toss, one side is always a winner. In this case, either side alone is a loser.

As for that niggling question which gave impetus to the idea of purgatory in the first place, it's yet another two-sided coin. In this world, where the temptations of the flesh reach out moment by moment to entice us, we find ourselves struggling to respond in kind to God's perfect holiness. But in the spiritual realm on the other side, our bodies, our awareness, and our surrounding environment will be so dramatically transformed that the present, arduous process of sanctification will be brought immediately and gloriously to fruition. When that final coin is flipped in the presence of a holy and pure God, there won't be any question of our tainting heaven with our past imperfections. At the portals of eternity, this life's *present*, imperfect tense will have become *future perfect*!

In the meantime, we have those who dreamt up the idea of purgatory to thank for reminding us that our sanctification is just as important as our justification–that we need to be more and more intentional about becoming a holy people fit for heaven. But any thought that such a place as purgatory actually exists ought to be forever purged from any doctrine calling itself Christian...no matter how painful that might be.

Anchor Verse - Mark 10:14-15

"Let the little children come to me, and do not hinder them, for the kingdom of God belongs to such as these."

Chapter Preview

Although Catholicism takes no official position on the eternal destiny of unbaptized infants, many of its theologians have speculated that these souls go into a state of existence known as "limbo." This hypothesized afterlife fixture exposes flaws in the underlying fundamental assumptions–widely held by both Catholics and Protestants–that infants are tainted by original sin and that children are proper subjects for baptism.

Because spiritual jeopardy assumes a mature understanding of sin and its consequences, there is no moral accountability for sin at the point of conception, nor in the mother's womb, nor at the moment of birth, nor as a toddler, nor as a young child just learning his way through the moral maze.

11

LIMBO—A THEOLOGY IN SEARCH OF COHERENCE

Necessity is the mother of invention.

—Anonymous

By Catholic doctrine, unborn fetuses, the stillborn, and newborn infants are all automatically under the condemnation of original sin inherited from Adam and Eve. Also by Catholic doctrine, no unbaptized person can enter into heaven; but neither does hell seem to be appropriate for those who have not had the opportunity or knowledge to commit an actual sin. Hence the theological problem: With neither heaven nor hell available, what happens to unbaptized "baby souls" when they die? (For similar reasons, the question also arises regarding the unbaptized souls of the mentally disabled, the autistic, and others unable to understand the nature of sin.)

Although Roman Catholicism takes no official position on their eternal destiny, many of its theologians and clergy have speculated over the centuries that these souls go into a state of existence known as "limbo." The word itself is derived from the Latin *limbus*, meaning edge, fringe, or border. The idea, then, is that limbo is neither heaven nor hell, but someplace in-between.

Interestingly, if limbo more closely "borders" either place (in some kind of geographical sense), traditionally it is thought to be nearer to hell than heaven. Yet, that itself is problematic, since limbo is widely thought to be an eternal state of perfect happiness where God is both known and loved. (How, in that event, limbo differs significantly from heaven is not clearly articulated.)

History of the notion

Historically, there has been no clear-cut unanimity regarding the nature and effect of limbo. The view of the early Church Fathers may be reflected in the statement by Gregory of Nazianzus (ca. 329-ca. 390) that infants dying without baptism "will neither be admitted by the just judge to the glory of Heaven nor condemned to suffer punishment, since, though unsealed [by baptism], they are not wicked."[1]

Under Augustine's influence, the Council of Carthage (A.D. 418) rejected the concept "of any place...in which children who pass out of this life unbaptized live in happiness." According to the Catholic Encyclopedia, "St. Augustine and the African Fathers believed that unbaptized infants share in the common positive misery of the damned, and the very most that St. Augustine concedes is that their punishment is the mildest of all."[2] From the time Thomas Aquinas (ca. 1226-1274) dissented from that decree until relatively recent times, the general consensus has favored the existence of a felicitous existence in limbo, not damnable torment in hell.

Without specifically referring to limbo, the Catechism of the Catholic Church (CCC 1261) currently declares: "As regards children who have died without baptism, the Church can only entrust them to the mercy of God, as she does in her funeral rites for them. Indeed, the great mercy of God, who desires that all men should be saved, and Jesus' tenderness toward children, which caused him to say, 'Let the children come to me, do not hinder them' [Mark 10:14, cf. I Tim 2:4], allow us to hope that there is a way of salvation for children who have died without baptism. All the more urgent is the Church's call not to prevent little children coming to Christ through the gift of holy baptism."

Not just infants

Beyond mere hopeful sentiment on behalf of these unfortunate innocents, there has been an almost necessary linkage between their destiny and that of all the righteous souls who lived prior to the Christian era. Having taken the position that no unbaptized person could enter into heaven, the Church faced a similar dilemma regarding what to do with the righteous ancients, from Abraham, Isaac, and Jacob to the thief on the cross–none of whom, of course, were ever

1 Orat., XL, 23.
2 R. C. Broderick, Ed., *The Catholic Encyclopedia*, 349-350.

baptized. Since logic forbade consigning them to hell, yet strictly-interpreted doctrine demanded excluding them from heaven, limbo became the first available staging area. Of course, it meant that if those righteous souls (some specifically listed in the roll call of the faithful) could not conceivably be in torment, then neither could the unbaptized children who shared space with them in limbo.

Yet strangely, it seems, not all limbo is limbo. In the "limbo of the Fathers," the souls of the righteous dead before the Christian era may have won a place in heaven, either through their holiness in life or perhaps through the discipline of purgatory, but they must remain in limbo until the final judgment. By contrast, in the "limbo of children" heaven is only a wistful hope of the Church. Absent God's mercy, the souls of infants could just as easily remain forever in limbo, even after the final judgment.

From the perspective of the Reformers

For anyone looking from outside Catholicism, virtually every aspect of limbo appears to be in a muddle. It must be said, however, that Protestant thinking on the subject has its own lack of coherence. For example, Calvin rejected the idea of limbo, but primarily as an *a priori* conclusion necessarily following his belief in predestination, whereby God arbitrarily chooses in advance which souls will be saved and which will be lost. Given that premise, Calvin could only surmise that what's true for adults is also true of children: some would go to heaven; others would end up in hell.

Ulrich Zwingli agreed that there was no such place as limbo, but primarily because he opposed the "necessity of baptism to infant salvation." Since, therefore, he believed that all children who die in infancy are saved, there was no need for limbo.

Still another "take" on the issue comes from the Presbyterian Church, U.S.A.'s 1903 Declaratory Statement, which professes: "We believe that all dying in infancy are included in the election of grace, and are regenerated and saved by Christ through the Spirit, who works when and where and how He pleases." (If the latter clause affirming God's sovereignty is correct, then what necessarily assures the former clause? What prevents Calvin's conclusion that God will consign children to hell just as he will adults? Why, apart from sentimentality, should dying infants–as a group–automatically be exempt from predestination of the wicked? Indeed, were *all infants* exempt, there could be no *adults* predestined to perdition!)

Oh what a tangled web...

Unfortunately, space in this volume does not allow for a full discussion of the numerous theological issues raised at this point, about which untold volumes already have been written. Suffice it to say that the notion of limbo–wholly unknown to Scripture–raises serious questions about the dubious theological assumptions which desperately need such a place as limbo in order to keep their shaky theological house of cards from collapsing.

Original sin is the original troublemaker

The first problem with limbo's underlying theology is the fundamental assumption–widely held by both Catholics and Protestants–that every child, born or unborn, is tainted with the sin of Adam and thus automatically under condemnation. In so limited a discussion, one can only suggest that David was using hyperbole when (thinking specifically about his clearly *adult* sin with Bathsheba and the cover-up murder of her husband) he lamented: "Surely I was sinful at birth, sinful from the time my mother conceived me" (Psalm 51:5). And that Ezekiel reminds us it is the soul that sins who dies–not the son for the father's sins, nor the father for his son's sins (Ezekiel 18). And that, although Paul speaks in Romans 5:12 of sin entering the world through Adam, he hastens to add: "in this way death came to all men, *because all sinned*."[3] And that Jesus himself–without the slightest mention of baptism–said, "Let the little children come to me, and do not hinder them, *for the kingdom of God belongs to such as these*" (Mark 10:14-15).

---

3 Since the state of infants is not under discussion, but rather the contrast between the problem of sin (of which Adam is the icon) and its divine solution (for which Christ Jesus is the icon), nothing forces the assumption that Paul is necessarily including fetuses, the still-born, and newborn infants along with mature adults who clearly are responsible for having sinned. And the same applies to Paul's statement that "all have sinned and fall short of the glory of God" (Romans 3:23). Would we automatically include infants when hearing someone say, "Everyone should vote"; or "All are invited to participate in the debate over original sin"?

Indeed, one must also be careful to distinguish our participatory "acts of sin" from the passive "taint of sin" assumed by the doctrine of original sin. Adam and Eve's sin was certainly the *original* sin, but nothing in Scripture suggests that Cain and Abel inherited their parents' sin as if it were a biological defect transmitted genetically. If sin were passed on in that way to everyone emerging from the womb, then the same would have to be said of the Son of Man, himself. That this logically follows explains why Catholicism has been forced to contrive the Immaculate Conception of Mary so that she herself would be sinless and thus unable to pass on Adam's sin to Jesus.

The problem with infant baptism

The second problem with limbo's theology is the assumption that children are proper subjects for baptism. As even a quick reading of Acts and the Epistles will confirm, baptism was never intended for infants, nor administered to them in the primitive church.[4] The fact that Christian immersion was for the forgiveness of sin (Acts 2:38) begs the earlier question about the spiritual state of newborns. If they are not sinful by fiat, there's no reason to baptize them by fiat. Moreover, since baptism was always a personal response to God in recognition of one's lost condition and the need for Christ's saving grace, the vicarious expression of faith by parents on behalf of their children robs any supposed baptism of its most essential element. As Peter tells us, baptism is "the pledge of a good conscience toward God" (1 Peter 3:21)–a pledge which must surely be made with mature awareness of the commitment being undertaken.[5]

That no actual mental assent by the infant is required for the efficacy of his baptism reveals much about a sacrament in which form trumps substance. In what amounts to baptismal regeneration, salvation comes through the sacrament itself, *ipso facto*, even without any faith on the part of the child. While it is true that in the apostolic church there was no such thing as an "unbaptized Christian," neither was there such a thing as a "baptized non-believer"–nor, for that very reason, infant baptism.

Confusing two separate covenants

The third problem (specifically with the so-called "limbo of the Fathers") is the biblically-unfounded assumption that the righteous prior to Christ's death on the cross were subject to Christian bap-

---

4 That entire households were baptized, as in the case of the Philippian jailor, tells us nothing either way as to whether young children were included among those receiving baptism. To say, for example, that "their whole family is coming over to eat and then discuss the issue of infant baptism" wouldn't suggest to many that the toddlers in the family would be expected to join in the adults' weightier conversation.

5 As elsewhere, Catholicism is here again forced to invent a remedy for an antecedent theological blunder. The practice of Confirmation–experienced at a more mature age when one who is already "baptized" ratifies that act by expressing personal faith–merely serves to confirm that the most essential element of Christian baptism was missing in the first place. The odd result of this time-delayed, bifurcated sacrament is that there is baptism without faith on the first occasion and faith without baptism on the second.

It's yet another discussion...but, since biblical *immersion* is typically replaced by *sprinkling*, it cannot faithfully be said that there is a "Christian baptism" even in the first instance. Interestingly, sprinkling replaced immersion largely because children were involved; and children became involved only because an assumption about their lost condition had already replaced the apostolic assumption that young children were neither in eternal jeopardy nor capable of the mental assent required for adult, faith-responsive baptism into Christ.

tism, or for any other reason to be penalized with some afterlife consequence for not having been baptized. However, this assumption fails to take into account the two separate and distinct covenants through which God has shown his grace to mankind. Although we are reminded by the Hebrew writer that Christ's covenant is in every way superior to God's former covenant with the Jewish nation (Hebrews 8:6-13), the fact remains that those who lived and died under that covenant were bound only by its particular requirements.

As for the patriarchs of old, the miraculous taking up of Enoch and Elijah ought to put to rest any notion that a failure to be baptized prior to the institution of Christian immersion prevents one from going into the presence of God.

It is true, of course, that the faithful men and women of God in the pre-Christian era must wait until the day of the Lord's appearing to enter their heavenly home, but this is equally true of the dead who have been baptized into Christ. "These [righteous predecessors] were all commended for their faith, yet none of them received what had been promised. God had planned something better for us so that *only together with us would they be made perfect*" (Hebrews 11:39-40). That "something better" was Jesus' blood, which flowed both forward and backward from the cross.

As we saw in earlier chapters, none of the saved will get to heaven before any others. We will all arrive at the same time. Nor is there any need to speculate about some unrevealed "limbo," when we already have an abundance of scriptures identifying *sheol-hades* as the intermediate "waiting room" of all the dead–the righteous and the wicked; the baptized and the unbaptized; the young and the old; the born and unborn.

No need for parental panic

Though Catholicism today has largely abandoned the notion of infant damnation (and speaks more and more quietly about limbo), the average parishioner doesn't seem to have gotten the message. Mothers and fathers may not have a clue about the theological in's and out's of original sin, but they still bring their babies to be baptized, fearing the spiritual consequences for any child who might die unbaptized. On that score, of course, many Protestants aren't far behind. While Protestants generally have rejected any notion of limbo, the widespread belief in the taint of original sin has caused all sorts of consternation about the eternal destiny of children who die before they have matured sufficiently to submit their lives to Christ.

Indeed, a similar dilemma presents itself to parents who reject the theology of original sin, but who accept that children commit sin from very early ages. Among fellowships insisting on adult, faith-responsive immersion, actual practice often reflects earlier and earlier baptisms. Official church doctrine may be adamantly opposed to infant baptism, but early-youth baptism easily becomes the norm. Why? Because of the same nagging fear which haunts Catholic parents: that, should death suddenly intervene, young souls are in as much spiritual jeopardy as the souls of mature adults.

Have we forgotten that children are children?

It's another book, but such fears have no basis in Scripture.[6] There is no question that from early ages children lie, cheat, and steal. They are often selfish and unsharing, and are notorious for disobeying their parents. But none of that makes children unholy or spiritually impure. Nor would their misconduct send them to hell in the event of an untimely death. As with our own criminal justice system, blameworthiness always assumes moral accountability, which presupposes a certain degree of moral awareness and responsibility. Following on from this rudimentary truism, the law recognizes not only the defense of insanity but also the defense of infancy.

Certainly, a child may know right from wrong at an elementary level in the earliest stages of development. However, spiritual accountability requires knowing, not only the nature of one's act, but also the quality of it. In terms of sin, this would entail appreciating the spiritual consequences of one's conduct–including, of course, how it might affect one's eternal destiny. Since the degree of awareness about such weighty issues will vary with each child, the exact age at which one becomes accountable cannot be known with any precision. But clearly there is no moral accountability for sin at the point of conception, nor in the mother's womb, nor at the moment of birth, nor as a toddler, nor as a young child just learning his way through the moral maze.

6 For a fuller discussion, see F. LaGard Smith, *Baptism–The Believer's Wedding Ceremony* (Nashville: Gospel Advocate Publishers, 1993), Chapters 9 and 10.

One of the key biblical passages in this regard is Moses' rebuke of the Israelites who, as the result of their sins, were not to be permitted entrance into the land of promise. By contrast with those who were old enough to have known better, Moses says of the children: "The little ones that you said would be taken captive, *your children who do not yet know good from bad*–they will enter the land" (Deuteronomy 1:39). We don't know how old these children were, but they likely were old enough to know right from wrong on at least some level. Even so, their lack of moral maturity gave them immunity from the spiritual consequences which were about to be enforced against those who were old enough to be spiritually accountable.

So it is with all children. Should death occur before they reach an age of sufficient moral awareness as to be held spiritually accountable for their thoughts and actions, there is no reason to fear for their eternal destiny. Like Israel's young, they will enter the land! To those whose afterlife theology casts doubts on the fate of the young, let Jesus' words ring forth again: "Let the little children come to me."

An issue larger than limbo

Why include a lengthy discussion of limbo in this book if Catholicism no longer gives it prominent play? First, because everyone keeps asking about it! Limbo is such a part of our common language now that folks use it with reference to anything whatsoever that is "betwixt and between"; and, even if they know little else, are not oblivious to the fact that limbo is thought to be a place where some people go when they die. So, when a book about afterlife is being written, limbo stubbornly insists on imposing itself into the conversation.

Just as important, however, is the fact that limbo is one of the best examples possible for demonstrating how afterlife issues become a litmus test of the legitimacy of underlying theological assumptions. Whenever any afterlife scenario lacks coherence with other clear biblical teaching regarding what happens after death, red flags are raised immediately as to the validity of any doctrines upon which that afterlife theology is based.

According to a well-known legal maxim, "hard cases make bad law"–which is to say that any law framed primarily with difficult, exceptional cases in mind is likely not to be a good law generally.

When it comes to afterlife issues, that maxim gets turned on its head: bad doctrine makes for hard cases. Does it make any sense that an aborted fetus should be consigned to hell? Or that an unbaptized day-old infant should be excluded from heaven? When those unacceptable conclusions present themselves, instead of inventing limbo out of rarefied air it's time to query how we ever reached those conclusions in the first place. As with context, context, context, it's also doctrine, doctrine, doctrine!

Time to reexamine our beliefs

Nor is this a uniquely Catholic problem. If tomorrow the Catholic Church categorically renounced limbo but maintained allegiance to the underlying doctrines, Catholicism would be in no better a position (and no worse) than most Protestants who share much of the underlying theology.

For Protestants who believe in the universal taint of original sin, there are only so many options for what happens when an infant dies. Either they will go to hell (the most logical conclusion); or some will go to hell and some to heaven, at God's option (Calvin's position); or they'll automatically be lumped in with "the elect" (an arbitrary and inconsistent imposition on God's sovereignty); or be saved from hell through an artificial sacrament making no sense for its subjects (such as infant baptism); or, in a desperate clutching for straws, be entrusted hopefully to the mercy of God at the last day (which is the current Catholic fallback position).

When, by contrast, eternal damnation is solely based upon one's personal, conscious, and deliberate rebellion against God as a mature, responsible individual, then there need be no panicked machinations to avoid disagreeable alternatives. Hell is unquestionably a fit place for those who have chosen their fate accordingly. End of story. Which *matches* the story–perfectly fitting what the Scriptures teach, both with regard to the afterlife and, more importantly, with regard to the nature of sin and personal accountability.

God is not a God of confusion. Heaven only knows why, but confusion is a mantel we have presumed to take on ourselves. If anything is in limbo, it's our own betwixt-and-between theology, doomed to a desperate search for coherence.

Anchor Verses - Luke 17:20-21; John 18:36

"Once, having been asked by the Pharisees when the kingdom of God would come, Jesus replied, 'The kingdom of God does not come with your careful observation, nor will people say, "Here it is," or "There it is," because the kingdom of God is within you.'"

Jesus said, "My kingdom is not of this world. If it were, my servants would fight to prevent my arrest by the Jews. But now my kingdom is from another place."

Chapter Preview

The current most popular afterlife scenario among Evangelicals is a two-part belief in a thousand-year "millennial reign" of Christ on earth at the end of the world, preceded by a Rapture of all Christians, living and dead, who, after being caught up into heaven, return to rule with Christ. The Millennium is said to make possible God's program for the Jews, both to complete unfulfilled covenant promises and to provide opportunity for "all Israel" to be saved.

The Rapture/Millennium hypothesis is cobbled together from an overly-literal rendering of Revelation 20's "thousand-years"; a misunderstanding of Daniel's seventieth "week"; and an abuse of context in 1 Thessalonians 4:17, which, correctly understood, is describing what happens to Christians at the one and only, final resurrection and judgment of both the righteous and the wicked. Not only have God's covenant promises to the Jews already been fulfilled in Christ, through whom also "all Israel" can be saved through faith, but Christ's kingdom is spiritual and eternal, not political or temporal, not even for a limited thousand-year period.

12

RAPTURE, AND OTHER BEST-SELLING FICTION

Better the disappointment of truth than the fair but false promise of error.

−W. J. Eerdman

Perhaps you're wondering why we've not mentioned the Rapture up to this point. From the best-selling "Left Behind" series[1] to almost hourly coverage on Christian radio and television, no single feature of popular end-times prophecy is the subject of more excited discussion than the Rapture. For anyone who has just now arrived from another planet and might not be familiar with the term, "Rapture" is the soon-to-be-expected cataclysmic moment when those who are in Christ will suddenly disappear from the earth. Together with the resurrected dead in Christ, they will have been taken up into heaven. Hence the bumper sticker: "In case of Rapture, this vehicle will be unmanned."

The word (from the Latin *rapio* or *rapturi*, meaning "caught up" or "snatched away") does not itself appear in Scripture. It is derived from Paul's description of events in 1 Thessalonians 4:17, in which those Christians who are alive at the time will be "caught up...in the clouds to meet the Lord in the air." As we will see momentarily, the particular spin put on this passage by proponents of the Rapture is radically different from what we have seen in earlier chapters.

In order to better appreciate the concept of Rapture, one must understand a broader end-times framework, drawn principally from Revelation 20. The initial rapture of all Christians, living and dead,

---

1 By Tim LaHaye and Jerry B. Jenkins, Tyndale House Publishers

and the much-later resurrection of the lost are seen as separate bookends to a "millennial" reign of Christ on earth. Whereas the Rapture takes place even before the Millennium begins, the resurrection of the lost must wait for a thousand years.

Because the Millennium is thought to be inaugurated by a seven-year period of extraordinary suffering and turmoil known as the Tribulation, the sequencing of the Rapture becomes somewhat more complicated. While all its proponents agree that the Rapture will occur prior to the Millennium, they are split over whether it will take place before or after the Tribulation, or even half-way in the middle. But whether it occurs pre-Trib, mid-Trib, or post-Trib (most accept the pre-Trib scenario), the Rapture will pave the way for the Millennium, during which time all those who have been caught up and clothed with immortality will return to earth to reign with Christ.[2]

These Christians, arrayed in their new incorruptible bodies, will be joined in that millennial reign by the "Old Testament saints" who will have been resurrected during a 45- or 75-day period (depending on one's interpretation) between the end of the Tribulation and the beginning of the Millennium.[3] Presumably, they too, along with the previously-raptured Christians, will be clothed in their immortal bodies. Less certain is the status of those who may have been converted to Christ during the Tribulation. Whether they will participate in the millennial reign and what kind of bodies they might have remains a matter of debate.

The millennium-rapture connection

What is unquestionably clear for many, if not most, Evangelicals today is the bottom line: that eternal life in heaven will not begin until Christ has reigned on earth for a thousand years. The prevail-

---

2 In the case of post-trib Rapture, there will have to be an incredibly quick costume change off-stage. "The Christians (living and dead) will be swooped up in resurrected bodies to meet Jesus in the sky ('the rapture'), and then they will all parade down to earth together to establish Christ's kingdom ('the second coming'). The rapture and second coming will be separate events, but will happen in immediate succession." Bruce Bickel and Stan Jantz, *Guide to the End of the World* (Eugene: Harvest House Publishers, 1999), 172.

3 Calculating from Daniel 12:11-12, there are those who believe that the interim between the end of the Tribulation and the Millennium will be 45 days (1335 days minus 1290). Most millennialists believe that the interim will be 75 days, calculating from Daniel 12:12 together with Daniel 12:7 (where "time, times and a half time" represents three and a half years, which–assuming 360 days per year–would be 1260 days).

Interestingly, a footnote to 1 Thessalonians 4:17 in the Scofield Bible (1917 edition) rejects any distinction between Old Testament saints and church saints, saying: "Not church saints only, but all bodies of the saved, of whatever dispensation, are included in the first resurrection (see 1 Cor. 15:52, *note*), as here described...."

ing view, which believes that Christ will return to earth at the beginning of that millennial reign, is known as "premillennialism." A minority view, known as "postmillennialism," believes that Christ will return only after a loosely-defined "millennium" of world-wide evangelism and the ultimate triumph of good over evil.[4] (Denying both of these doctrines, "amillennials" do not believe in any theologically-significant thousand-year period, contending instead that the "thousand years" of Revelation 20 is a symbolic, non-temporal term representing the perfect completeness of salvation already experienced in Christ in a present and eternal spiritual kingdom.)

What's crucial to understand is that, under the prevailing, premillennial view, belief in the Rapture and belief in the Millennium are inextricably tied together. In the absence of the Millennium, there would be little purpose for a premillennial Rapture. While it is possible to believe in the Millennium without also believing in the Rapture, it is meaningless to believe in the Rapture if the Millennium idea itself is rejected.

Historically, of course, the idea of a last-days Millennium has cropped up from time to time over the centuries–from Irenaeus (ca. 130-ca. 200), who believed that Christ's return would herald a "hallowed seventh day" millennium; to the apocalyptic beliefs which fueled the Crusades between 1097 and 1270; to Joachim of Fiore (ca. 1135-1202) and his culminating "Age of the Spirit"; to the myth that German ruler Frederick II (1220-1250) was going to usher in the Millennium as the "Emperor of the Last Days"; to Christopher Columbus' belief that he was predestined to fulfill prophecies leading to the end of the world. As Paul Boyer notes in his encyclopedic history of prophetic belief, "Modern prophecy scenarios are in fact updated versions of very ancient ones."[5]

---

4 This view was especially popular in the heady days of antebellum America when many viewed the New World as the New Jerusalem. Among frontier evangelists in the Restoration Movement (which spawned the Disciples of Christ, the Christian Church, and the Churches of Christ), Alexander Campbell, in particular, was optimistically postmillennial. His periodical, titled the *Millennial Harbinger*, reflected a belief that restoration of primitive New Testament Christianity would usher in a golden era of unexcelled conversion, Christian unity, and national righteousness which would pave the way for Christ's coming. However, there were others in the movement who were more pessimistic and apocalyptic, including Barton W. Stone and his heirs in the faith, David Lipscomb and James A. Harding, the latter actually professing belief in a premillennial Rapture. See, Richard T. Hughes, *Reviving the Ancient Faith* (Grand Rapids: Eerdmans Publishing Company, 1996), 3;124-127; 137-167.

5 Paul Boyer, *When Time Shall Be No More* (Cambridge: Belknap Press of Harvard University Press, 1992), 55. Of course, the more Rapturists attempt to show a historical chain of millennial expectation, the more they must face the implications of multiple millennial disappointments over the centuries.

There are also rare hints of Rapture-like thought, including the early eighteenth-century view of American evangelist Increase Mather that the saints would be "caught up into the air" before the earth's destruction by fire.[6] Yet Rapture proponents generally acknowledge that the idea of the Rapture first took flight during the dispensationalist movement of the nineteenth century. Initially articulated in 1830 by John Nelson Darby, an Irish Anglican who became a leading influence among the Plymouth Brethren, dispensationalism holds that the New Testament "church age" is merely a parenthesis between God's covenant promises to the Jews and the future fulfillment of those promises in the Millennium. It was Darby who joined the Millennium and the premillennial Rapture in a lasting theological marriage, and first championed the idea of separate end-times tracks for Jews and Gentiles—all under the dispensational umbrella.

That fully-packaged Rapturist/Millennialist view found a ready audience through the *Scofield Reference Bible*, published in 1909 by C. I. Scofield (especially after its 1917 revision). Dispensationalism was further developed in the 1960's by Charles C. Ryrie, with his *Dispensationalism Today* and *The Ryrie Study Bible*. Even more popular was Hal Lindsey's phenomenal *The Late Great Planet Earth*, published in 1970, which fueled both an end-times frenzy and widespread acceptance of an imminent Rapture. Lindsey's popularization of the Rapture has been matched only by the current "Left Behind" series.

Resurrecting familiar problems

Although arguably not devoid of historical precedent, in terms of classic Christian doctrines, both dispensationalism and the Rapture are relative newcomers. While first-century Christians generally believed that Christ's return was imminent in their own day, nothing in Scripture suggests that they anticipated a special, Christians-only Rapture or a thousand-year earthly reign before the final resurrection and judgment of all the dead. During his ministry, of course, Jesus himself had never mentioned anything about a thousand-year reign, nor had Paul suggested such a distinct period of time.

It cuts both ways, certainly, but the fact remains that it was not until the third chapter from the end of the Bible—in the final book to be written in the closing years of the apostolic era—that anything in

6 Boyer, 75.

Scripture even suggested a literal reign on earth for a thousand years. Little wonder, then, that the apostolic church prior to John's *Apocalypse* would not have been focused on a millennial reign or a premillennial Rapture. The real wonder is that, even after Revelation 20 was written, such dispensational notions did not take root for almost eighteen centuries.

Why it took so long has been argued to be a matter of unfolding revelation to man regarding how God is working out his eternal plans in our modern era. Current events in the Middle East since the establishment of the nation of Israel in 1948 certainly have spurred dispensational expectations. However, the fact that centuries of Christian thinking did not give literal interpretation to the apocalyptic language in Revelation 20 undoubtedly is best explained by overriding theological reasons. Coherent biblical teaching along a broad front would automatically rule out dispensationalism, regardless of whatever political events might unfold. Even more would that be true of millennialism's afterlife implications which spawned the idea of Rapture.

Ironically, the Rapture scenario for Evangelicals suffers precisely the same defects as the purgatory scenario for Catholics: 1) It is based on shadowy inferences from a paucity of direct scriptural support; 2) It depends upon suspect logic and gross abuse of context; 3) It does not fit within the clear teaching of Scripture about other afterlife events and their sequence; and 4) It perpetuates misguided theology—especially regarding the nature of Christ's kingdom and God's covenant relationship with the Jews.

More on the Jewish connection momentarily, but note how even the language of purgatory is related to the Tribulation. Explaining the purpose of the Tribulation, one dispensationalist author tells us: "God will use the Tribulation to purge the Jewish people. He will put the nation of Israel into a vice grip from which there is no earthly hope of deliverance. The rebellious nation will be refined by the fires of tribulation."[7]

Beyond even the similarity of language, just as we saw with purgatory, once you throw a millennial reign into the mix of afterlife events, you have to do a lot of pushing and shoving to make room for it. And that is precisely what the Rapture thesis has done. Whereas Scripture speaks of but one universal resurrection and

---

7 Mark Hitchcock, *101 Answers To the Most Asked Questions About the End Times*, (Sisters: Multnomah Publishers, 1999), 170.

judgment of both the righteous and the wicked on the Last Day, dispensationalism's tangled web gets ever so complicated.

Surprise appearances and resurrections

First off, according to the Rapture scenario there are two appearances of Christ: one secret appearance in the air (often referred to as "the Parousia," as if that "coming" is somehow separate and distinct from Christ's so-called "Second Coming") and one universally-witnessed return to earth (the "Second Coming" itself). This, despite the assurance given to John that when Christ comes again "every eye will see him" (Revelation 1:7). It is important to note that nowhere in his *Apocalypse* does John make mention of a secret mission for Christ to gather his own. In all of Revelation, there's not a single hint of Rapture.

In order to come up with the concept of Rapture, you've got to mix together Revelation's "thousand years" and Daniel's "seventieth 'week'" (for the Tribulation) in a theological cocktail with 1 Thessalonians 4:17. Blatantly extracted from its context, this keystone Rapture verse in fact describes how those who are in Christ will be resurrected and transformed when "the Lord himself will come down from heaven, *with a loud command, with the voice of the archangel and with the trumpet call of God....*" Hardly a stealth operation!

Just how many resurrections will there be?

Second, according to the Rapturists there are also at least three resurrections: 1) the dead in Christ at the Rapture; 2) the "Old Testament" saints at the end of the Tribulation; and 3) the final resurrection at the end of the Millennium for the unsaved of all time.[8] That's even one more than the "two resurrections" of Revelation 20:4-6, which—if taken literally—would auger well for there being more than one resurrection.

I saw thrones on which were seated those who had been given authority to judge. And I saw the souls of those who had been

---

8 No ready answer is provided by Rapturists as to which of the (presumably) first two resurrections will apply to infants who die prior to the Rapture. (As with adults, a strange contradiction arises when it is held that children immediately go to heaven when they die.) On the issue of whether infants living at the time of the Rapture will be taken or left behind, Rapturists are of three opinions: 1) that no unbelievers, including children, are eligible for the Rapture; 2) that *all* infants and children will be included in the Rapture; and 3) that the children of believers will be raptured along with their parents, but that the children of unbelievers will be left behind.

> *beheaded because of their testimony for Jesus and because of the word of God. They had not worshiped the beast or his image and had not received his mark on their foreheads or their hands. They came to life and reigned with Christ a thousand years. (The rest of the dead did not come to life until the thousand years were ended.) This is the first resurrection. Blessed and holy are those who have part in the first resurrection. The second death has no power over them, but they will be priests of God and of Christ and will reign with him for a thousand years.*

Given the explicit language of this passage, there is a clear choice to be made: Either this apocalyptic passage is to be interpreted literally (at the expense of treating non-apocalyptic passages figuratively); or the non-apocalyptic passages are to be accepted with their straightforward meaning, and this passage is to be understood as speaking figuratively about the first resurrection.[9]

If we take the former approach, which would be consistent with the dispensationalist view of the end times, then those who come to life in the first resurrection are those who "had not worshiped the beast" or "received his mark on their foreheads," things which, say Rapturists, will have taken place during the Tribulation. Accordingly, this resurrection (and the subsequent reign with Christ) would apply only to those who had been martyred during the Tribulation–not to the whole church as claimed. How, in any event, could these Tribulation saints be raised in the *first* resurrection, when supposedly the whole church has already previously been raptured?

Don't forget our spiritual resurrection in Christ

If we take the second approach, what we have is a perfect apocalyptic parallel to the words of Jesus recorded by John in his earlier gospel (in John 5:24-29). Consistent with the view that the "thousand-year" reign represents the spiritual kingdom of God, we see that the first resurrection is the *spiritual* "resurrection" experienced by all Christians, which is then followed by a future *physical* resurrection of both the righteous and the wicked (John 5:24-29).

---

9 This dilemma is but a corollary of the general rule of interpreting the obscure in light of the clear, rather than the clear in light of the obscure.

I tell you the truth, whoever hears my word and believes him who sent me has eternal life and will not be condemned; he has crossed over from death to life. I tell you the truth, a time is coming and has now come when the dead will hear the voice of the Son of God and those who hear will live....

Do not be amazed at this, for a time is coming when all who are in their graves will hear his voice and come out—those who have done good will rise to live, and those who have done evil will rise to be condemned.

The first part of this passage obviously refers to a soul-reviving transformation of the *spiritually* dead, whose spiritual "resurrection" *has already come*. The second part of the passage clearly refers to the end-of-the-world, simultaneous resurrection of both the righteous and the wicked.

It's easy to forget that John's *Apocalypse* was specifically addressed to first-century Christians in the seven churches of Asia—the very ones facing the pressure of worshiping "the beast and his image" in their own day. For that very reason they are being exhorted again and again throughout the *Apocalypse* to "overcome." In that light, compare Revelation 2:11 ("He who overcomes will not be hurt at all by the second death") with Revelation 20:6 ("Blessed and holy are those who have part in the first resurrection. The second death has no power over them...."). Clearly, then, it was these beleaguered saints who, like all Christians, had already experienced the "first resurrection," having submitted their lives to the risen Christ and thereby "crossed over from death to life." It was these same first-century martyrs who, both in life and in death, were sharing in the "thousand-year," perfectly-complete spiritual reign of Christ.

If this "spiritualized interpretation" seems strained (as it surely must to anyone who is already committed to a dispensationalist view of Revelation 20), put the idea on hold for a moment as we consider further how the millennial scenario creates yet more complications.[10] At the very least, a spiritualized "first resurrection" is no

---

10 The mix of spiritual and literal resurrections is not unlike John 6:49-50, where Jesus compares the spiritual eating of his body with the literal eating of the manna in the desert, which in turn reflects parallel comparisons between spiritual life and physical death. See Kenneth L. Gentry, Jr.'s discussion in *Four Views on the Book of Revelation*, C. Marvin Pate, Ed. (Grand Rapids: Zondervan, 1998) 85-86.

more strained than the Rapturists' notion of three distinct earth-to-heaven resurrections, all the while assuring us that–at the moment of death–"for Christians it's *on to heaven–no waiting*....Christians who die will go directly to the presence of the Lord"![11]

A whole lot of judging going on!

Most striking of all the incongruities flowing from a dispensational perspective is the matter of multiple judgments. Just as the doctrine of purgatory necessitated the invention of a "particular judgment" and a "general judgment" unknown to Scripture, dispensationalism is forced to come up with, not two, not three, but *five* separate judgments. First, is the "Judgment Seat of Christ," before whom raptured Christians will be given their reward. Second, is the judgment of Israel when it is regathered in the second half of the Tribulation (supposedly from Matthew 25:1-30 and Ezekiel 20:30-39). Third, is the so-called "sheep and goats judgment" of the Gentiles who have survived the Tribulation (supposedly from Matthew 25:31-46). Fourth, is the judgment of Old Testament and Tribulation saints (Daniel 12:1-3; Isaiah 26:19; Revelation 20:4). And fifth, the "Great White Throne Judgment" of the lost (Revelation 20:7-10).[12]

That Rapturists would cite these particular scriptures begs belief. In the two primary passages, especially, it requires taking a theological meat cleaver to neatly divide what is obviously intended to describe a single, universal judgment.[13] Consider again Daniel 12:1-3, which concludes: "Multitudes who sleep in the dust of the earth will awake: some to everlasting life, others to shame and everlasting contempt." Does that sound like multiple resurrections and multiple judgments? And, as we saw earlier in John 5:29, we have Jesus' own final word on the matter: "A time is coming when all who are in their graves will hear his voice and come out–those who have done good will rise to live, and those who have done evil will rise to be condemned."

Could the simultaneous nature of the rising and judging possibly be any clearer? Only, perhaps, in Matthew 25:31-46 where Jesus plainly speaks of his future coming, together with his angels, to judge all nations–rewarding the righteous with their inheritance and banishing the wicked to their eternal punishment. It's simply not

---

11 Bickel and Jantz, 245
12 Hitchcock, 272-275.
13 See, e.g., Douglas Moo's discussion in *Three Views On the Rapture*, Stanley N. Gundry, Ed. (Grand Rapids: Zondervan Publishing House, 1996), 162-163.

good enough to talk about "foreshortening of two events," or "tele-scoping of events," or "the opening phase of the Day of the Lord." There is but one resurrection of the dead and only one judgment which every soul will face together.[14]

Just as we saw earlier with the rationalization of purgatory, in order to bolster the initial miscue (in this case a literal thousand-year reign on earth), necessity gives birth to invention (the Rapture), which begs yet another invention (multiple judgments), and on and on it goes (including interminable debates over pre-Trib, mid-Trib, and post-Trib details). As always, get the theology wrong and practical problems pile up like dead bodies on the plain of Armageddon.

Literally confusing!

In fairness, it must be said that, unlike the illusory passages cited in support of purgatory, at least in Revelation 20 there is a challenging text which forces us to think long and hard about what's being said. Words referring to a "thousand-year reign" of *some kind* are right there in undeniable black and white in your Bible and mine. Any child of eight asked to read Revelation 20 could tell us that, in John's vision, Satan was bound in prison for "a thousand years," and that the souls of those who had been beheaded came to life and reigned with Christ "for a thousand years."

Was that for five hundred years? "No, a thousand!"

Then again, any child of eight reading Revelation 19 would also tell us that someone named Faithful and True, riding a white horse, had a sharp sword coming out of his mouth.

"Cool!"

And also (from Chapter 1) that Christ was making known to John at least something that would be happening right away.

You mean a long, long time from now? "No way!"

What child of eight is going to appreciate that words can be symbolic? Not just figurative, but *symbolic*. Children can pick up on figures of speech early on, but deeper meaning and symbolism general-

---

14 Compare our earlier discussion of the Olivet Discourse (Matthew 24) wherein we suggested that Jesus was answering two separate questions–first about events soon to take place in Jerusalem, and then about events at the end of time. This two-part prophecy not only answered two distinctly different questions being asked, but was a type of "incarnational prophecy" in which one, more-immediate event graphically pictures and heralds another, more-distant event. By contrast, the blatant attempt of dispensationalists to force a thousand years between the resurrection of the righteous and the wicked in these passages has no similar hermeneutical justification.

ly eludes them. As adults appreciate, there are words, and then there are *words*–as in this very sentence, where the same word "words" has two different connotations. Such a distinction would be lost on most eight-year-olds. So to insist from Revelation 20 that Christ is to have a literal thousand-year reign on earth may be to see the obvious, but also to overlook the obvious.

Feasting at a smorgasbord

It is also to capriciously pick and choose which words will be taken literally. No Rapturist seems to take that sword coming out of Jesus' mouth literally; nor those decidedly non-futurist words: *soon*, or *near*. And few would suggest we ought to take as literal fact that Jesus will descend from heaven literally riding a literal white horse. Or that when Satan is bound for a literal thousand years it will be with a literal chain. As one dispensationalist knowingly nuanced it, they were "...chains such as are necessary to contain a spiritual being...."[15] (Literally, of course, there was only *one* chain–"a great chain.")

With a straight face, the same author tells us that "A literal interpretation of the 144,000 servants of God in Revelation 7:3-8 sees them as ethnic Israel, physical descendants of Abraham, Isaac, and Jacob."[16] He is apparently oblivious, first of all, to the fact that he is reading into the passage words which literally aren't there. (Perhaps once you insinuate the words "on earth" into Revelation 20, it's easier to supply words wherever else it's convenient.)

More incredible still is that–even if he were right about the "servants" in question being Jews–any rendering which is as literal as that used for the "thousand years" of Christ's reign would require there to be *solely* and *precisely* 144,000 of those Jewish servants. Not one more, nor one less. It should be obvious, of course, that such a figure could not possibly include all of Abraham's descendants, who (to be taken literally?) were promised to be "as numerous as the stars in the sky and as the sand on the seashore" (Genesis 22:17). Where does it all end?

As it happens, dispensationalism's vaunted literalism comes to a screeching halt at Daniel's "seventy weeks" (Daniel 9:24-27, KJV). Were one to take those *seventy weeks* as literally as Revelation's *thou-*

---

15 Robert L. Thomas, *Four Views on the Book of Revelation*, C. Marvin Pate, Ed. (Grand Rapids: Zondervan, 1998), 205.
16 Thomas, 196.

sand years (or even as literal as the "week" in Daniel 10:2-3), then much of Rapture theory would disintegrate on the spot. Suddenly, the seven years of the Tribulation would have to be reduced to a single, seven-day week![17]

How literal is "literal"?

Perhaps we are talking past each other when we speak about taking the text "literally" as the grammatical-historical approach to biblical interpretation requires. That it was never meant to end up as a self-serve smorgasbord in which we can whimsically pick and choose to our heart's content should go without saying. The question is not whether we are interpreting *words* literally, but their literal *meaning* within scriptural context and historical setting. The idea, surely, is to get a true sense of the meaning the words were intended to convey. Even figurative words have a true sense—a sense which, once properly understood, can be taken literally.

If we're honest, all of us end up with a fair amount of inconsistency when choosing between a rigid, seemingly-mindless literalness which ignores context, and a context-driven appreciation for figurative language which is taken at face value for what it is. However, most of our seemingly capricious choices are dictated, not so much by pesky inconsistency, but by our underlying theological assumptions. Whether, for example, the "thousand years" of Revelation 20 should be understood any differently from God's "cattle on a thousand hills" (Psalm 50:10) is most likely to be determined by our understanding of two genetically-related theological issues: the nature of the kingdom and the status of the Jews in God's plan. That crucial point of disagreement is the true fork in the road, not hermeneutical quibbling somewhere down the line over whether a certain word or phrase should be taken literally or figuratively.

Becoming enslaved to literalism

Do you not find it ironic that dispensationalists, who pride themselves in literal faithfulness to the text, end up being far more symbolic when applying their literal interpretations to current and future

---

17 That the New International Version banishes "weeks" to a remote footnote and enthrones in its place a linguistically ambiguous "Seventy 'sevens'" is not exactly a violent overthrow of the root word *heptad*, given the context. But it should be a gentle reminder to dispensationalists that one of their keystone beliefs (the Millennium) demands wooden literalism, whereas another of their core beliefs (a seven-year Tribulation) would suffer from such wooden literalism.

events? The literal "beast out of the sea" *has to be a malevolent person....* The literal "woman clothed with the sun" *is a figure of speech pointing to national Israel....* The literal seven mountains *represent....* And so on.[18] By contrast, those who see the thousand-year reign as symbolic of a present spiritual kingdom (very much literal but by no means political) are not forced to burn late night candles desperately reaching for some sensational current event to justify taking every detail of the *Apocalypse* to the absurd.

It's kind of a "pay me now or pay me later" syndrome. If you take symbolism at face value, you can sit back and relax, comfortable in the knowledge that you have grasped the literal meaning being conveyed. But the more literal you insist symbolic language to be, the more strained applications you inexorably will be forced to find.

Separating fact from fantasy

When it comes to meaningful symbolism, adults decidedly have the edge on children. But what adult can match a child's fascination of *fantasy*? Although children are pretty savvy about fantasy's not being strictly *real*, there's no question that, from *Fantasia* to *Star Wars* to *Harry Potter*, children find fantasy absolutely rapturous! It's a world in which their imaginations can run wild–where they can dream impossible dreams and float to the moon!

Though divinely inspired, in a literary sense John's *Apocalypse* is like that–sheer fantasy, complete with a great dragon, a ten-horned, seven-headed beast crawling out of the sea, flying angels, a mystery woman, and a "Darth Vader" Beast. For its original readers, who were facing imminent suffering and death because of their faith, it captured the imagination...and was meant to! For fearful, vulnerable saints of God, it was the escapist movie of its day–a time for Christians sitting in a darkened world to see on the big screen the fantastic, hopeful future which lay ahead. To imagine the unimaginable. To dream big dreams as they emerged back into the blinding light of their condemning culture. In a world where persecution was far from fantasy, a graphically-depicted apocalypse in which the good guys win was a dream worth dying for.

Dare we ask an eight-year-old emerging from the theater to assign some literal, factual meaning to each detail of *Star Wars* or

---

18 Thomas, 199, 200, 203.

Harry Potter? Is it not the *story* that makes the fantasy come to life? And yet, with great irony, the "fantasy" elements of Revelation have been assigned (from all sides) creatively imagined meanings which are more speculative and fanciful than the original "fantasy" itself. Fantasy times fantasy is fantasy squared!

Despite more caution, speculation still thrives

From a review of current dispensational literature, one gets the feeling that serious dispensationalists have just about learned their lesson regarding overly-specific end-times prophecies. Now that confident predictions about Hitler being the "Antichrist" have ended with a single bullet to his brain; and that assurances of the former Soviet Union's role in the Tribulation have been eclipsed by dramatic changes in the political landscape; and that *88 Reasons Why Jesus Will Return in 1988* went out of print on January 1, 1989–Rapture and Millennium prophecies have become almost as generic as horoscopes. We don't know who, exactly, the Antichrist will be, but he'll definitely be a suave political leader who will broker a Middle East peace accord, then renege on it. And, at the Rapture, we'll all know who he is because the number of his name will be 666 (whatever that turns out to be!).

Of course, there can be no doubt that the time for the Rapture is near, because there are earthquakes in California (news flash!); cataclysmic events in the sky (like the Hale-Bopp comet?); wars and rumors of war (read any newspaper); famines (say...in Africa?); an increase in knowledge (it's the Information Age); movement toward a one-world government (thank goodness we now have the European Union to point to!); and a global economy (merely think of McDonald's). Despite increasing caution about the details, the temptation to find dispensational significance in current political and cosmic events seems altogether irresistible.

Likewise, for every reasonable question, it seems there is always a ready answer no matter how contrived. For example, if all believers are raptured up to heaven before the Tribulation begins, how will those who are left behind be evangelized? "One possibility," we are told seriously, "is that they could come to faith in Christ through Bibles and Christian books, videos, tapes, curriculum, software, and music that are left behind."[19] And, when it comes to the battle of Armageddon,

---

19 Hitchcock, 178.

aren't we a bit beyond wars waged by soldiers on horseback? Haven't nuclear weapons and computer technology made that kind of warfare archaic? "Well, it is quite possible that the calamities of the tribulation will destroy most of the world's technology."[20] Or, as oil crises worsen, the Russians, who have seventy percent of the world's horses, will fall back on horsepower![21] What can one say?

Everybody's playing the game

Unfortunately, this game of end-times "I Spy" is not Solitaire. At the opposite extreme, preterists (who believe that virtually everything in the Olivet Discourse and in John's *Apocalypse* was fulfilled in the A.D. 70 destruction of Jerusalem) also seem to get carried away with making even the most minor details fit their scenario of choice. For example, make no mistake: "The rider on the white horse 'bent on conquest' (Revelation 6:2-3) represents the victorious Roman march toward Jerusalem to engage the Jewish war in the spring of A.D. 67. The rider on the red horse who takes the 'peace from the earth' (6:4; cf. Matthew 24:6-7), speaks of the surprising disruption of the famous *pax Romana*, an enforced peace that prevailed throughout the Roman empire for many years."[22]

And what about the infamous six seals of Revelation? They "represent the early stage of the Jewish war, wherein Vespasian fought his way through Galilee toward Jerusalem." And the four trumpets? "The burning up of one-third of the trees of 'the land' (Gk. $h\_$ $g\_$; 8:7) reminds us of the Romans' setting villages on fire in conjunction with their denuding the land of its trees."[23]

And what could be more certain than that "666" is unquestionably a reference to Nero? "As scholars note, a first-century spelling of Nero Caesar's name (NRWN QSR), written in Hebrew characters, adds up to that exact value."[24] Nor is there the slightest doubt that

---

20 Bickel and Jantz, 201.
21 Boyer, 132.
22 Gentry, 53.
23 Gentry, 56, 58.
24 With equal passion, dispensationalists formerly identified Hitler as the Antichrist, noting that if A is given the value 100, B 101, C 102, and so on, Hitler's name adds up to 666! See, Boyer, 108. With equal numeracy legerdemain, others have identified 666 with the Pope, Oliver Cromwell, King George III, and Napoleon. Not even John F. Kennedy was left out, keen prophecy observers noting that he had received 666 votes at the 1956 Democratic convention. Not to be overlooked, there's also Henry Kissinger (whose name in Hebrew adds up to 111–or 666 divided by 6) and Ronald Wilson Reagan (whose three names each have six letters). See, Boyer, 275-276.

"The beast's 'war' with the saints for 'forty-two months' (13:5-7) refers to the Neronian persecution." Maybe. Sounds good. But if these historical references were really that foolproof, why is there still such vigorous debate?

When it comes to creative imaginations, the minds of the preterists can be as fertile as those of the dispensationalists. In terms of speculation, the only real difference between these two schools of thought is that one works overly hard forcing historical events to fit within a particular mold, while the other is working overtime interpreting (and reinterpreting) their own scheme, depending on the morning headlines or evening news. Neither side is served well by overplaying its hand.

Nor, apparently, is either side all that bothered by John's warning, not once but twice, that interpreting and understanding his unique *Apocalypse* demands caution. "This calls for wisdom," John says with reference to the number of the beast, "666" (13:18). Has that stopped some folks from pontificating the beast's precise identity? And again, "This calls for a mind of wisdom," with reference to the beast ridden by the woman (17:9). Seems like there are always plenty of people who are eager to display their "minds of wisdom."

What is there about being "in the know" regarding arcane and esoteric secrets which so intrigues? That countless mystery cults and squirrelly religious movements thrive on little more than insider information for the initiated ought to make us think twice when any belief system becomes top-heavy with the obscure rather than the obvious. Scripture was never meant to be a top-secret Bible code which we must spend a lifetime deciphering.

So what *is* Revelation all about?

The truth is that both extremes seem to have lost the plot, literally. Can we just take a deep breath, calm down, and go off into a quiet corner to re-read Revelation as if we'd never heard of the debate over preterism, dispensationalism, the Millennium, or the Rapture? In fact, you may want to put down this book long enough to do just that. As you read (either now or sometime later), ask yourself the obvious questions: To whom is the *Apocalypse* directed, and why? In what way does it address their needs? What is the book's central, overarching theme? If there are aspects we might not understand, what *can* we understand? And, finally, what lessons can you take away from Revelation for your own comfort, edification, or perhaps even admonishment?

Once you've gone through that process, here in a nutshell is what you probably will have discovered. (Feel free to scream out loud if you disagree!)

The purpose of the book seems to be twofold. First, it's to encourage Christians in the seven churches of Asia to have "patient endurance" in the face of persecution and potential martyrdom (1:9; 13:10; 14:12). Whether Jew or Gentile, Christians were under pressure (possibly from the Nicolaitans–2:6, 15) to compromise with blasphemous worship, as seen most likely in "worship of the beast and his image."

The second main purpose of John's writing is to warn these Christians to repent of their ongoing sins which were inviting God's fierce judgment: idolatry (especially, again, "worshiping the beast and his image"), the practice of magic arts, sexual immorality, lying, and–curiously–even murder (9:20-21; 21:8; 22:15).

First-century meaning for a first-century audience

As for the basic theme-line, would we be far off to suggest, first of all, that Revelation is about Christ's imminent coming in judgment regarding their struggles with persecution and moral sin? (1:1,3; 2:16; 3:11; 14:15; 22:6-7, 10, 12, 20). That, just as God has always done, Christ is coming in judgment against their persecutors, but will also hold them accountable for their own sins? If any of this is to have any meaning at all for John's readers, there simply have to be some heavy-duty first-century implications.

Yet there's that pivotal passage where John is told to write down all that he sees–both "what is *now* and what will take place *later*" (1:19). Is that not reminiscent of the two separate questions Jesus was addressing in Matthew 24 (about when the temple would be destroyed and when the disciples could expect the end of the age)? As seen previously in similar "incarnational prophecy," *soon* always begins in the near future, but extends forward to the distant future as well, the former typifying the latter. So it's obvious there are going to be long-term implications flowing from their present persecution, dependent in large measure upon how faithful they are as God's people.

For those whose faithfulness leads to martyrdom, there is special assurance. Those who are persecuted in this way will form a great multitude wearing white robes who stand before the throne in front of the Lamb, having emerged from their great tribulation (6:9-11; 7:9-17); heaven will rejoice because they did not shrink from death (12:11-12); they will be redeemed from the earth and sing a new song, with the names of God and Christ on their foreheads (14:1-5); they will be blessed with rest for having died in the Lord (14:30); they will be avenged for their blood when their enemies have been destroyed (16:5-7); they can rejoice over the destruction of "Babylon" who martyred them (18:20, 24; 19:2); and their souls, having come to life, reign with Christ as priests of God for that controversial "thousand years," whatever we might believe that represents (20:4,6).

Christ, of course, is shown as the ultimate martyr—the resurrected Lord who himself has overcome. "I am the First and the Last. I am the Living One; I was dead, and behold I am alive for ever and ever! And I hold the keys of death and Hades" (1:17-18). If Jesus could be killed on a cross and yet live forever, so could these martyrs (2:8). Holding the keys to death and Hades, Christ has the power to bring the dead back to life at the resurrection (22:13). So, in Christ, the day is coming when there will be no more death to fear (22:14). What better news could there be for people who are staring death in the face simply because they are Christians?

Taking the book at face value

When you read Revelation in this straightforward way, you begin to appreciate that its apocalyptic symbolism is to be taken, not literally, but at face value. For example, an ocean of ink has been spilled over the identity of the "144,000." Some say they represent national Israel. Others, that it's a group of Jews specially commissioned for evangelism. Still others, that it's "the church" as a collective whole. Why not simply take the text at face value? Tell us, John. We're dying to know! Who are these 144,000?

These are those who did not defile themselves with women,
for they kept themselves pure. They follow the Lamb wherever he
goes. They were purchased from among men and offered as first-

*fruits to God and the Lamb. No lie was found in their mouths;
they are blameless. (See Revelation 14:1-5)*

There's no mention at all, here, about Jews as opposed to Gentiles;
nor anything whatsoever about "the church"–just one individual
Christian after another who looked temptation in the face and turned
away. Just one courageous Christian after another who went to his or
her death rather than do obeisance to "the beast and his image."

Tie John's own explanation together with his specific warnings
about sexual immorality and idolatry and lying, and what you have
is a perfect match with those individual Christians within the seven
churches who would "overcome" everything this world could throw
at them. Focus on what John actually tells us. (Read again, in particular, Revelation 21:6-8 which summarizes the entire book.) He's talking about those who would steadfastly follow the Lamb; and about
those who would keep themselves morally pure, fit for a holy kingdom. Where's all the mystery? What's all the fuss?

A special warning!

More to the point, perhaps, how can there be such wildly speculative interpretation of this book by so many people who seem to want
it to say so much more? Have we forgotten that a day is coming when
God will bring the severest judgment upon anyone who has added to
or taken away from the words in John's *Apocalypse* (22:18-19). That
this is the only book in all the Bible with such a user warning label
attached ought to give us all pause. (Rapturists, especially, may want
to reconsider their unauthorized insertion into John's *Apocalypse* of
the word "Antichrist," which nowhere appears in the text.[25])

---

25 Dispensationalists have tacked on the name "Antichrist" to the "beast" of Revelation
and given him a whole persona such that now, even among secular folks, "Antichrist" is the
definitive word describing any evil person. In the New Testament, the word itself is mentioned
only five times, all in four verses of John's epistles: (1 John 2:18, 22; 4:3; 2 John 7). A quick
review of those verses will show that no single person–past, present, or future–is referred to as
the Antichrist. In speaking of the "antichrists," John is specifically addressing a doctrinal error
in his own day in which some were denying the fleshly humanity of Christ. It was thus that
they were *anti*-Christs–those who were *against* Christ. Who were the "*many* antichrists" (plural)? "They went out from us [meaning they had been counted among the Christians]." Who
did John call liars? "It is the man who denies that Jesus is the Christ. Such a man is the
antichrist–he denies the Father and the Son." When will he come? "This is the spirit of the
antichrist, which you have heard is coming and *even now is already in the world.*" John describes
these first-century Gnostic-thinking former believers as "liars," "false prophets," "deceivers,"
and "antichrists." Call the beast "the Beast," if you wish, but John's Revelation knows nothing
of a powerful "Antichrist" who is supposedly coming during the Tribulation.

Falling out over a serious misunderstanding

Suppose for a moment that the dispensationalists are absolutely right in taking the "thousand-year" reign literally–that Christ is really and truly going to descend back down onto the Mount of Olives and slay the armies gathered in league against him. That he will then rule the world from Jerusalem for literally a thousand years before judging the lost and ushering the saved into eternity. Would there be anything particularly unseemly about that? To say the least, if that's what God wants to do, who are we to say otherwise?

Of course, it raises a thousand questions, not the least of which is how Christ could possibly come "like a thief in the night" when the seven-year clock of Tribulation would have started ticking from the moment of the Rapture. And one wonders why Jesus didn't just set up an earthly kingdom immediately after his resurrection, as he well could have. And why a thousand years is such a magic number, as opposed to, say, a hundred or a million? Why, for that matter, have a heaven at all, especially since some folks think heaven is going to be right here on a rejuvenated earth in any event. If, on the other hand, the Millennium is a time to remove the curse of sin from the earth and restore creation to its original, Eden-like glory, what's the point if–at the end of a thousand years–the earth and everything in it will be burned up, as Peter tells us?

Granted, there are just as many questions about why God created us in the first place; and why he put us on this particular planet in this particular solar system; and why he allows evil to exist, or Satan to have any influence whatsoever. And on and on. So we simply have to acknowledge that God has every right to order the events at the end of the world as he pleases, even if that were to include a literal thousand-year reign on earth. Without question, God would have his reasons.

What's far more troubling are the reasons given by Rapturists....

A deeply disturbing theology

Just as the purgatory thesis exposes the weak underbelly of a number of other, far-more-significant doctrinal fallacies which make its existence necessary, so too the Rapture thesis would never exist were it not for a gross misunderstanding of the doctrine which underlies the concept of a millennial reign. What, purportedly, is the purpose of Christ's future earthly reign? First and foremost, it is to fulfill the covenants and promises made with Abraham, David, and the nation of Israel which, so it is said, were never fulfilled either before or during Christ's earthly ministry. Of the various covenants and promises cited, the three most central are: 1) the establishment of Israel as a nation; 2) the occupation of its promised land; and 3) the everlasting perpetuation of David's throne in Jerusalem.

Covenant promises already fulfilled

As a matter of historical fact, Abraham's descendants did become the nation of Israel and entered the land of promise, just as God had said. Had that not happened, there never would have been a throne of David in the first place. What's more, God's promise to Abraham that all the nations would be blessed through his descendants was wonderfully and completely fulfilled in the coming of the Savior of the world, Jesus of Nazareth, the Messiah, the Anointed One, the Christ!

For dispensationalists, however, all that is not enough. Even if there is a spiritual kingdom of an eternal nature (which dispensationalists readily acknowledge), "God's program for Israel" remains incomplete. They believe there is yet unfinished business, as reflected in the words "everlasting" and "forever" which are associated with the various covenant promises and apocalyptic prophecies (see especially Ezekiel 37-39).

Yet, if conceivably those words give birth to the idea of some future grand fulfillment, they also resoundingly militate against that very idea. For if "everlasting" and "forever" are to be understood as literally as the "thousand years" itself, it would mean, first of all, that God has already reneged on his promises. David's throne, for example, has not been occupied now for scores of centuries. And even if Christ were to re-establish David's throne in some future millennial reign, that "Davidic reign in Jerusalem" would last no longer than a thousand years–not *forever*.[26] You can't play it both ways.

What did Daniel see?

When Daniel interprets Nebuchadnezzar's dream (Daniel 2:31-45), it is almost universally agreed that what Daniel sees is the future

---

26 See Luke 1:32-33, in which a literal reading, if applied to the Millennium, would mean that Christ's reign on earth would *never* end. In point of fact, it is Jesus' *spiritual* reign on "David's throne" that will never end.

coming of the kingdom of Christ. Dispensationalists insist that this kingdom–still to come at least two thousand years beyond the cross–is to be "a complete *replacement* of present conditions on earth with a new world wide and multinational world order."[27] Yet, Daniel says of that rock cut out of the mountain: "In the time of those kings, the God of heaven will set up a kingdom that will never be destroyed, nor will it be left to another people. It will crush all those kingdoms and bring them to an end, but it will itself endure forever" (vs. 44).

As compared with the rise and fall of earthly kingdoms (especially those leading up to the first century), this radically-different kingdom will never end. Which kingdom? The one that was to be established "in the time of those kings," which we've all agreed is during the Roman era when the Messiah-King, Jesus of Nazareth, came to live among his people as the incarnate Christ. So how could there possibly be a hiatus of over two thousand years now in which there supposedly has been no ongoing fulfillment of Daniel's promise?

More thought-provoking still, how could such an enduring kingdom be reduced *ad absurdum* to some presumed thousand-year phase which more greatly resembles the very earthly kingdoms over which it already has triumphed? The very reason Daniel's kingdom of prophecy will never end, is that it is the eternal kingdom of God–not a political kingdom in a time-delayed, realized Jewish utopia on earth.

Repeating the mistake of first-century Jews

Have we not learned any lessons from the Jews of Jesus' own day who rejected him for the very reason that he did not match their expectations of a political ruler and national savior? Interpreting Ezekiel 37-39, Daniel 2, Isaiah 2, and Micah 4 in precisely the same way as do dispensationalists today, they *missed him*! What, no national resurgence? No triumphant occupation of the ancient boundaries of Israel? No golden era of Davidic rule from Jerusalem where every man will sit under his own fig tree and swords will be turned into plowshares? If you're not going to be that kind of Messiah, Jesus, well, then..."We have no king but Caesar!"

These are carefully measured words, but after a century and a half of millennial madness the time has come to speak frankly. If Jesus had

---

27 Craig A. Blaising, *Three Views on the Millennium and Beyond*, Darrell L. Bock, Ed. (Grand Rapids: Zondervan Publishing House, 1999), 193.

set up the kind of Zionist millennial reign described by today's dispensationalists, Jesus would never have hung on a Roman cross. The Jews would have been absolutely ecstatic with their restored, glorified kingdom, and the Romans would have been wiped right off the map! As it was, Jesus refused to be the earthly, political king which a strictly-literal interpretation of the prophets' apocalyptic language would have demanded. Little wonder that the dispensationalists of Jesus' day were so furious that the sign above the cross read, "The King of the Jews." In contrast to the familiar hymn, their hope was built on nothing less than a political reign and Jewishness.

The disciples, themselves, missed the point

Even more amazing than Jesus' rejection by Israel's politicized religious leaders is the fact that, despite being told over and over again about what "the kingdom of heaven is like," even Jesus' chosen Twelve intractably wore nationalist blinkers. Up until the very last days of Jesus' ministry, the Twelve were still arguing over who would be highest in the political pecking order in the restored kingdom. Until the Holy Spirit imbued them with a radically different understanding following Jesus ascension, here they were—Jesus' closest disciples—and they just didn't get it! Sadly today, millions of professing Christians still don't get it. Throughout dispensational literature there is more than a whiff of talk about preferential power-sharing during the millennial reign.

Incredibly enough, only moments before Jesus ascended into heaven, his disciples were still asking: "Lord, are you at this time going to restore the kingdom to Israel?" (Acts 1:6). His answer pointed, not to some future millennial reign, but to that coming day of Pentecost when his power would be fully manifest among them. "It is not for you to know the times or dates the Father has set by his own authority. But you will receive power when the Holy Spirit comes on you...."

"Objection, Your Honor. Non-responsive."

"Sustained!"

Rather than respond to the question put to him, which reflected the disciples' misinformed Messianic mind-set, Jesus turned their question on end, redefining altogether the nature of the kingdom they were expecting. In their own way, Jesus' own disciples were first-century "dispensationalists," eagerly anticipating a golden age for Israel in fulfillment of apocalyptic prophecies and the Davidic promise. It is not without significance, therefore, that Jesus' very last words on earth were pointing away from a restored national Israel and, instead, toward an altogether new and different kind of kingdom.

Jesus tried to tell them!

That so many people in Jesus' day misunderstood the true nature of the kingdom of heaven wasn't for lack of Jesus trying to tell everybody otherwise. There is that occasion, for example, when the Pharisees sneeringly asked Jesus when the kingdom of God would come. In a context, the latter part of which is a favorite of dispensationalists (Luke 17:20-37), Jesus could not have been more pointed: "The kingdom of God does not come with your careful observation, nor will people say, 'Here it is,' or 'There it is,' because *the kingdom of God is within you.*"

The Pharisees were thinking in terms of an external, physical, political *realm*, not an internal, spiritual, eternal *reign*. For all the talk today about a future millennial *reign*, it is a future millennial *realm* which has become all the rage–a realm complete with national boundaries, a capital city, economic prosperity, a judicial system, and a perfect health care program. That's the kind of kingdom you can *observe*, and the kind of futuristic kingdom you can *predict*, saying: "The signs of the times definitely indicate it's going to be here any day now." "It will be centered where the modern state of Israel is located." "Jerusalem will be Jesus' headquarters." And so on.

Were we not listening to what Jesus just said?

A kingdom not of this world

And then there's that conversation (in John 18:33-37) in which Pilate asks Jesus: "Are you the king of the Jews?" Jesus' response goes to the very heart of the matter: "*My kingdom is not of this world,*" he said. "If it were, my servants would fight to prevent my arrest by the Jews. But now *my kingdom is from another place.*" Even Pilate recognized it was a non-denial denial. "You are a king, then!" he insisted. To which Jesus responded: "You are right in saying I am a king. In fact, for this reason I was born, and for this reason I'll be coming back into the world, bringing my raptured servants with me to fight the battle of Armageddon, after which I'll reign on David's throne right here in Jerusalem for a thousand years in order to fulfill the Zionist dream."

You and I both know this was not Jesus' answer, nor anything close to it. Jesus said he came "to testify to the truth"–the truth about a kingdom which is not of this world; about a kingdom without a fighting army, or boundaries, or rulers over cities; about a kingdom whose king wore a crown of thorns soaked in blood; about the King of kings and Lord of lords who–even now–is seated at God's right hand "in the heavenly realms, far above all rule and authority, power and dominion, and every title than can be given, not only in the present age but also in the one to come" (Ephesians 1:20-21). What more could anyone wish of a kingdom?

Christian Zionism

Surprisingly, the dispensationalist answer to that question is: "the reinstitution of Israel's national life;" and not just that, but "the preeminence of Israel in the future kingdom.[28] Are you aware of the call for preferential Jewish status during the thousand-year reign? Responding to a position statement which posited that there would be no distinction between Jewish and Gentile Christians in the Millennium, one scholarly dispensationalist makes the breath-taking argument: "These words apparently advocate an equality by which all the redeemed share equally in the same kingdom roles, with no distinction between Israel and the body of Christ. This would mean that Israel will no longer be a special people and special recipients of the Old Testament promises made to them."[29] And so we discover that during the thousand-year reign, some Christians–namely, Jewish Christians–will be more equal than others!

Just when you thought it couldn't get more outrageous, the same author contends that, in the eternal kingdom following the Millennium (which is to say, heaven), Israel's distinctiveness will remain. "The church is separate from Israel throughout the New Testament. This will not change in Christ's eternal kingdom."[30] While his courageous consistency is to be applauded (not many other dispensationalists seem to have even thought through the "eternal kingdom" implications), his

---

28 Thomas, 198, 207.
29 Thomas, 207-208.
30 Thomas, 210.

outspoken Zionist perspective simply underscores what's really going on behind the whole Rapture/Millennium hypothesis.

Reverting to the beggarly elements of the Law?

To address but two of the scores of points begging for rebuttal, take a closer look at Ezekiel 37:24-28. If dispensationalists are correct that this is a literal picture of Christ's millennian reign, the first thing we learn is that the laws of Moses and the whole of the Jewish ceremonial system will be in force during that thousand years. What else would Jewish readers conclude when the word of the Lord tells Ezekiel: "They will follow my laws and be careful to keep my decrees"? Naturally, this raises embarrassing questions about the purpose of sacrificing animals in the newly-built temple there in the center of millennial Jerusalem (which dispensationalists assure us will happen).

Why reinstitute animal sacrifices during the Millennium? Says one author (reflecting the party line held by other Rapturists): "These sacrifices will serve as a powerful memorial to the final sacrifice for sin, Jesus Christ. They will serve, like the Lord's Supper today, as a vivid reminder of the holiness of God, the awfulness of sin, and the death the Savior died in our place."[31] Say again? The memorial bread and the cup of the *new covenant* replaced by memorial animal sacrifices under the *old covenant*? The blood of bulls and goats, which could never take away sin, soon to be transformed into a fitting memorial to Christ, whose blood alone is our atonement for sin? Are we not treading dangerously close to the line of blasphemy here?

And yet, why else rebuild the temple and restore national Israel if not to bring back into play every part of the Jewish system, including its priests, its ritual feasts, its Passover and festivals, and its kosher dietary laws. And if all these, then surely also circumcision. And if circumcision...(you know what follows)...then we are obligated to keep every jot and tittle of the law! (Galatians 5:3-6).[32] Are

---

31 Hitchcock, 215.

32 Dispensationalists claim that fulfillment of the Abrahamic, Davidic, and land covenants do not require that the complete Mosaic covenant law be restored. The most they will concede, as articulated by the oft-quoted J. Dwight Pentecost, is that "the form of worship in the Millennium will bear strong similarity to the old Aaronic order." And that, "While there is mention made of the five great offerings in force under the Aaronic order, yet, in the millennial age, these offerings are given a different emphasis." See J. Dwight Pentecost, *Things To Come* (Grand Rapids: Academie Books, Zondervan Publishing House, 1958), 519, 522.

The fact remains that dispensationalists insist there will be a reinstitution of the priesthood, and—with the exception only of the Day of Atonement—the system of blood sacrifices which were the central core of the Mosaic covenant system. Their "cake and eat it too" attempt to *have*, and then *not have*, a Levitical system during the Millennium is disingenuous.

Gentile dispensationalists fully aware of these Jewish aspects of the Millennium? More serious yet, are they prepared to distinguish their modern version of Christian Zionism from the Judaizing teaching which threatened to undermine first-century Christian doctrine?[33]

Emptying the new covenant of its power

The second point of rebuttal arising out of Ezekiel 37 is its reference to a new "covenant of peace." As we have seen, the very centerpiece of dispensationalism is the future fulfillment of those "eternal" and "everlasting" Abrahamic and Davidic covenant promises. And yet in Jeremiah 31:31-34 we see that, even while those covenants were in force, God was planning for a new covenant with Israel:

> *"The time is coming," declares the LORD,*
> *"when I will make a new covenant*
> *with the house of Israel*
> *and with the house of Judah.*
> *It will not be like the covenant*
> *I made with their forefathers*
> *when I took them by the hand*
> *to lead them out of Egypt,*
> *because they broke my covenant,*
> *though I was a husband to them,"*
> *declares the LORD.*

That this passage is quoted virtually verbatim in Hebrews 8:8-13 as having already been fulfilled in Christ, should put an end altogether to Christian Zionism. "By calling this covenant 'new,'" says the Hebrew writer, "he has made the first one obsolete; and what is obsolete and aging will soon disappear."

In view of Christ's own blood sacrifice, the former covenant is not *unfulfilled*, but *obsolete!* "For this reason Christ is the mediator of a new covenant, that those who are called may receive the promised eternal inheritance—now that he has died as a ransom to set them free from the sins committed under the first covenant" (Hebrews 9:15).[34]

---

33 See Galatians 2:14; 5:1-12.

34 On this point, renowned dispensationalist author John Walvoord equivocates. At one point he concedes: "The fact that these promises were made to Israel, forming a New Covenant replacing the Mosaic covenant, is further evidence that those who put their confidence in the Mosaic Covenant are trusting something which is already antiquated." Yet he concludes: "Today it is still necessary to carry the Gospel to one's neighbor for all do not know the Gospel. This is evidence that the New Covenant with Israel is not now being fulfilled." See, John F. Walvoord, *The Prophecy Knowledge Handbook* (Wheaton: Victor Books, 1990), 502.

Still think that God needs a future earthly reign to fulfill expectations of his ancient covenant with the physical descendants of Abraham?

It's hard to ignore Hebrews

One of the most remarkable features of more populist Rapturist literature, in particular, is the relative rarity of reference to any part of the book of Hebrews. It is, of course, a textbook response to dispensationalism. Anyone who can read Hebrews 8-10 and still think that God has unfinished covenant business with the Jews has just made a huge statement about the inefficacy of Christ's blood and the new covenant which it has sealed "once for all." Once for all time. Once for all people, Jew and Gentile alike.

As the book of Hebrews indicates, the idea of biblical dispensations is not a completely wrong-headed notion. While Rapturists are wrong to insist that there are two Jewish dispensations divided by a third, "Church age," there are indeed three distinct dispensations spoken of in Scripture: 1) the patriarchical dispensation; 2) the Mosaic dispensation; and 3) the Christian dispensation, which encompasses salvation for Jews and Gentiles alike.

The "all Israel" myth

For most dispensationalists, the millennial reign is necessary to implement not only unfulfilled covenant promises, but also Paul's statement (in Romans 11:26) that "all Israel will be saved." Because there has been no mass conversion of ethnic Israel to this point in history, there's no particular reason to believe it will happen in the future–unless the dispensationalists are right about the horrors of the Tribulation turning all Israel to Christ.[35]

Immediately, of course, there is the problem of how literal "all Israel" is to be understood. It doesn't take long to discover that, in this case, dispensationalists are sufficiently astute to fudge on absolute literalness–one writer telling us, for example, that Tribulation events "will bring the majority of Jews to faith. This is John's apocalyptic way of saying what Paul had earlier said–all Israel

[35] One wonders how much more of a purging the Tribulation could be than the Holocaust, in which six million Jews were "refined by fire" in the ovens of Dachau and Auschwitz and Buchenwald. And yet, far from turning to Christ, surviving Jews became even more skeptical about a God who would permit such a "tribulation" to happen.

will be saved."[36] (Which must be something akin to saying, "a majority have sinned and fallen short of the glory of God.")

Of course, this "majority" would only apply to those Jews who were living at the time of the Rapture and were left behind to experience the Tribulation. What percentage of Jews who have lived since the first century would likely be alive on the actual day the Rapture occurs? How many Jews are we talking about? Come to think of it, how many out of that number will survive the widespread Tribulation slaughter long enough to be converted? (We're told "more than half the earth's population will be killed during the judgments of the Tribulation."[37])

If only a majority of fortuitous Jewish survivors out of one particular generation in history is all we're dealing with, suddenly "all Israel" is but a shadow of its former self. Why must there be a millennial reign in order to facilitate "all Israel's" being saved when, in fact, only a tiny fraction of ethnic Israel even remotely could be affected? And if God truly wishes to save "all Israel," why is there no program to save the millions of Jews who will have missed out on the Tribulation and Millennium? Surely, we're not being asked to believe that "all Israel" will be granted salvation at the final judgment, despite the fact that not "all Gentiles" will be saved...*are we*?

In so short a space, we can hardly begin to plumb the depths of Paul's thesis in Romans 9-11 in order to get the right context for his statement about "all Israel." Suffice it to say simply that Paul is responding to the "problem" of how Israel possibly can be blessed through a Messiah whom they have largely rejected. Paul's answer makes a crisp distinction between prophecies directed to Israel *as a nation* and prophecies directed to Israel as *the people of God*.[38] Hence Paul's point that "It is not as though God's word had failed. For not all who are descended from Israel are Israel" (9:6). Moreover, "it is not the natural children who are God's children, but it is the children of the promise who are regarded as Abraham's offspring" (9:8).

Because of that crucial distinction, "there is no difference between Jew and Gentile—the same Lord is Lord of all and richly

36 C. Marvin Pate, *Four Views on the Book of Revelation* (Grand Rapids: Zondervan, 1998), 170.

37 Bickel and Jantz, 192.

38 See Douglas J. Moo, *Three Views on the Rapture*, Stanley N. Gundry, Ed. (Grand Rapids: Zondervan Publishing House, 1996), 207.

blesses all who call on him, for, 'Everyone who calls on the name of the Lord will be saved'" (10:13). So "Did God reject his people" by extending his grace to Gentiles? "By no means!" (11:1). Even now "there is a remnant chosen by grace" (11:5). Yes, but what about the vast majority of Jews who so far have rejected Christ? "Did they stumble so as to fall beyond recovery? Not at all!" (11:11). As a Jew himself, Paul says, "I make much of my ministry in the hope that I may somehow arouse my own people to envy and save some of them" (11:13-14). Only *some of them*, Paul? Didn't you say, famously: "all Israel will be saved"?

What I said, says Paul, is that "Israel has experienced a hardening in part until the full number of the Gentiles has come in. And so all Israel will be saved...." just as God promised in Jeremiah 31:33-34. That's not all Israel *as a nation*, but all Israel as *the people of God*. All Israel who were once cut off because of their rebellion but have *now* received mercy. "For God has bound *all* men over to disobedience so that he may have mercy on them *all*" (11:30-32). Right now. Already. *All* who turn to Christ in obedient faith will be his righteous remnant. In terms of Israel, the Jews will be saved one believer at a time—not *all ethnic Jews*, or even a *majority*, at some future time.

As train conductors used to say: "All aboard who are getting aboard!" The "mystery" is that "all Israel will be saved" in precisely the same way: not *as a nation*, but as *the people of God* who have individually accepted his saving grace.

Whatever else might be said of Romans 9-11, and whatever other interpretation might be given to "all Israel's being saved," of one thing we can be certain: there is not the first word from Paul about a millennial kingdom in which all Israel will be saved as part of a revived Jewish nation-state in the promised land. As we are wittily reminded, "These omissions...are tantamount to Sherlock Holmes's dog that did not bark. What better place for Paul to mention the millennial reign from Jerusalem? But Paul is deafeningly silent."[39]

Coming full circle

So, what's the point of all this eschatological palaver? Simply to raise the obvious questions about the popular, neo-orthodox Rapture hypothesis. As we have seen, not only is the Rapture itself a

39 Gentry, Jr., 133.

contrived theory which defies clear, coherent afterlife doctrine concerning the coming resurrection and judgment of the dead, but it is based on seriously misguided theological assumptions. (In turn, the Rapture/Millennium hypothesis has given rise to a highly-politicized, church-energized Christian Zionism which could hardly be further from the biblical notion of Christ's apolitical, spiritual kingdom.[40])

Rapturists are right, of course, to remind us that Jesus is coming again soon. Few of us (including, we dare say, Rapture's most ardent defenders) live our lives as if we really and truly believed that Christ might return at any moment—that his appearing is *always imminent*.[41] Yet, what Rapturists have missed by a mile is *why* he is coming. The proposition that some kind of a millennial reign is required to complete God's special program for the Jews is not only a return to "weak and beggarly elements" unworthy of the doctrine of Christ but also a gross reductionism of the nature of Christ's kingdom.

Why, then, is Jesus coming again?

Naturally, human logic would ask, Why else would Christ come back to earth if he's not actually going to do anything while he's here? But don't you see? That's the very beauty of it. Unlike earthly kings, our King isn't just going to sit on his throne and issue a summons for our appearance. Praise God, we have a King who is coming all the way down from his heavenly throne just to meet us in the air!

Isn't that what Jesus said? "In my Father's house are many rooms; if it were not so, I would have told you. I am going there to prepare a place for you. And if I go and prepare a place for you, I will come back *and take you to be with me that you also may be where I am*" (John 14:2-3). Mind you, that's not just for seven years (or three-

---

40 Somebody simply has to say it before the very stones themselves cry out. At some level, dispensationalists who politically and financially support the Zionist aims of the State of Israel in order to hasten the coming millennial kingdom must share responsibility for the carnage and suffering resulting from the Zionist conflict. When the Rapture/Millennium hypothesis becomes politicized to the point of welcomed conflict (almost as proof itself of the thesis), it is no longer simply a matter of academic doctrinal debate but a deadly serious moral issue.

41 That even the matter of Christ's "imminent" coming has spawned the often-fierce debate between pre-trib and post-trib millennialists is testimony to the confusion generated when dispensationalists insist, on one hand, that the Rapture is a matter of Christ's "any-moment" return, yet press with equal insistence that a series of prophesied events will precede the Rapture. It's difficult for someone to *watch* for an imminent appearing if he is told that other predictable and recognizable events will necessarily come first. Were there no millennial reign and attendant Rapture, of course, this difficulty would never arise. We could simply take at face value Jesus' repeated teaching that his one and only, Day-of-the-Lord reappearing would be without prior warning, as a thief in the night.

and-a-half years, or only for an instant) before he herds all of us back down to a restored, good-as-new earth where—according to Rapturists themselves—not all Utopia is Utopia.

Other scenarios make no sense

Are we, for example, to enjoy the perfect bliss of heaven only to re-experience an earth where we are surrounded by people—maybe even our loved ones—who struggle with disease (before Christ heals them), and even die (despite Christ's healing power)? And to go from not being married in heaven back to what surely would be an awkward reunion with a former spouse who was an unbeliever left behind at the Rapture? And to be surrounded by mortals who still sin (despite the absence of temptation)?[42] And to have to do battle with Satan when he is let out of the Abyss?[43]

Whatever happened to the no-more-tears heaven of sin-free, disease-free, death-free existence we knew during those seven blissful years in the very presence of God? And what sense does it make to live back here on earth for a literal thousand years when we've already tasted of the eternal realm where time itself is no more? For those who are gloriously caught up to heaven while flying in an airplane or walking the dog, today's "best-selling" Rapture scenario quickly becomes a farcical "now-you-see-it, now-you-don't" climb-down![44]

---

42 J. Dwight Pentecost affirms that sin during the Millennium will be the ultimate proof of man's depravity, yet suggests, curiously, that the resurrected righteous "can have no rightful place on the earth at that time" (538-539). This comes as part of his answer to the overall question about how raptured souls in their immortal bodies can mingle in a millennial society where non-raptured souls are still in their mortal bodies. Pentecost explains the conundrum with a two-tiered millennial Jerusalem–the one on earth and the "heavenly Jerusalem." "The fulfillment of Israel's national promises would be realized, not in resurrected [raptured] individuals, but rather in natural saved Israel who are living at the second advent" (546).

Where are the Old Testament saints who have been raptured just prior to the second advent? And where are raptured Christians during the Millennium? In the "heavenly city," says Pentecost–not the one that *is* heaven, but the one that comes down *out of heaven.* "This heavenly city will be brought into a relation to the earth at the beginning of the millennium, and perhaps will be made visible above the earth. It is from this heavenly city that David's greater Son exerts His Messianic rule, in which the Bride reigns, and from which the rewarded Old Testament saints exercise their authority in government."

And with this ingenuous "hovering heavenly city," the tangled web gets even more tangled....

43 See, Bickel and Jantz, 229, 231. Also, Hitchcock, 217-219.

44 Because we are told that Christians go straight to heaven when they die, are we to believe in a kind of "yo-yo eschatology" whereby first-century Christians will have been in heaven for two thousand years before being resurrected from their graves in the Rapture, only to be caught back up to heaven for seven years before being returned to earth for a thousand years before being taken back up into heaven for the third time at the "Second Coming" and the destruction of the world?

Surely, somebody's just not fully thinking through what they purport to believe. At the end of the day, does any of this cobbled-together hypothesis make any sense? One is tempted to say, "No, no, a *thousand times*, no!" In that same hyperbolic sense, the "thousand years" of Revelation 20 wasn't meant to be understood with blindfolded literalness, but was an apocalyptic, symbolic way of expressing the perfect completeness of Christ's spiritual kingdom. And 1 Thessalonians 4:17 is not at all talking about a secret rapturing up of Christians, but about their being caught up to glory at the trumpet-heralded, "every-eye-shall-see-him" Coming of the Lord–the same Day of the Lord on which every soul who has ever lived will meet his Maker and be judged for the deeds done in the body. Nor is Daniel's seventieth "week" about Tribulation, but consummation! It is the mystery "week" which lasts for "a thousand years"–the fulfillment of every promise given to the Jews in the eternal kingdom of God, in which all Jews and all Gentiles will be saved–one by one–through their faith in him who alone reigns supreme, now and forevermore.

Want to take something literal? Try this: *Christ is coming back to pick us up!* We can count on it! But the time is long overdue to come to our senses about the Great End-times Distraction. Best-selling or not, the Rapture/Millennium scenario is pure fiction which, once and for all, ought to be left behind.

APPENDICES
Three Enigma Variations

Revelation is like a glassy pool in which expositors find mirrored their own interpretive preconceptions.

–Paul Boyer

Dispensationalism's skewing of biblical afterlife teaching has affected not only mainstream Evangelical thinking, but also religious fringe groups with whom Evangelicals would have little in common otherwise. Three in particular–the Seventh-day Adventists, the Jehovah's Witnesses, and the Mormons–share a belief in dispensationalism's key feature: a thousand-year millennial reign of Christ. One major difference is that, for the Adventists and Jehovah's Witnesses, there is no special millennial role for the Jews; nor, for the Mormons, any talk of fulfilling the land promise for Israel. To that extent, the very *raison d'etre* of Darby/Scofield-type dispensationalism is undermined. In all three groups, their unique brands of millennialism reflect idiosyncratic, historically-based interpretations, especially of Daniel and Revelation.

Without duplicating fully our earlier analysis of the pertinent passages, the brief discussions which follow should suffice to indicate how millennial thinking has been mixed together with various other suspect doctrines to produce three enigmatic variations on the general theme we explored in the final chapter.

Anchor Verse: Galatians 1:8-9

"But even if we or an angel from heaven should preach a gospel other
than the one we preached to you, let him be eternally
condemned! As we have already said, so now I say again:
If anybody is preaching to you a gospel other than what
you accepted, let him be eternally condemned!"

Preview of Appendices

Seventh-day Adventists have a unique slant on the Millennium, believing that during that period of time the saved will remain in heaven, while the earth is completely empty and lifeless until the end of the thousand years. At that point, the Holy City will descend to the earth, and "heaven" will be a glorified life on this planet forever. Adventists believe that there is no distinction between body and soul, and therefore that nothing of the person exists between death and resurrection except for any memory of the saved which remains in the mind of God.

Jehovah's Witnesses share with Adventists that basic belief in the non-existence of the soul following death, but take it one step further, holding that, unless God specifically chooses to raise certain of them, the wicked simply cease to exist at the point of death. Jehovah's Witnesses also hold to a different view of the millennium, during which time, an elite cadre of 144,000 who are taken up into heaven—and are its only residents ever—will be co-regents of the earth, exercising kingdom rule toward the perfection of mankind. At the end of the millennium, the earth will be returned to its original, paradisiacal state for life on earth throughout eternity.

Claiming to have received modern revelation, Latter-day Saints (Mormons) believe in the pre-existence of souls in heaven before one is born, and a form of universalism in which all but a very few will experience some degree of afterlife glory in three separate kingdoms. LDS practice baptism for the dead on behalf of those who receive the Gospel in the postmortal spirit world beyond death. The LDS view of the Millennium is uniquely linked with a dubious American connection in which Independence, Missouri will serve as one of two captials, along with Jerusalem, and in fact will be the site of the millennial temple.

The Afterlife Beliefs of Seventh-day Adventists

Historically, Seventh-day Adventists have end-times roots going back to the 1830's and early 1840's when up to fifty thousand fervent followers of William Miller (1782-1849) excitedly anticipated an immediate fulfillment of Christ's Second Coming. From Daniel 8:14, Miller had calculated that the Lord would return in 1843 and set up a millennial reign, exactly 2,300 years after Artaxerxes I of Persia authorized Ezra to rebuild the temple in Jerusalem in 457 B.C. (In the words of Daniel's vision: "It will take 2,300 evenings and mornings; then the sanctuary will be reconsecrated.") When Miller's much-publicized prediction failed to materialize, some of the Millerites—realizing that Miller had forgotten to account for there being no year "0" between B.C. and A.D.–reset the date for the Lord's return to be October 22, 1844 (corresponding to the Jewish Day of Atonement).

As one might guess, that "Great Disappointment," as the Adventists refer to it, dampened future enthusiasm for specific date-setting. It also led to Miller's fading influence and to the rise of a Millerite remnant whose study of the book of Hebrews, in particular, led them to believe that the temple cleansing of which Daniel prophesied was not to be on earth, as Miller had thought, but in heaven. Their continuing study of the "heavenly sanctuary" eventually led these fledgling Adventists to be convicted about the need to observe the Sabbath–leading, in 1860, to their present designation: "Seventh-day Adventists." Among this remnant, the 17-year-old Ellen G. White, began to have visions which verified–so she and others claimed–the conclusions of their study. All of this ultimately culminated in the establishment of the Seventh-day Adventist Church in 1863. (On a wider scale, the Millerite fiasco gave impetus to modern dispensationalism's focus, not on historically-based dating methods, but on the increasingly popular interpretation of current events supposedly pointing to the coming Millennium.)

Adventists' view of the Millennium

Having been spawned in large part by the Millerite experience, Seventh-day Adventists never traveled far beyond their millennialist roots. Along with dispensationalist evangelical seminaries, Bible institutes, and scores of charismatic and independent Bible churches, Seventh-day Adventists regularly conducted Bible Prophecy seminars—principally, in the case of the Adventists, as a proselytizing opportunity.[1] Little surprise, then, that the Adventists' view of the afterlife is largely defined in millennial terms.

According to the Adventists' Fundamental Beliefs (number 26): "The millennium is the thousand-year reign of Christ with his saints in heaven between the first and second resurrections. During this time the wicked dead will be judged; the earth will be utterly desolate, without living human inhabitants, but occupied by Satan and his angels. At its close, Christ with his saints and the Holy City will descend from heaven to earth. The unrighteous dead will then be resurrected, and with Satan and his angels will surround the city; but fire from God will consume them and cleanse the earth. The universe will thus be freed of sin and sinners forever. (Rev. 20; 1 Cor. 6:2,3; Jer. 4:23-26; Rev. 21:1-5; Mal. 4:1; Eze. 28:18,19.)"[2]

You may have noticed a crucial distinction between the Adventists' view of the Millennium and the more-popular dispensationalist view. Whereas premillennialists typically believe that the church saints are raptured prior to the Millennium and then descend with Christ to reign with him on earth for a thousand years, Adventists have a rather different slant. Speaking not of the "Rapture" but of "the first resurrection," Adventists see the saints as being caught up into heaven and remaining there—*in heaven, not on earth*—for a thousand years. With the wicked having been wiped out at the Second Advent of Christ, "the earth stands for a time without human inhabitants."[3] To be precise, for a thousand years.

Three distinct judgments

By Adventist understanding, there are three distinct divine judgments. The first, known as the "pre-Advent investigative judgment," is said to be a "premillennial judgment" already begun in 1844 and continuing even now. Regarding the need for such a preliminary judgment, Adventists explain: "A judgment is needed—*before* the sec-

---

1 Boyer, 7.

2 Ministerial Association, General Conference of Seventh-day Adventists, *Seventh-day Adventists Believe...A Biblical Exposition of 27 Fundamental Doctrines,* (Hagerstown: Review and Herald Publishing Association, 1988), 362.

3 Ministerial Association, 365.

ond coming of Christ–to sift the true from the false and to demonstrate to the interested universe God's justice in saving the sincere believer."[4] When one searches the Scriptures for such a judgment and its supposed rationalization, the doctrine seems to appear completely out of thin air. [5]

The second judgment, the so-called "millennial judgment," or "Review Phase," takes place during the Millennium. While still in the celestial realm, the resurrected saints will sit on thrones judging the world and the angels–meaning, they will examine, or audit, the "books" of the wicked. "The judgment in which the righteous participate serves the purpose of answering any questions the righteous may have as to why the wicked are lost."[6]

Certainly, this novel concept provides a comforting answer for those who wonder how the saved could possibly enjoy their own salvation knowing that their loved ones, having been eternally damned, will be destroyed forever. Yet it begs the further question why such an audit of the judgment books for that purpose is never once mentioned in Scripture. Is it not enough simply to trust that God will resolve this human dilemma as he deems fit in heaven? Then again, once you accept that there's to be a literal thousand years in which the resurrected saints are dwelling in heaven above a barren earth, there must be *something* for them to be doing during that time.

The third and final judgment, known as the "executive judgment," comes at the end of the Millennium. "When God's enemies have surrounded the city and are ready to attack it, God sets up His great white throne. As the entire human race meets around this throne–some secure inside the city, others outside, terrified in the presence of the Judge–God will carry out the last phase of judgment," including the opening of the Book of Life. Whereupon, "the very surface of the earth outside the city appears to melt, becoming a vast lake of fire for the 'judgment and perdition of ungodly men' (2 Peter 3:7)....and "immedi-

---

4 Ministerial Association, 326.

5 One could be forgiven for suspecting that the obvious link between this nebulous, wholly unbiblical "judgment" and the year 1844 is a convenient cover for the notorious Millerite miscue. Admitting the discouragement which followed the "Great Disappointment," Adventists nevertheless claim that "Their mistake–and that of all interpreters of that time–was in their understanding of what event was to take place at the end of that prophetic period....Their [new, more in-depth] study of Biblical teachings on the sanctuary revealed that in 1844 Christ came to the Ancient of Days and began the final phase of His high-priestly ministry in the heavenly sanctuary," a significant part of which is the pre-Advent investigative judgment. (Ministerial Association, 324.)

6 Ministerial Association, 366-367.

ately upon their sentencing, Satan, his angels, and his human followers receive their punishment. They are to die an eternal death."[7]

In the end, a faux hell

It is often said that Adventists believe in the usual concepts of both heaven and hell, but that they hold to an annihilationist view of hell. And certainly that would appear to be correct, given Adventist teaching that: "hell is the place and state of punishment and destruction, by eternal fire in the second death, of those who reject God and the offer of salvation in Jesus Christ."[8] However, it is clear that this statement, taken in a vacuum, is somewhat misleading. As we have just seen, Adventists do not, in fact, believe that the souls of the wicked are annihilated in hell, as that term is typically used. Rather, they believe that the wicked are destroyed prior to (and apart from) any great Day of Judgment and subsequent hell. By Adventist doctrine, destruction of the wicked comes at the end of Christ's thousand-year reign as God sweeps the present earth clean of all wickedness in a fiery conflagration.

As thus presented, the destruction of the wicked is pretty much a repeat of what happened to Sodom and Gomorrah, with literal fire raining down on the earth and consuming them. So to say that Adventists are "annihilationists" in their view of hell, as some claim, does not take into account their unique end-of-the-Millennium version of hell. Nor, more importantly, does the Adventists' millennial scenario equate with what Jesus taught (in Matthew 10:28) about fearing the one who will "destroy both body and soul *in hell.*"

The distinction here is significant, especially given the fact that the Adventists' end-of-Millennium rain of fire precludes an opportunity for God to punish the wicked in hell prior to their destruction, should that be God's intention. Nor, of course, does it align with Jesus' teaching about the Day of his coming, on which Day both the righteous and the wicked are simultaneously raised and judged (John 5:28-29; Matthew 25:31-46). Just as Rapturists do, the Adventists insist on inserting a thousand years between the resurrection of the righteous and the wicked.

Raising similar difficulties as those we saw earlier with dispensationalism, it is the same ill-conceived millennial concept which

---

7 Ministerial Association, 368-369.
8 *SDA Encyclopedia*, rev. ed., 579.

necessitates having two different resurrections a thousand years apart, as well as three separate judgments; and the same millennial concept which–in the Adventist scheme of last things–has the wicked being destroyed in an earthly, military-like battle outside the walls of the Holy City, rather than in a spiritual hell.

Heaven on earth

But the differences don't stop with their millennialist understanding of "hell." It is an equally difficult stretch to say that Adventists believe in anything like the traditional notion of heaven. For Adventists, heaven will be right here on a rejuvenated planet. "Over and over the Bible declares that this eternal home of the redeemed will be a real place, a locality that real people with bodies and brains can see, hear, touch, taste, smell, measure, picture, test, and fully experience. It is on the new earth that God will locate his real heaven."[9]

For Adventists, the new earth is not just a matter of the Holy City descending from heaven down onto this planet. In their vision of heaven on earth, "The redeemed will not be confined within the walls of the New Jerusalem. They will inherit the earth. From their city homes the redeemed will go out into the country to design and build their dream homes, to plant crops, and harvest and eat them (Isa. 65:21)."[10] And, coming as little surprise from *Seventh-day* Adventists, "Week by week the saved will meet together for Sabbath worship."[11]

This reductionist, earth-bound rendition of God's eternal spiritual realm suffers from its lack of attention to 2 Peter 3:3-13, wherein Peter plainly tells us that, at Christ's coming, the earth and the firmament will be completely and totally destroyed–not simply renovated, nor yet be the designated landing site for a Holy City coming down, flying-saucer-like, out of heaven. It also appeals to a mind more geared to carnal appetites (building dream homes) than to spiritual longings (where Jesus prepares "heavenly mansions" for us and then comes back to take us there).

No soul distinct from the body

Worth noting, finally, is the Adventist perspective on the state of the dead prior to resurrection. Believing as they do that God will com-

---

9 General Conference, 375.
10 General Conference, 377.
11 General Conference, 380.

pletely and totally destroy the wicked in "the second death," Adventists seemingly go overboard trying to demonstrate that man is not naturally or inherently immortal. By the doctrine of "conditional immortality," Adventists assert that man is wholly mortal unless and until immortality is granted him at the resurrection. It is thus the belief of Adventists that "the soul has no conscious existence apart from the body, and no scripture indicates that at death the soul survives as a conscious entity." What's more, "according to Solomon, at death there is no difference between the spirits of man and beast....There is no indication that the spirit, or breath, was a conscious entity separate from the body."[12]

The Adventists are adamant that the Bible "does not teach that man comprises two separate parts. Body and soul exist together; they form an indivisible union."[13] "Body and soul" is shorthand for saying that it is impossible for there to be a soul existing separate and apart from the physical body following death. Adam was no more a living soul after his death than he was a living soul before he was created. And the same, supposedly, is true of us. Yet, contradiction abounds in Adventist teaching. Having denied the existence of the soul beyond death, Adventists are nevertheless forced by Scripture to concede defensively that "Death is not complete annihilation; it is only a state of temporary unconsciousness while the person awaits the resurrection. The Bible repeatedly calls this intermediate state a sleep."[14]

How a person who no longer exists can be said to "sleep" in an "intermediate state" is an illogical conundrum which only serves to expose the Adventists' overstatement about man's animal-like cessation at death. To say that the soul has no *conscious* existence is not to rule out the soul's having an *unconscious* existence, for which the apt metaphor is "sleep." Nothing is lost by acknowledging what Scripture plainly teaches: that the soul lives on beyond the grave, resting unconsciously in sheol/hades until the Resurrection. At that point, God still has it within his power to completely destroy the wicked in hell; and immortality for the saved is still a matter of God's grace, conditioned upon our response to his loving offer of eternal life.

Major doctrinal concerns

If the debate over *unconscious existence* versus *unconscious non-existence* seems trivial (the implications regarding Jesus' own death make

12 Ministerial Association, 353.
13 Ministerial Association, 352.
14 Ministerial Association, 352.

it *not* trivial), there are far greater concerns. Surely, something is seriously awry when the Adventists' eschatology ends up with an extra resurrection (at the cost of inserting a gratuitous time gap between Jesus' own words in Matthew 25:31-33 and John 5:28); two biblically-unknown, strangely-conjured judgments in addition to the one, universal Judgment on the Day of the Lord; a "hellish," Millennium-ending battle which turns out to be no hell after all; and a cheapened, marked-down "heaven" where time continues to be counted in weeks, and building dream houses in the country is somehow still alluring.

What accounts for all these unauthorized end-times felonies? By now it should be familiar suspect: A masked millennial intruder which robs Scripture of its clarity and assaults the beauty of its simplicity.

Appendix II

The Afterlife Beliefs of Jehovah's Witnesses

Established in 1884, the Watch Tower Bible and Tract Society (whose current members are better known as Jehovah's Witnesses) shares a similar history with the Adventists. The original Watch Tower's founder, Charles Taze Russell, having notoriously predicted the end of the world in 1914, died two years later but left a spiritual legacy which later transformed itself into one of the fastest-growing religious groups worldwide, the Jehovah's Witnesses. Both in his book, *Millennial Dawn* (1886), and in his *Watch Tower* magazine, Russell espoused his own peculiar interpretation of Daniel and Revelation, which was adamantly Zionist in sharp contrast to the present Watchtower Bible and Tract Society.

Only an elite cadre in heaven

Today's Jehovah's Witnesses believe that the 144,000 "sealed servants" of Revelation are not Jews, or even the church generally, but specially-chosen people "selected from among the followers of Christ, starting with the faithful apostles."[15] These chosen few will be the only people who actually enter heaven...*ever!* "Jehovah will give each one of these resurrected ones a spirit body so that they can live in heaven....The vast majority of those who have died, however, will be resurrected to life on earth....The heavenly government of Christ Jesus and his 144,000 associates will progressively bring obedient mankind back to the perfection that our original parents, Adam and Eve, lost."[16]

According to Watchtower doctrine, "It was never God's purpose for the human family in general to die and to populate heaven via the grave." The renovated, cleansed earth will be "transformed into a productive paradise with abundance for all." Indeed, "the Kingdom will educate its subjects in a peaceful way of life while at the same time raising them to the very pinnacle of human perfection (John 17:3; Romans 8:21). All of that is made possible because the earth

---

15 Watch Tower Bible and Tract Society of Pennsylvania, "What Happens to Us When We Die?" (Brooklyn, Watchtower Bible and Tract Society of New York, 1998), 27.

As it happens, the total number of 144,000–gathered over the past 2000 years–is now virtually complete, the only contingency being whether the last eight thousand or so, who are presently living, remain faithful unto their deaths. Should any of these eight thousand lose their esteemed position, others will be chosen to take their place.

16 Watchtower, 27.

"will be ruled by the Kingdom of God. Ruling from heaven, this Kingdom will be earth's sole government (Daniel 2:44; 7:13,14)."

Watchtower literature deftly sidesteps John 14:2-3, where Jesus told his disciples he was going away to prepare a place for them, and would come back to take them there. Nor does it convincingly address the obvious import of 2 Corinthians 5:1-5, which speaks of God's eternal plan for man to be translated from mortality in a physical world to immortality in a spiritual world. Certainly, there is not the slightest hint in Scripture that some elite cadre of 144,000 will be singled out for special Kingdom rule over the rest of God's people. Indeed, there is something theologically sinister about the idea of Kingdom subjects being brought to "the pinnacle of human perfection" in a new earth. God's final sanctification of the righteous comes through Christ's shed blood, not some millennial "nanny" state.

A thousand years of kingdom rule

Briefly summarizing the details of their millennial understanding, Jehovah's Witnesses believe that the battle of Armageddon will begin any time now. Under Jehovah's divine rage, Jesus will execute vengeance on those who may profess to be Christians but are not faithful Witnesses, and also on those in other religions of the world, represented by "Babylon the Great." After the world is purified in this way, God's Kingdom will be established as a theocracy on earth for a thousand years. During that time, those who have survived Armageddon and the Tribulation will be joined by all the "worthy dead" who will be resurrected to inhabit a transformed, utopian earth.

Unlike those who believe that the end of the Millennium will herald eternal life in heaven, Jehovah's Witnesses believe in an eternal paradise on earth, apparently for all but the 144,000, who will remain in heaven with God. While the whole purpose of the Millennium is to bring about perfection for those who are on earth, that perfection is not universally achieved. At the end of the Millennium, those who rebel against Kingdom rule during that thousand years will be destroyed in *gehenna*, the lake of fire in which Satan and his angels will also be destroyed—not to be confused, surprisingly enough, with hell.

Nonexistence, unless special resurrection

For Jehovah's Witnesses, "hell" is an interchangeable term for *sheol, hades,* and "the grave"–all of which refer to the state of the dead, whether righteous or wicked. In order to make sense of that odd linguistic linkage, one must first understand that Jehovah's Witnesses have a view of human nature which excludes man's having a soul that survives death of the body. They believe that man's spirit is no different from the "breath of life" which animates the animals (a force they compare to the electric current which makes appliances function). Similar to Adventists, they contend that "Death is a state of nonexistence." To that extent, *everyone* is extinguished in "hell"–which is to say, in *sheol,* or *hades,* or "the grave." The only question after that point is whether God chooses to resurrect any who have died.

Jehovah's Witnesses make much of the phrase "memorial tombs" which is seen in their unique translation of John 5:28-29 (where other versions speak only of the "grave"). The reason for this unusual emphasis in translation is seen in their position statement that "Jesus Christ promised that all those in Jehovah's memory will be resurrected, or brought back to life. Among them will indeed be those who have pursued a righteous course as Jehovah's servants. But millions of other people have died without showing whether they would comply with God's righteous standards. Either they did not know about Jehovah's requirements or they lacked sufficient time to make needed changes. Individuals of this sort are also in God's memory and will be resurrected, for the Bible says: 'There is going to be a resurrection of both the righteous and the unrighteous.' –Acts 24:15."

Carefully sidestepped within that statement is the *relative number* of the "individuals of this sort" who will cease to exist at death, yet nevertheless have the prospect of resurrection. Contrary to what a superficial reading might suggest, only those *specially-selected* unrighteous ones who are in God's memory will be resurrected and given an opportunity during the Millennium to turn to God. As for all the other wicked who are *not* resurrected during that time, the barely-publicized fact is that they will *never* be resurrected–not to a second chance in the Millennium, nor to formal Judgment, nor to a "hell"–as typically defined–where they might ultimately be annihilated.

To put it succinctly: unless God happens to give Hitler a second chance during the Millennium, he simply ceased to exist the moment his life-force ebbed away. In effect, Hitler destroyed himself, with no lingering spiritual consequences whatsoever. Instead of "annihilating" Hitler as part of a divinely-imposed punishment, God just chose not to resurrect him. Even more amazing, apparently God doesn't even remember him!

Just as with Hitler, the same fate would be true of most of the wicked who have ever lived: Death has cheated both Resurrection and Judgment. The message of Hebrews 9:27–that it is appointed unto man to die and then to face judgment–seems not to have a place in Watchtower doctrine, at least for those wicked whom God never resurrects.

To say, as many have done, that the Jehovah's Witnesses are "annihilationists" with regard to hell is to misunderstand the subtle nuances of Watchtower doctrine. Not only do Jehovah's Witnesses distinguish (strangely) between "hell" and *gehenna*, but they also deny the existence of a soul apart from the body which could be "annihilated" in the way that Jesus spoke of the soul's destruction in Matthew 10:28. For Jehovah's Witnesses, death is death is death–whether that death occurs now (even for the righteous) or at the end of the Millennium (for those who rebel against God during that thousand years). The most that can be said is that if an unrighteous person is "resurrected" (by re-creation from God's memory) during the Millennium but "selfishly refuses to change his wicked ways," then he will be destroyed in the lake of fire (*gehenna*) along with Satan and his angels. (Interestingly, Jehovah's Witnesses deny that Satan and the angels could ever be in "hell," because "hell"–having been equated with *sheol* or *hades*–is not for spirit beings, only for dead humans.)

Nonexistent, but asleep!

To appreciate yet another oddity, turn back for a moment to Watchtower's understanding of what happens to us at the point of death. "Those asleep in the grave but who are in God's memory will be resurrected...," says Watchtower's literature with not a wink or a nod. It may be small potatoes to some folks, but the fact that Jehovah's Witnesses employ the word "sleep" for what happens to the dead before they are resurrected is curious, to say the least. As with Adventists, it apparently has not occurred to Jehovah's Witnesses that there is a crucial distinction between "sleeping" (even as a metaphor) and nonexistence. Yet, the question seems obvious by analogy: When we are sleeping at night, are we nonexistent?

Despite their reference to the dead being "asleep," there is for Jehovah's Witnesses no such thing as a soul which lives on beyond death, and thus no intermediate state of the dead in which one would be capable of "sleeping." (Nor, incidentally, do the Jehovah's Witnesses feel any compelling need to take Daniel 12:2–about the multitudes who are sleeping in the dust of the earth–as literally as they interpret the rest of Daniel, which provides the foundation for much of their millennial belief system.)

Even apart from all the "sleep" terminology, there is obvious inconsistency when Jehovah's Witnesses affirm that: "Jesus, who knew the truth about what happens to the soul at death, believed that Lazarus was unconscious, nonexistent."[17] Like nonexistent sleep, "unconscious nonexistence" is a philosophical oxymoron. To be totally nonexistent is to be neither conscious nor unconscious. Or to put it the other way around, if someone is lying "unconscious" in a hospital bed, is he nonexistent?

Implications regarding the nature of both Christ and man

There is grand irony that, in attempting to prove the fact of nonexistence at death, Jehovah's Witnesses cite Luke 23:46, where Jesus called out from the cross, "Father, into your hands I entrust my spirit." Says Watchtower teaching: "At the time of his death...Jesus confidently left his spirit in his Father's hands, fully trusting in Jehovah's ability to bring him back to life." Of course, that's Watchtower code for saying that, at the moment of his death, Jesus ceased to exist altogether, and therefore would have to be re-created from God's memory three days later. That's okay for some, especially Jehovah's Witnesses, who don't believe that Jesus was *the* Son of God, or God wrapped in human flesh. But in the face of Scripture's unambiguous assurance that Jesus of Nazareth was God incarnate, the claim that Jesus was even temporarily nonexistent sheds interrogation-level lighting, not only on their rejection of the tripartite nature of God, but also on their rejection of the tripartite nature of man.

Indeed, it is the very fact that Jesus was *resurrected* and not merely *re-created from God's memory* which best demonstrates that we our-

17 Watchtower, 24.

selves are more than simply animated physical bodies and minds subject to an earthly, existence-ending death. We are not *just dust*, snuffed out like a candle beneath six feet of dirt. Our inmost essence having been made in the image of God, we are living, surviving souls over whom physical death is powerless. Speaking specifically of those who had long since died, Jesus himself affirmed that God "is the God of the living, for to him all are live" (Luke 20:38). No suggestion here that God is the God of the nonexistent! Of one thing we can be sure: When Jesus raised Lazarus from the grave (the beloved friend Jesus said was "asleep"), Jesus didn't re-create a nonexistent Lazarus from memory, but *called him forth!* Indeed, he *stood him up*, the very meaning of the word resurrection!

When Jehovah's Witnesses (and Adventists) tell us that man's soul cannot exist apart from his body, it is because they have reduced man to flesh and bones plus breath and animation. When the breath expires and the animation ceases, the body dies and there is nothing that remains. If they are right...if that's all there is...then there is nothing intrinsically which separates us from animals. In light of biblical teaching that, unlike animals, we are created in the image of God–a little lower than the angels–this reductionist perspective of an animated but soul-less man is not just a quibble about the intermediate state of the dead, but a fundamental misunderstanding of the nature of our humanity.

On wings of doubtful doctrine

As we have seen before, time and again, aberrant teaching about the afterlife inevitably has a way of exposing aberrant underlying doctrine. To believe there is no soul apart from animating breath which survives death; that most of the wicked throughout the centuries will never face judgment; that others who are still unrighteous at the time of their deaths will be given a second chance during the Millennium; that only 144,000 specially-chosen followers of Christ will go to heaven to rule over all the other saints; and that eternal life will be nothing more than living forever on a face-lifted version of this present earth speaks volumes about the false foundational doctrines which Jehovah's Witnesses repeatedly bring to our doorsteps. That the rest of us are nowhere near as committed to sharing from house to house the *true* gospel of Christian life and afterlife is to our eternal shame.

Appendix III

The Afterlife Beliefs of Mormons

When a church's afterlife beliefs are based on perceived modern-day revelation in addition to the Bible, and those beliefs are linked directly with a supposed "premortal" life in heaven before we were ever born, something tells you you're about to encounter a very different perspective. Of all the major religious groups claiming Christian connections, the Church of Jesus Christ of Latter-day Saints (LDS) is the only one which believes we had a robust life with God long before we were born here on earth. In that belief, Mormons have much in common with eastern religions which espouse reincarnation, right down to the shared belief that a "veil of forgetfulness" prevents our *remembering* our life-before-life on the other side.

When you combine this belief in a heavenly preexistence with a millennial view of the end times, along with a Catholic-like purgatorial progression in the spirit world and what fundamentally amounts to universalism at judgment–the resulting doctrinal maze is the most complex set of afterlife beliefs among any group affirming allegiance to Jesus Christ. In the limited space available, one can only trace the briefest outline of LDS afterlife teaching. Even diagraming a flow chart of all the different intermediate states, resurrections, judgments, and ultimate afterlife destinies is itself a daunting task–and an unmistakable object lesson regarding what happens when a group embraces the notion of continuing divine revelation. With each new revelation, the already-ailing patient experiences more and more complications.

When the Bible plays second fiddle

Relative to the Bible, Mormon scholars speak candidly about the primacy of the Book of Mormon, Doctrine and Covenants, Pearl of Great Price, and living prophets. "Latter-day Saints are not dependent upon the Bible alone for doctrine, church organization, or standards of living," writes Robert L. Millet, former dean of Religious Education at Brigham Young University. Indeed, "Latter-day Saints feel no need to 'prove' their positions from the Bible...."[18] In such a case, of course, there is no possible basis on which we can have a biblical discussion of any kind, whether about the afterlife, or salvation, or even marriage–which Mormons believe can be eternal. More

18 Robert L. Millet, *The Mormon Faith* (Salt Lake City: Shadow Mountain, 1998), 187.

troubling still is the LDS view, not only that the Bible is secondary in importance to supposed latter-day revelation, but that not even the words of Jesus are sacrosanct. Referring to Joseph Smith, Millet says: "The Prophet quoted the Savior about many mansions and said: 'It should be–"In my Father's kingdom are many kingdoms, in order that ye may be heirs of God and joint-heirs with me.'"'"[19]

Joseph Smith...*presuming to correct the text regarding what Jesus said?*

And it only gets worse. As Millet relates the incident, Joseph Smith and his scribe, Sidney Rigdon, were translating John 5:28-29 (in the KJV) where Jesus says the time will come when the dead will come forth from the graves: "They that have done good, unto the resurrection of life; and they that have done evil, unto the resurrection of damnation." Says Millet, "The Prophet felt impressed to alter the text as follows: 'And shall come forth; they who have done good, in the resurrection of *the just*; and they who have done evil, in the resurrection of *the unjust*.'"[20] Whereupon Millet observes: "The alteration in the text, though interesting, is not earthshaking or overwhelming. But truly, 'out of small things proceedeth that which is great' (D&C 64:33)."

In truth, of course, seemingly insignificant changes to Jesus' words invariably lead to serious error, never better illustrated than in this instance. What followed immediately on the heels of this unauthorized alteration to the biblical text was what is known to Latter-day Saints as the "Vision of the Glories," in which Christ's reference to "many mansions" was transformed into the "three degrees of glory" now forming the bedrock of LDS afterlife doctrine.[21] That which Latter-day Saints accept with such confident assurance as modern prophecy not only nullifies the words of our Lord himself, but thereby (not surprisingly) charts a path leading to incoherence, contradiction, and what appears to an outsider as a crucial need for additional, stop-gap revelations.

Postmortal spirit world

At death, by LDS teaching, the human spirit enters immediately into a postmortal spirit world, either into paradise (the abode of the faithful) or into hell (the realm of the wicked), both being in the

19 Robert L. Millet, *Life After Death* (Salt Lake City: Deseret Book Company, 1999), 37.
20 Millet, *Life After Death*, 22.
21 Doctrine and Covenants 76.

same sphere known variously as sheol, hades, or "spirit prison." Intriguingly, that postmortal spirit world is closer than one might imagine. President Brigham Young answered the question, "Where is the spirit world?" saying simply: "It is right here."[22] In 1916, President Joseph F. Smith had already declared that our loved ones who have passed through the veil can see us and know us. "We live in their presence, they see us, they are solicitous for our welfare, they love us now more than ever."[23]

Curiously, too, we are told that in the postmortal world "spirit beings have the same bodily form as mortals except that the spirit body is in perfect form....They have the same appetites and desires that they had when they lived on earth." Moreover, "all spirits are in adult form...even if they die as infants or children (see Joseph F. Smith, *Gospel Doctrine*, p. 455)."[24] How this can be true when other LDS doctrine declares these same deceased children will later be resurrected in their original *non-adult* bodies, requires some dextrous explaining, to say the least.[25]

Presumably even the wicked are endowed with conscious, active spirit bodies in the postmortal world. In the LDS pre-resurrection version of hell, "the very wicked" are subject to confrontation and suffering. Yet hell is by no means limited to the worst of the worst. There are other, "good people" in hell who did not accept the gospel while on earth but who may develop spiritually in their postmortal state. Although hell is a time of painful awareness and repentance, there is also opportunity for being taught the gospel.

In fact, the residents of hell can cross the crucial divide into paradise if they accept the gospel being taught to them, and if the ordinance of baptism is performed by proxy through Latter-day Saints still on earth. (It is this practice, incidentally, which explains the enormous LDS interest in genealogies. Family lineage is meticulously researched in aid of their acting on behalf of generations long since deceased to assure covenant blessings for them through vicarious acts of immersion, confirmation, endowment, and even temple marriages.)

Prior to 1918, it was steadfastly maintained from 1 Peter 3:19 that Jesus personally preached the gospel to the whole spirit

---

22 *Gospel Principles*, (Salt Lake City: Church of Jesus Christ of Latter-day Saints, 1978–1997), 290.
23 Millet, *Life After Death*, 114-115.
24 *Gospel Principles*, 290.
25 See Millet, *Life After Death*, 16, 54, 81.

world–the righteous and wicked alike–while his body lay dead in the tomb. But many, including President Joseph F. Smith, queried how that could be. As Millet tells it, "While pondering the question of how the Savior could have taught the gospel to so many in the spirit world in so short a time, perhaps no more than thirty-eight to forty hours, President Smith received what may be the most significant doctrinal insight of the entire vision." That insight was the notion that when the Savior visited the inhabitants of the spirit world, he did so only indirectly, preaching to the righteous himself, but choosing to organize and empower messengers to preach the gospel on his behalf to the wicked.[26]

Of course, whether done personally by Jesus or subsequently through the efforts of others, the very notion of postmortal evangelism of any kind is repugnant to genuine revelation. It will take more than claimed latter-day visions to counter the obvious teaching point of the rich man and Lazarus (that there are no second chances beyond death), not to mention the clear import of Hebrews 9:27–that death leads to judgment, not redemption of the dead through some hadean salvation.[27]

Two major resurrections and several minor ones

According to LDS teaching, the postmortal spirit world will come to an end for the righteous when the Lord returns and resurrects them. (Those in hell will have to wait for the end of the Millennium.) Yet it is also believed that already there have been a number of preliminary resurrections, all of which are part and parcel of the First Resurrection. "After Jesus rose from the dead," says the LDS primer, *Gospel Principles*, (somewhat out of sync with the timing indicated by Matthew 27:52-53) "other righteous people who had died were also resurrected. They appeared in Jerusalem and also on the American continent....This was the beginning of the First Resurrection. Some people have been resurrected since then.[28] (While it is said that these "resurrected" people did not die again, the nature of their transforma-

---

26 Millet, *Life After Death*, 85-87.

27 It is strongly argued by some Mormon scholars that postmortal evangelism is not a doctrine of second chances–that, for many, the playing field was simply not level the first time around. Yet if that were the case, surely Jesus himself would have taken such circumstances into account. Whatever other leniency God might show on the Day of Judgment, Christ's teaching still stands. Call it what you wish, postmortal evangelism is simply not taught by Jesus or the apostles. Any supposed latter-day revelation to the contrary is simply that: *contrary to biblical teaching*.

28 The identity of this group of people is not known, but the assurance is given by an LDS spokesman that "There wouldn't be many of these."

tion from people walking around on earth into heavenly beings of a kind is obscure. Nor is there much detail about the "entire society of ante-diluvians" who, according to Joseph Smith, were translated direct-ly from earth into the bosom of God.[29])

Those yet to be resurrected in the First Resurrection include the righteous who will be caught up to meet Christ at his coming (in the "Resurrection of the Just") and a class of people who, at the beginning of the Millennium will be raised to receive a "terrestrial glory" (more on that in a moment). "When all these people have been resurrected, the First Resurrection will be completed."[30] At the end of the Millennium—in line with classic dispensational millennialism—comes the Second Resurrection (the "Resurrection of the Unjust").

Presumably at both major resurrections, "every limb and joint shall be restored to its body...."[31] According to latter-day prophets, the resurrected body will be the exact same one that was buried in the grave, "whether young or old; there will not be 'added unto their stature one cubit,' neither taken from it....[32]" Unless, of course, it's a matter of missing hands or legs or eyes, for "physical deformities will not be a part of the resurrected body."[33]

As for children who die before adulthood, there seems to have been some evolution of understanding. Although Joseph Smith taught that "children will be enthroned in the presence of God and the Lamb with bodies of the same stature that they had on earth,"[34] in 1918 President Joseph F. Smith (who himself had lost little ones to death) declared that, following their resurrection, children "will be nurtured and reared to physical maturity by worthy parents."[35] (As suggested above, this view of resurrected children seems patently incongruous with the adult spirit bodies that deceased children are already given in the postmortal world.)

Events at Christ's coming

Like other premillennialists, Latter-day Saints believe that tumul-tuous wars and cataclysmic events will precede Christ's coming.

29 Millet, *The Mormon Faith*, 105. It is said that these are the "people of Enoch," though Hebrews 11:5 speaks only of Enoch himself.
30 *Gospel Principles*, 279.
31 Millet, *Life After Death*, 16.
32 Joseph Smith, *Teachings of the Prophet Joseph Smith*, 199-200.
33 Millet, *Life After Death*, 16.
34 Smith, *Teachings of the Prophet Joseph Smith*, 199-200.
35 Joseph F. Smith, *Improvement Era*, May 1918, 570.

Unlike other premillennialists, Mormons believe that near the time of the Lord's appearing "the faithful Saints will build a righteous city, a city of God, called the New Jerusalem. Jesus Christ, himself, will rule there." The big surprise is that, "The Lord said the city will be built in the state of Missouri in the United States (see D&C 84:3-4)"[36]—specifically, "in the western boundaries of the State of Missouri."[37] Of course, that is not a surprise to anyone familiar with the distinctly American thread running throughout all of Mormon doctrine, beginning with the LDS belief that "After Jesus was resurrected, he visited the people in America and organized his church among them."[38] As we shall see in more detail, the "American connection" has a specially high-profile significance with the LDS as it relates to the future coming of the Lord and his millennial kingdom.

The dubious American connection aside, at Christ's second coming the wicked on earth will be destroyed and sent into the postmortal world for the duration of the Millennium. It will also be a day wherein every corruptible thing, whether man or beasts or birds or fish, will be consumed by fire. When asked whether that fire would be literal, Joseph Fielding Smith responded strangely: "Oh, no, it will not be literal fire any more than it was literal water that covered the earth in the flood."[39]

The unique LDS Millennium

As the thousand-year earthly reign begins, the cleansed earth will be transformed. "At the beginning of the Millennium, the earth and all things upon it will be quickened, made alive, and transfigured—lifted to a higher plane for a season. The earth will be transformed from a telestial to a terrestrial glory, to that paradisiacal condition that prevailed in Eden before the Fall."[40]

Those who survive the earth's cleansing at the Lord's coming will remain on the earth, having been "partially changed" but not made immortal until they shall have lived for a hundred years (the "age of man"[41]), at which time they "will pass through death and be

---

36 *Gospel Principles*, 268.
37 Doctrine and Covenants 84:3
38 *Gospel Principles*, 105.
39 *The Signs of the Times* (Salt Lake City: Deseret Book Co., 1942), 41; Millet, *The Mormon Faith*, 157.
Also note: If the waters of the Flood, in which eight persons were saved (1 Peter 3:20), were not literal, then what does it say of the literal waters of baptism in which Mormons and others are immersed, consistent with 1 Peter 3:21?
40 Millet, *The Mormon Faith*, 158.
41 Isaiah 65:20

changed instantly from mortality to resurrected immortality."[42] Earth's millennial residents will build houses, have children, and go about life as normal, except that there will be no poverty or crime. Children born during the Millennium will "grow up without sin unto salvation," their fallen nature having been eradicated at the earth's renewal.[43]

As with other millennial theories, LDS doctrine teaches that resurrected Saints—at least "those who have lived from the time of Christ's resurrection to the time of his second coming"—will come to earth with the Lord.[44] (Mormon consensus holds the belief that those from the pre-Christian era who received the gospel and were baptized were resurrected at the time of Christ's resurrection, and that the "first resurrection" will *resume* at the time of Christ's coming in glory.) During the thousand years, mortals who were living at the time of Christ's coming will live alongside resurrected immortals. Oddly, though, "Joseph Smith explained that Jesus and the resurrected Saints will probably not live on the earth all the time but will visit whenever they please or when necessary to help in the governing of the earth."[45] (Where Jesus and the resurrected Saints will "reside" when not on the earth is seemingly a mystery.)

If, as dispensational millennialists believe, Israel is to be gathered for one last fulfillment of God's covenant promises to Israel, the LDS put a peculiarly chauvinistic twist to that popular notion. For LDS, there will be, not just one but two capitals for the millennial kingdom—one in Jerusalem and the other (by now predictable) in the "New Jerusalem" here in Missouri.[46] Having two capitals only makes sense, given LDS teaching that, "The tribes of Ephraim and Manasseh will be gathered to the land of America. The tribe of Judah will return to the city of Jerusalem and the area surrounding it. The ten lost tribes will receive from the tribe of Ephraim their promised blessings."[47]

---

42 Millet, *The Mormon Faith*, 156.

The fate of those on earth who, at the age of a hundred, are still unbelievers is ambiguous. Some believe that these rebellious souls will descend into hell until the end of the Millennium in order to learn repentance.

43 Millet, *The Mormon Faith*, 158.

44 Millet, *The Mormon Faith*, 159.

45 *Gospel Principles*, 283, citing *Teachings of the Prophet Joseph Smith*, 268.

46 Somehow this will be the case despite the fact that during the Millennium, "There will not be different continents as we have now, but the land will be gathered in one place as it was in the beginning." See *Gospel Principles*, 284.

47 *Gospel Principles*, 274.

For Latter-day Saints, there is yet more detail. During the Millennium "there is a center place, a place where the chief temple shall stand, a place to which the Lord shall come, a place whence the law shall go forth to govern all the earth in that day when the Second David [Christ, the Millennial King] reigns personally upon the earth. And that center place is what men now call Independence in Jackson County, Missouri, but which in a day to come will be the Zion of our God...."[48] (At that time, LDS headquarters will shift from Salt Lake City to Independence.)

The millennial temple is important, because it is believed that temple work will be more important than ever during the thousand-year reign on behalf of those who are still in hell awaiting the Second Resurrection. "There is too much work to finish before the Millennium begins, so it will be completed during that time. Resurrected beings will help us correct the mistakes we have made in doing research concerning our dead ancestors."[49]

One altogether fascinating part of LDS teaching is that "in the millennium men will have the privilege of being Presbyterians, Methodists or infidels, but they will not have the privilege of treating the name and character of Deity as they have done heretofore. No, but every knee shall bow and every tongue confess to the glory of God the Father that Jesus is the Christ."[50] Indeed, "eventually everyone will accept Jesus Christ as the Savior."[51] Yet apparently that universal conversion will break down at the end of the Millennium, LDS doctrine telling us that "there will come a time at the end of the thousand years when 'men again begin to deny their God' (D&C 29:22)," and openly rebel along with Satan and his armies in the "Battle of Gog and Magog."[52]

As the Millennium comes to an end, 1) there will be a final cleansing and celestialization of the planet; 2) those who have been in hell will be resurrected;[53] 3) the Day of Judgment will follow; and 4) the children of God will be assigned to one of three kingdoms of glory–celestial, terrestrial, or telestial. Only the relatively few "sons of perdition" (those who blaspheme against the Holy Ghost by denying Christ and who,

---

48 Millet, *The Mormon Faith*, 110, citing *A New Witness for the Articles of Faith*, p. 595.

49 *Gospel Principles*, 283.

50 Millet, *The Mormon Faith*, 159, citing Brigham Young in *Journal of Discourses*, 12:274.

51 *Gospel Principles*, 283, citing Daniel H. Ludlow, ed., *Latter-day Prophets Speak*, 261-262.

52 Millet, *The Mormon Faith*, 161.

53 Purgatory-like, "Even the spirits who have committed the greatest sins will have suffered sufficiently by the end of the Millennium (see Acts 2:25-27). They will then be resurrected." *Gospel Principles*, 292-293.

with their eyes wide open, reject the plan of salvation will be cast into outer darkness–or the eternal hell–where there is no glory. ("The particulars of the fate of the sons of perdition have not been revealed.")[54]

Celestial glory

For Mormons, the celestial kingdom will be inherited by those who receive the covenant gospel, participate in the necessary sacraments or ordinances (including the endowment and celestial marriage), and remain faithful throughout their lives. It will also include "those who did not have opportunity to receive the gospel fulness, including little children who die before the age of accountability, but who would have done so if that opportunity had been extended to them."[55] (This might be said to be the "Alvin exception," given the fact that Joseph Smith's brother, Alvin, died unbaptized, seven years before the organization of the church[56]).

LDS doctrine holds that there are three degrees of the celestial kingdom, and one cannot enter the highest degree unless one has entered into the new and everlasting covenant of marriage performed within the temple.[57] There is no further explanation of the lower two degrees. It is believed that all celestials will receive the presence of the Father and the Son. In fact, "they will have everything that our Heavenly Father and Jesus Christ have–all power, glory, dominion, and knowledge." What most distinguishes those of the highest degree is the prospect of divinity. "They will become gods."[58]

"Gods" they may be, but they will live on a material (if celestialized) earth, with celestial, yet material, bodies qualitatively different (in some way "more refined") than those who inherit either the terrestrial or telestial kingdoms. And they will continue to have children (presumably forever[59]), and enjoy heaven on earth with "lands, houses, cities, vegetation, rivers, and animals; with thrones, temples, palaces, kings, princes, priests, and angels; with food, raiment, musical instruments, etc., all of which are material."[60] All in all, a strange

---

54 Millet, *Life After Death*, 28, citing D&C 76:45-48.

55 Millet, *Life After Death*, 30.

56 One cannot help but wonder if this "revelation" ever would have surfaced had it not been for the need to resolve Alvin's special situation. See *Life After Death*, 50-52.

57 *Gospel Principles*, 242; *Doctrine and Covenants*, 131:1-4.

58 *Gospel Principles*, 302. See also D&C 76:58.

59 By LDS belief, celestials have the power to produce spirit offspring, which is to say, to create a whole new pre-existence leading to physical births in worlds yet to come, in perpetuity. That these births should occur, not in heaven, as before, but on a celestialized earth, adds a further complication to an already complicated scenario.

60 Millet, *Life After Death*, 37; *The Mormon Faith*, 162.

ending indeed for people who supposedly began their existence in the premortal spiritual realm of heaven and became part of a material life on earth only in order to be purified and tested for advancement to a greater spiritual reality.

Terrestrial glory

It is believed that the terrestrial kingdom will be inherited by four distinct groups of otherwise honorable people, including 1) those who, in the postmortal spirit world, finally accepted the testimony that Jesus is the Savior, but who thereafter had no further interest in accepting the gospel in full; 2) those who knew Jesus in the mortal world, but were not valiant enough to receive the fulness of the gospel–which is to say, join the Church; 3) those who joined the Church of Latter-day Saints but were not valiant in their testimony; and 4) those who died "without the law"–meaning, the pagan nations.[61]

No clear explanation is given as to why the "Alvin" exception (those who *would* have received the gospel fulness if the opportunity had been given them) does not apply to the pagan nations. All that is said is that, though "any who repent may obtain celestial glory," the "great bulk of them shall only obtain terrestrial glory."[62] Even that seems to contradict LDS President Lorenzo Snow's belief that when the gospel is preached in the postmortal spirit world, "there will be very few indeed of those spirits who will not gladly receive the Gospel when it is carried to them."[63]

Those who inherit the terrestrial glory will receive the presence of the Son, but not of the Father. Although they will have their same earthly bodies (glorified only in some unexplained "terrestrial" sense), they will not be married or be part of eternal families. In fact, it is not even known where they will be! The only thing certain is that they will *not* be on the celestialized earth, which is fit only for celestial bodies.

Telestial glory

It is something of a surprise that those who inherit the telestial kingdom (as "heirs of salvation," no less) will receive any glory at all, for among them will be murderers, liars, sorcerers, adulterers, and

---

61 Millet, *Life After Death*, 31-32.
62 Millet, *Life After Death*, 32.
63 Millet, *Life After Death*, 88, citing *Collected Discourses: Delivered by President Wilford Woodruff, His Two Counselors, The Twelve Apostles, and Others*, 3:363.

whoremongers. Along with these quintessentially immoral reprobates will be those who "received not the gospel, neither the testimony of Jesus, neither the prophets, neither the everlasting covenant."[64] However, there are others (said to be in a separate part of the telestial kingdom) who seem not to have been either vile, or wicked, or hard-hearted, but simply those of dual loyalties, as if between God and Mammon. Apparently there will be some awfully surprised people who thought they were "for Jesus, for Peter and Paul, and even for Luther, Calvin, and the Pope." But in their mixed professions of allegiance, it appears they never really and truly received the gospel of Christ, as indicated in this bit of visionary poetry by Joseph Smith:

> *These are they that came out for Apollos and Paul;*
> *For Cephas and Jesus, in all kinds of hope;*
> *For Enoch and Moses, and Peter and John;*
> *For Luther and Calvin, and even the Pope.*
>
> *For they never received the gospel of Christ,*
> *Nor the prophetic spirit that came from the Lord;*
> *Nor the covenant neither, which Jacob once had;*
> *They went on their way, and they have their reward.*[65]

Whether vilely wicked, therefore, or simply disloyal by virtue of split allegiances, the consequences befalling all of the above saved-but-third-class-telestials include being without God and without Christ, worlds without end[66] (though it is said that "they will be visited by the Holy Ghost").[67] While those in this basement kingdom may manage to advance to the highest level of telestial glory, there is no hope of their ever being promoted to either the terrestrial or celestial glories. Wherever they are (and, here again, all we are told is that they won't be on earth), their bodies are the same bodies as in the mortal world, only with a "telestial glory," whatever that is.

And how many people will end up in this lowest of the three glories? According to *Doctrine and Covenants* 76:109, "These people are as numerous as the stars in heaven and the sand on the seashore,"

---

64 *Doctrine and Covenants*, 76:82, 99-101, 103.

65 Millet, *Life After Death*, 33, citing Smith, *Times and Seasons* 4 (1 February 1843): 85, stanzas 70-71.

66 *Doctrine and Covenants*, 76:109, 112.

67 *Gospel Principles*, 298.

once again calling into question President Snow's ebullient optimism about the overwhelming reception to postmortal evangelism. Also once again causing one to wonder how those who have rejected outright the gospel of Christ both on earth and in the spirit world could possibly receive anything even remotely described as "salvation," "exaltation," and "glory."

Summing up

How the afterlife can become so muddled and unbiblical is perhaps best explained by Joseph Smith's revealing admission: "I do not believe the Methodist doctrine of sending honest men and noble-minded men to hell, along with the murderer and the adulterer....I have an order of things to save the poor fellows at any rate, and get them saved; for I will send men to preach to them in prison and save them if I can."[68] Say again? "*I have an order of things...?*" "*I will send men...?*" "To save them if *I* can...?" Once Joseph Smith arrogated to himself the right to overturn not only Methodist afterlife doctrine but clear biblical teaching about salvation and judgment, he ended up devising a perplexing and incoherent scheme in which not even the murderer and the adulterer will end up in a post-resurrection hell, and in which innumerable honest and noble-minded men are said to be "saved," yet will spend eternity outside the presence of the Father, and perhaps even the Son.

That the exemplary personal morality and wholesome family life of Mormons have become admirable hallmarks of a people dedicated to God cannot be denied. Would that all people everywhere would follow that example. Yet even those virtues are betrayed by an overarching system of beliefs which reveal a mixed allegiance in which (paraphrasing the Prophet's own poem) Mormons are "for Jesus and also for Joseph Smith; for Paul and also for Brigham Young." For Latter-day Saints, the risks are enormous. Which shall they choose to believe: Brigham Young's statement that, "Should the Lord Almighty send an angel to re-write the Bible, it would in many places be very different from what it now is;" or Paul's ominous warning: "But even if we or an angel from heaven should preach a gospel other than the one we preached to you, let him be eternally condemned!" (Galatians 1:8)?

---

68 Millet, *Life After Death*, 37, citing *Teachings of the Prophet Joseph Smith*, 366.

Afterlife View Presented in this Book

Death	Christ's Coming	Eternal Life or Death
Souls of both the righteous and the wicked are "sleeping" unconsciously in Sheol/Hades until the Resurrection	Resurrection of both the righteous and the wicked (Dead in Christ are raised— Those alive in Christ join them in the air—) ——— Judgment of both the righteous and the wicked ——— Earth totally destroyed	For the righteous, life eternal in the ethereal, heavenly realm ——— For the wicked, eternal condemnation in hell (Possible conscious punishment followed, sooner or later, by destruction of both soul and resurrection body)
	Single Resurrection	
	Single Day of Judgment	

Two Traditional Views of the Afterlife

Death	Christ's Coming	Eternity
1. The righteous go immediately to heaven* (or) 2. The righteous in paradise of conscious bliss while awaiting Resurrection ——————— 1. The wicked go immediately to hell (or) 2. The wicked in realm of conscious torment while awaiting Resurrection	Resurrection of both the righteous and the wicked (Dead in Christ are raised– Those alive in Christ join them in the air–) ——————— Judgment of both the righteous and the wicked ——————— Earth totally destroyed	Heaven for the righteous ——————— Never-ending, conscious torment in hell for the wicked
	Single resurrection	
(Implied Judgment?)	Day of Judgment	

* This belief becomes problematic in light of subsequent Resurrection and Judgment

Roman Catholic View of the Afterlife

Death	Christ's Coming	Eternity
Some (few) righteous souls enter heaven immediately Purgatory for final cleansing of the remaining righteous ——— (unofficially) "Limbo," for unbaptized infants and "Limbo of the Fathers" for the righteous ancients The wicked are bound over to Judgment and Hell	Resurrection of both the righteous and the wicked ——— Judgment of both the righteous and the wicked ——— Earth totally destroyed	Heaven for the righteous, both "baptized" Christians and righteous ancients ——— (unofficially) "Limbo," for unbaptized infants ——— Hell for the wicked
	Resurrection of the body	
1. "Particular Judgment"	2. "General Judgment"	

Pre-tribulation Rapture

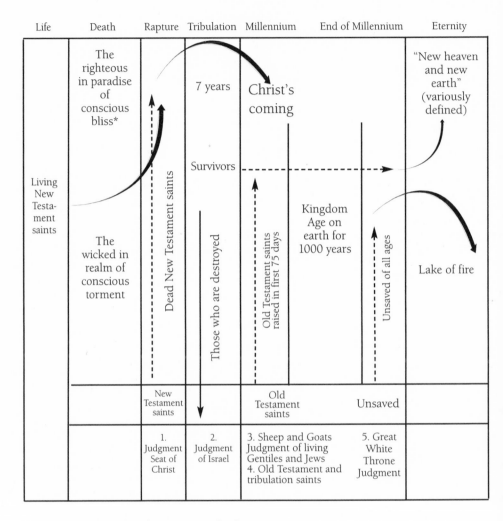

Life	Death	Rapture	Tribulation	Millennium	End of Millennium	Eternity
Living New Testament saints	The righteous in paradise of conscious bliss* / The wicked in realm of conscious torment	7 years / Christ's coming	Survivors	Kingdom Age on earth for 1000 years		"New heaven and new earth" (variously defined) / Lake of fire
		New Testament saints		Old Testament saints	Unsaved	
		1. Judgment Seat of Christ	2. Judgment of Israel	3. Sheep and Goats Judgment of living Gentiles and Jews 4. Old Testament and tribulation saints	5. Great White Throne Judgment	

(Labels within chart: Dead New Testament saints; Those who are destroyed; Old Testament saints raised in first 75 days; Unsaved of all ages)

* It is often said that the righteous go immediately to heaven, which obviously becomes problematic

310

Mid-tribulation Rapture

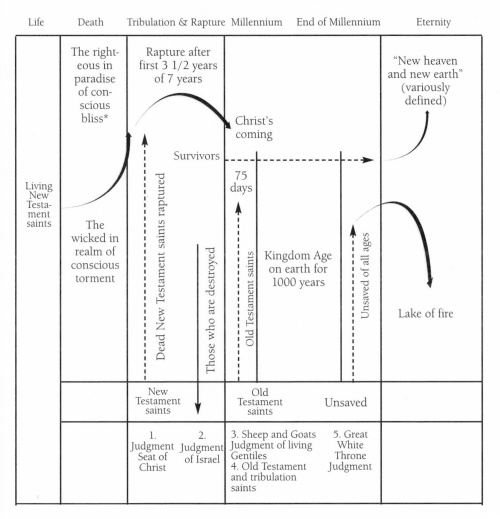

| Life | Death | Tribulation & Rapture | Millennium | End of Millennium | Eternity |

The righteous in paradise of conscious bliss*

Rapture after first 3 1/2 years of 7 years

Christ's coming

Survivors

"New heaven and new earth" (variously defined)

Living New Testament saints

The wicked in realm of conscious torment

Dead New Testament saints raptured

Those who are destroyed

75 days

Old Testament saints

Kingdom Age on earth for 1000 years

Unsaved of all ages

Lake of fire

New Testament saints

Old Testament saints

Unsaved

1. Judgment Seat of Christ

2. Judgment of Israel

3. Sheep and Goats Judgment of living Gentiles
4. Old Testament and tribulation saints

5. Great White Throne Judgment

* It is often said that the righteous go immediately to heaven, which obviously becomes problematic

Post-tribulation Rapture

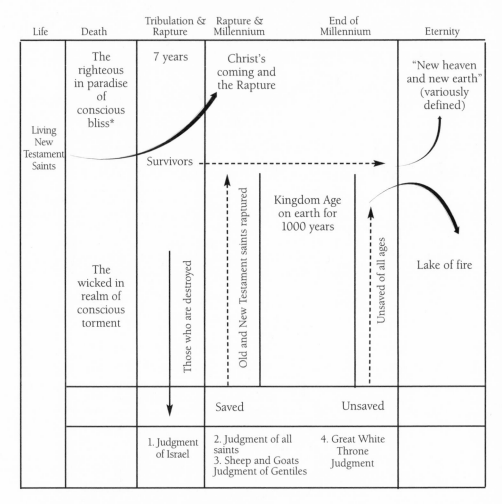

Life	Death	Tribulation & Rapture	Rapture & Millennium	End of Millennium	Eternity
Living New Testament Saints	The righteous in paradise of conscious bliss*	7 years	Christ's coming and the Rapture		"New heaven and new earth" (variously defined)
		Survivors			
		Those who are destroyed	Old and New Testament saints raptured / Kingdom Age on earth for 1000 years	Unsaved of all ages	Lake of fire
	The wicked in realm of conscious torment				
			Saved	Unsaved	
		1. Judgment of Israel	2. Judgment of all saints / 3. Sheep and Goats Judgment of Gentiles	4. Great White Throne Judgment	

* It is often said that the righteous go immediately to heaven, which obviously becomes problematic

Seventh-day Adventists

Life	Death	Christ's Coming	Heavenly Millennium	End	Eternity
	Nothing of the soul exists beyond death until the Resurrection	Saints raised	Saints in heaven with Christ (in Holy City) for 1000 years — As Holy City descends to earth, the wicked are raised	But then destroyed in fiery battle	No heaven — Earth transformed into rejuvenated planet for "heaven on earth" forever — No hell
			Earth is desolate. No humans, only Satan and angels		
		First Resurrection	Second Resurrection		
1. Pre-Advent investigative judgment (premillennial judgment begun in 1844)			2. Millennial Judgment (Review Phase), during 1000 years 3. Great White Throne (executive) Judgment at end of Millennium		

Jehovah's Witnesses

Death	Pre-coming	Christ's Coming	Millennium	End	Eternity
(sheol, hades, grave, hell) Nothing of the soul exists beyond death ——— Righteous remain in memory of God until Resurrection ——— Wicked never resurrected unless God chooses to resurrect them for Millennium	Tribulation Battle of Armageddon Earth purified Survivors - - -	The "worthy dead" in God' memory will be resurrected	144,000 "sealed servants" in heaven, participating with God in governing the earth from heaven 1000-year Kingdom of God Planet transformed into utopian earth for all other righteous ones ——— (Those wicked who were raised along with the righteous have second chance to be faithful) Satan and those who rebel during 1000 years will be destroyed in gehenna		144,000 "sealed servants" only ones in heaven ——— Earth transformed into a paradise for all the other saved ones ——— No hell
		Resurrection of the righteous and selective resurrection of the wicked			
Judgment?					

Latter-day Saints (Mormons)

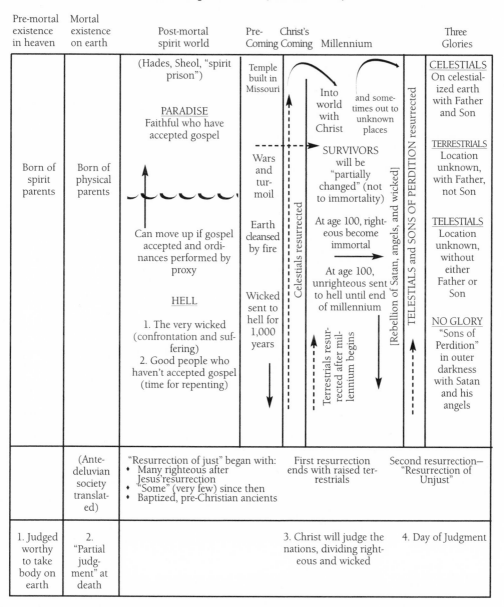

Pre-mortal existence in heaven	Mortal existence on earth	Post-mortal spirit world	Pre-Coming	Christ's Coming	Millennium		Three Glories
Born of spirit parents	Born of physical parents	(Hades, Sheol, "spirit prison") PARADISE Faithful who have accepted gospel Can move up if gospel accepted and ordinances performed by proxy HELL 1. The very wicked (confrontation and suffering) 2. Good people who haven't accepted gospel (time for repenting)	Temple built in Missouri Wars and turmoil Earth cleansed by fire Wicked sent to hell for 1,000 years	Celestials resurrected	Into world with Christ — and sometimes out to unknown places SURVIVORS will be "partially changed" (not to immortality) At age 100, righteous become immortal At age 100, unrighteous sent to hell until end of millennium Terrestrials resurrected after millennium begins [Rebellion of Satan, angels, and wicked]	TELESTIALS and SONS OF PERDITION resurrected	CELESTIALS On celestialized earth with Father and Son TERRESTRIALS Location unknown, with Father, not Son TELESTIALS Location unknown, without either Father or Son NO GLORY "Sons of Perdition" in outer darkness with Satan and his angels
	(Antedeluvian society translated)	"Resurrection of just" began with: • Many righteous after Jesus' resurrection • "Some" (very few) since then • Baptized, pre-Christian ancients		First resurrection ends with raised terrestrials			Second resurrection—"Resurrection of Unjust"
1. Judged worthy to take body on earth	2. "Partial judgment" at death			3. Christ will judge the nations, dividing righteous and wicked			4. Day of Judgment

315

INDEX OF SCRIPTURES

DISCUSSION QUESTIONS

Chapter 1
Frail Children of Dust, Made for Eternity

1. If Adam and Eve had not sinned in the Garden, do you think that they and their descendants would have lived forever on this earth? If so, was eternal life with God in heaven only an after-thought in the wake of their sin? Would you be content living forever in a sin-free, perfect earthly environment? More content than what you anticipate from eternal life in heaven?

2. Considering that heaven is the eternal spiritual realm of God, could man's everlasting existence in a temporal physical environ-ment ever have been anything more than a long-distance rela-tionship with God? Does God's presence in the Garden elimi-nate the problem? What do we learn, if anything, from the fact that angels in heaven rebelled against God, despite being in his very presence?

3. If mortality for all of mankind was the penalty for Adam's sin, why—in the face of that inevitability—were Adam's descendants continually reminded that sin would lead to death? With the penalty already in force, what would have been the point of those warnings? Do you take those same warnings seriously?

4. If physical death was meant as the penalty for sin, how did hell come about as an additional punishment? And why do you sup-pose that Adam's physical death was delayed so long if it was meant as a penalty?

5. If the penalty for sin was that the body would return to the dust from which it was taken, what was to happen to the soul? If it, too, came from dust, does this mean that the soul disintegrates at death along with the body? If so, wouldn't resurrection have to be more like a re-creation of the person—body and soul?

6. Are you as concerned about spiritual death as physical death? Do you ever specifically relate the sin in your life to spiritual death? What does "spiritual death" mean to you? Is it simply a theoretical separation from God which can be overcome through his grace, or is it possible that your soul literally could die in some way similar to your body's dying?

Chapter 2
That Great Gettin'-up Morning

1. If all who are in their graves at the Resurrection will come out, including both the righteous and the wicked, how could the righteous dead already have been in heaven, or the wicked already in hell? And what does it mean to be "in their graves"? Is the grave (or urn, or ocean) literally our resting place until the Resurrection?

2. Why do you suppose God did not provide the ancients with a clearer picture of resurrection, heaven, and hell? Does it help you, having a clearer picture than they had? Just how clear is your understanding of what will happen after you die? Are you bothered one way or the other about what will happen? Would you live your life differently if you knew more of the details?

3. Is it possible that we have unfairly read back into Old Testament passages a Christian view of various afterlife assumptions—such as Job's saying, "I know that my Redeemer lives?" Was he referring to Christ, as we tend to do? Did the Holy Spirit ever reveal concepts that would not have been understood by the prophets and writers of the Old Testament scriptures?

4. Why do you suppose Martha and the Pharisees had such a strong conviction about the resurrection, but that the Sadducees—equally familiar with the Scriptures—were equally convinced that there was no such thing? What kind of religion results when there is no clear belief in the afterlife, or the realm of the spiritual?

324

5. Is it reasonable to believe simultaneously that man is the result of a chance process of biological evolution and also that one day he will be resurrected for life in an eternal realm? Can the idea of a soul's purposely being created in God's image logically coexist with the evolutionary assumptions of natural selection and survival of the fittest? Are many Christians schizophrenic in holding to two competing fundamental assumptions?

6. What is the difference between resurrection and the examples we have of people being brought back from the dead? What difference with so-called "clinical deaths" and "near-death experiences?"

Chapter 3
A Most Mysterious Metamorphosis

1. Why do we insist on thinking that our resurrection body will be the same body we can touch and see at this very moment, when we know that it will totally disintegrate after we die? Are we really to believe that God is going to vacuum up all the sub-atomic particles, as it were, and re-assemble us just as we are now, except that he'll make our bodies immortal next time around? Are we overly attached to the "packages" in which our souls exist in this life?

2. If at the resurrection everyone gets the same basic body as on earth, are we to suppose that there will be aborted fetuses, still-born children, and amputees in heaven with those same physical forms, only glorified?

3. If, as some insist, man doesn't *have* a soul, but *is* a soul, would it also stand to reason that man doesn't *have* a body, but *is* a body? But if that were true, wouldn't the soul become extinct when the body decays?

4. If, as some say, a soul cannot exist without a body, what happens to the soul after the earthly body decays, and before the soul is resurrected with whatever body it will have on that day? If it is thought that the soul is immediately in heaven reclothed in its glorified, earthly body, what explains all the "earthly remains" which are still in the grave for some time following death?

5. If, as some say, both body and soul deteriorate in the grave, what continuity is there between the person who died–body and

soul–and the resurrected person? Without taking away God's power in the least, if something no longer exists, how can it be *resurrected*? Wouldn't it have to be completely *re-created*?

6. If the soul exists apart from a deteriorated earthly body, how do we explain the passages that speak of "bodies" rising from the dust or grave? Does it do violence to the text to see these passages as metaphorical? Is it possible that these "bodies" are referring to new, spiritual bodies in which souls are reclothed?

Chapter 4
It's All In the Timing

1. Does it disturb you to think that your deceased loved ones might not yet be in heaven? If so, why? Would it disturb you more, or less, to think they were in a kind of celestial "waiting room"?

2. Do you think the idea that Christians go straight to heaven when they die might possibly create a false sense of security for non-Christians who, taking their cue from Christians, think they too are going to heaven when they die? Does the prospect of a final Judgment somehow get by-passed along the way?

3. In what sense is it possible to already have life eternal before experiencing eternal life in the heavenly realm? Do you have a strong feeling that you are already experiencing life eternal?

4. Are you, like Paul, really and truly torn between your desire to leave this life and your desire to remain? Do you have an urgent sense of actually *wanting* to be on the other side?

5. On the scale of eternity, does it matter whether or not some people are already in heaven? Is there any risk to our faith if Christ did, in fact, take with him to heaven "captives" from the prison of hades? Can you think of any reason why it might be important to settle that thorny question if possible?

6. Do you regard the apparent silence of those who were raised from the dead as credible evidence that they had nothing to tell about life after life? Or is it possible that they were silenced by a "veil of forgetfulness"? What is the first question *you* would ask someone you knew who had been raised from the dead?

Chapter 5
Falling Asleep In the Waiting Room

1. Why is it so difficult for us to think of ourselves as existing apart from our physical body? Is the real problem that we can't think of ourselves as anything *but* our mind and body? How would you best describe your soul or spirit? Is there a difference between your soul and your spirit?
2. Why do you suppose God was so vague about what happens after death in the centuries before Jesus and the apostles filled in more of the details? In terms of carrot and stick, how important is it in your own life that you have a clear understanding about the nature of heaven and hell?
3. How do you feel about the prospect of existing in an unconscious state apart from your body between the day you die and the day of the Lord's appearing? If the intermediate realm of the dead turned out to be a state of consciousness, of what would you wish to be aware, and of what might you wish to remain unaware?
4. Do you accept that hades will be a place of sleep for the soul? Is "sleep" merely a euphemism? What so-called "soul sleep" theories seem to run counter to the Scriptures?
5. Apart from the concept of suddenly waking up after a long night of sleep, can you think of any analogies or explanations which might help reconcile the immediacy of being with the Lord with a period of waiting? Do relativity theories have anything to suggest, or novel concepts of time?
6. Having heard the arguments, what is your own understanding of the story of the rich man and Lazarus? Parable? Actual snapshot of hades? Graphic picture of hell? How important is this story to your own perception of life after death? Does the story, if taken as a literal picture of the afterlife, dovetail with what Jesus taught directly elsewhere about the afterlife?

Chapter 6
The Day To End All Days

1. What is your understanding of the meaning and purpose of apocalyptic language in Scripture? Why do you think this lin-

guistic form is used rather than more straightforward, easily understandable language? What rules of interpretation can help us chart our way safely through the confusing waters of apocalyptic language?

2. What are the strengths and weaknesses of the three main interpretations of the Olivet discourse? Can you think of any difficulties in assigning to Matthew 24 no meaning beyond the events of A.D. 70? Or in seeing Jesus' discourse primarily as a prophecy of cataclysmic events yet to come? Or in perceiving dual, overlapping prophecies encompassing both?

3. Did you find the concept of "incarnational prophecy" helpful in understanding Matthew 24? How would you describe its interpretative intent? How does it differ from dual or overlapping prophecy?

4. What do you think of when you see the words: *The Day of the Lord*? How were those words understood by the ancients? How, if at all, is *the Day of the Lord* different from *that day*? How often do you consciously and prayerfully think about either *the Day of the Lord* or *that day*: (A) Frequently; (B) Seldom; or (C) Never? What difference would it make one way or the other?

5. What implications follow from simultaneously linking together Christ's appearing, the Resurrection, Judgment, and the destruction of the universe? Are any afterlife theories put at risk by such close linkage?

6. What purpose will be served by the final Judgment? Will it be a trial or merely a sentencing, or perhaps something else altogether? Do you ever think seriously what it will be like to stand before the Judge on *that day*? Should you approach Judgment with confidence or fear?

Chapter 7
Give Me Heaven; You Can Have the Streets of Gold

1. What is your vision of heaven, and what has served most to shape that vision? How much is your vision of heaven influenced by what you see around you in this present world? Is it realistic to think that any vision we might have is anything near what heaven

will be like? Does it help to think of ourselves as babies still in the womb, unaware of the incredible world beyond the womb?

2. Are we capable of comprehending a heaven that is not a *place*, and stands outside of time? Can we ever get beyond thinking of eternity as time, simply stretched to the ultimate extreme? What is the difference between "forever," as time, and "eternal," as quality of existence?

3. What might have been Abraham's idea of heaven? Or David's? And, if heaven was so obscure to the ancients, how important is our own understanding of it? Could we be faith-filled, Christ-committed people with no understanding whatsoever of heaven? Or with no understanding of eternal life?

4. Do you find it ironic that God describes the eternal realm in patently materialistic terms? Is there not something inherently contradictory between the consummate spiritual realm and the desire for a *mansion* in the sky? Are you attracted, or influenced in your Christian walk, by the prospect of golden streets and pearly gates?

5. If you are brutally honest with yourself, do you really look forward to being "in heaven"? Does it sound fun, interesting, wonderful, or simply tedious and boring? Is your desire for heaven mostly in contrast to the unthinkable alternative? To what extent do doubts about the perpetual joy of a purely spiritual heaven drive the desire on the part of many for a "heaven on earth"?

6. What do you think of the idea that heaven is not about *doing*, but about *being*? Does that add to, or take away from, the prospect of life eternal? Does it suggest anything about the type of bodies we might have in heaven?

Chapter 8
The Tormenting Conundrum of Hell

1. What do you think of the idea that, at some point, the "fire" of hell will totally consume the souls of the wicked? Do you think ultimate destruction rather than endless torment diminishes the deterrent effect of hell? Do you think it lets the wicked off the hook and gives them an easy way out?

2. Would you be disappointed if hell turned out not to be ongoing, endless torment for the wicked? Would you feel that justice

would not have been done, or that God somehow had deceived us about hell's fire?

3. If you insist that the lake of fire burning forever is to be taken literally, do you also insist that the golden street and pearly gates of heaven be taken with equal literalness? If not, what for you is the difference between the two descriptions? How literal do you take the body that is to be burned with literal fire? Do you take Revelation's "thousand years" or "144,000" literally?

4. When the Bible speaks of fire in connection with God's judgment, which is overwhelmingly the result of that fire: torment or destruction? Which is more consistent with Jesus' warning to his disciples that they should fear the One who can destroy body and soul in hell? Which is more consistent with the character of God?

5. How does your concept of hell match up with statements like: "The soul that sins is the one who will die"; or "This is the second death"? As horrible as the prospect of ongoing fiery torment forever seems, can you envision what it would be like not to exist at all? Or do you think that not existing at all is preferable to pain and suffering? At what point would you say the same of pain and suffering in *this* life?

6. If the fire of hell is necessary to get people's attention, why didn't God paint a more vivid picture of hell for the Jews? Are the wicked today so fearful of the traditional view of hell that they eagerly turn to God? Are *you* fearful of hell; and, if so, have you ever consciously changed the way you live because of that fear?

Chapter 9
Living In the Eternal Present

1. Do you consciously live each day in view of eternity? Do you seriously consider that your eternal destiny could be put in jeopardy by decisions you make and actions you may take this very day? Or does that seem to put a damper on God's grace and the promises of salvation to God's children?

2. Given that we all will stand before God's judgment seat and give an account of ourselves, have you thought of what account will you give? Are we counting on God to remember that we are

dust? Or to have mercy on our souls because we are human and subject to sin? Have we rationalized our relationship with God by dividing sins into big and little, serious and not so serious?

3. Painfully aware of our sins–especially our secret sins–how can we have anything other than fear as we contemplate the throne of Judgment? At what point is there a valid distinction between wilful sins and sins of omission or ignorance? And can we honestly say our sins aren't wilful?

4. What do you think it would take for you to "fall away" to such an extent you that lost your salvation? Do you reject Calvinism's impossibility of apostasy in theory, only to depend upon it in practice?

5. Why do you suppose, in the face of repeated scriptural warnings to the saved against falling away, so many people are almost fanatical in their defense of Calvinism? In what way does the possibility of the saved losing their salvation deal a death blow to all of Calvinism's assumptions?

6. What gives you real hope for eternal life with God? What do you look to for encouragement when faced with a life of sin? In what way does the assurance of resurrection and life eternal allow you to face death with confidence?

Chapter 10
Purgatory–Slapping Grace In the Face

1. What do you think is the motivation behind the Catholic doctrine of purgatory? Is the primary concern really about how those who are not completely holy could ever enter the purity of heaven? Or is this doctrine the ultimate extension of a system of works salvation?

2. Will the saved ever be worthy to enter heaven on their own merit? If, in the end, salvation is always dependent upon God's grace, why is it not possible for God's grace to cover our unworthiness at the moment we die. Is the idea of purgatory centered on God's grace, or our own pain and suffering?

3. In what way is the pain of purgatory different from the spiritual discipline which we experience in this life? Is there a kind of "purgatory on earth"? In what way is the idea of spiritual purg-

ing a good idea? Have you ever consciously experienced true spiritual purging?

4. How can we believe that the blood of Christ purifies us from all sin when we know good and well that we keep on sinning, even as saved Christians? And if Christ's blood does in fact purify us from all sin, then was Calvin correct, after all, in pressing his belief in the unfailing perseverance of the saints?

5. In what way has Catholicism's doctrine of purgatory forced it to modify what the Scriptures tell us about the Judgment? If purgatory is a good illustration of how skewed doctrines (in this case about justification and sanctification) have a profound effect upon one's afterlife beliefs, does it not also demonstrate how false afterlife assumptions, in turn, can have serious implications for other doctrinal positions? Have you considered whether your own afterlife assumptions have forced you to compromise or accommodate other matters of doctrine?

6. If Catholic doctrine is wrong about purgatory and its role in the crucial process of sanctification, what can we learn regarding the *biblical* process of sanctification? Are you consciously allowing God to sanctify you in this life? To what extent, if any, has your reliance upon your justification (principally through ritual acts of obedience in becoming a Christian) made you take for granted your sanctification?

Chapter 11
Limbo—A Theory In Search Of Coherence

1. If a church has created a whole body of doctrine not found in Scripture (even informally), what likely course of action has the church already taken to get to that point? If you can see that process happening in the Roman Catholic Church, is it possible that there is any such parallel in your own fellowship?

2. How would you respond to the doctrine of original sin, the notion that babies come into the world tainted by sin? What is the biblical evidence which suggests it; and what scriptures would refute it? Is there any way at all in which the Fall has affected mankind since Adam and Eve?

3. In what way does infant baptism run counter to the baptism of first-century Christians? Is there any hard evidence from either Scripture or history to suggest that the primitive, apostolic church practiced infant baptism? What essential element of biblical baptism is missing in infant baptism?

4. How would you respond to the "limbo of the Fathers" which states that, unlike baptized Christians, righteous men and women living and dying before Christ must wait in limbo until the Resurrection? What is the first and most immediate misunderstanding entailed in that belief, relating to the timing of when one enters into heaven? What is the second misunderstanding, relating to the two different covenants God has made with his people?

5. In what way do many non-Catholic parents, who reject the doctrine of limbo in principle, actually live out the fears which lie behind this unbiblical teaching? When those who reject infant baptism nevertheless practice very-early-youth baptism, what larger statement is being made?

6. Why is doctrine so important? If most of God's people over the ages would have been ill-informed regarding the complexities of theology, is it so wrong that we might accept erroneous doctrine today? But if doctrine is unimportant, why do the New Testament writers give so much attention to doctrine? In what tangible way does doctrinal correctness and coherence play an important role in your faith walk?

Chapter 12
Rapture and Other Best-Selling Fiction

1. What is the most fundamental problem with perceiving of Christ's kingdom as a government on earth, as presented in the various millennial theories? Does the fact that the kingdom of God is within us necessarily rule out an earthly kingdom? Apart from concerns about unfulfilled covenants, what spiritual benefit would be derived from our being part of an earthly kingdom for a thousand years?

2. What scriptural and practical problems surround the notion that a millennial reign on earth is necessary to bring about the salvation of the Jews and the completion of covenants allegedly yet to

be fulfilled? How would you answer the argument that the land promise was never fulfilled, or that no descendant of David has yet sat on David's throne in Jerusalem forever as promised?

3. What part has the end-times Jewish connection played in Middle Eastern politics and the whole Israel question since modern Israel was established? Do believers who support the state of Israel as a necessary player in some apocalyptic end-times scenario bear any responsibility for the ongoing conflict in the region?

4. How has popular end-times literature maintained its credibility with so many people despite having to be reinvented with each new twist and turn in world politics? What is the allure of Rapture that makes it so popular? Do you agree with the suggestion that there could be an unworthy sense of pride attached to being part of "the special generation" to which Christ finally appears, or being included in the Rapture when others are "left behind"?

5. How can there be such major, even acrimonious, differences among believers regarding the role and nature of biblical prophecy? What tends to shape one's view of prophecy, and one's hermeneutic in approaching apocalyptic literature? Why do you suppose God gave us the book of Revelation, surely aware that it would become such a controversial book?

6. If you happen to reject the Rapture-millennial reign theory, do you nevertheless eagerly anticipate Christ's return? Do you have a sense of immediacy about his appearing, or does it seem unimportant that Christ would come soon? If Christ came today–this very day–would you be ready for his coming?

Other Books By F. LaGard Smith

The Narrated Bible

The Daily Bible

Baptism–The Believer's Wedding Ceremony

Male Spiritual Leadership

The Cultural Church

Meeting God In Quiet Places

Circles of Fellowship

Radical Restoration

30 Days With Jesus

Troubling Questions for Calvinists

Angels, Demons, and the Devil